Majestic is Thy Name:

Devotions from the Psalms

To Uncle Paul,

Love John

John Zehring

"O Lord, our Lord,

how majestic is thy name

in all the earth!"

Psalm 8:1, RSV

Introduction

Majestic is Thy Name contains 150 uplifting meditations and prayers, one for each Psalm. The book mines gems from the Psalms to pilot the reader into an encounter with the Divine. Praise and thanksgiving are key themes in the Psalms, raising the bar for our own prayers. The reflection for each Psalm provides language, lyrics, illustrations and quotations to lead us into a relationship with God with heighten praise. The Psalmist also speaks frequently of his enemies, which reminds us that it is in our valleys, challenges and difficulties that God is our refuge and our strength in times of trouble.

The hope, dear reader, is that you might keep this book by your bedside, reading table, or make it one of the first sites you connect with when you go online in the morning to start the day with an inspirational Psalm. For that day, this is your Psalm to meditate upon, to repeat or review as the day continues, and to think about in your closing thoughts of evening. Is that not a more fulfilling way to start a day than to connect with news, social media or emails – which is what everyone in the world seems to do? Rise above common routines of daily living to lift your spirit and thoughts to a higher plain. The selections, meditation and brief prayer for each Psalm pilot you to internalize Psalm, center upon it, remember it and make it your prayer for the day. You will likely find it more helpful to read and focus upon one chapter at a time than to attempt multiple chapters at one sitting.

The title of the book comes from the beautiful praise to God found in Psalm 8: _"O Lord, our Lord, how majestic is thy name in all the earth!"_ So many of the Psalms are about our personal I-Thou relationship with God, yet the Psalms lift us up out of our self-centeredness to a God-centeredness. The Psalms inspire us to initiate our day and elevate our thoughts with praise and gratitude to God, our Creator. First. First comes praise, then comes our need.

That is not the natural order, of course, which is why we turn to a resource outside of ourselves to change our way of thinking and seeing, from a "me first" prayer to a "God first" life goal. The Psalms inspire us as people of faith to seek to know God better and to love God more.

Many Psalms speak of God the judge extracting vengeance from the wicked and destroying the unrighteous, allowing the author of the Psalms to triumph over enemies. Once when I mentioned to a colleague about my affection for the Psalms, she asked what I did with all the writings about enemies, judgement, and violence. I have thought about her question over the years and see now that I can still love the Psalms, but have to read between the lines to lift the treasures from the Psalms out of their particular concern for the author's specific experience at that time, centuries ago. This is not so much an attempt to take them out of context, but rather to lift high the best of the Psalmist's writings that can apply to our experience today. And while we might not battle enemies the same way King David did, we battle our own enemies of problems, challenges, worries, difficulties, anxieties and even tragedies. For those experiences, the Psalms are a soothing balm.

While this is not a study of the authorship of the Psalms, biblical scholars agree that the Psalms were written by numerous authors. It was not an uncommon practice then for a writer to attribute his or her writings to another as an honor to them. There are a number of Psalms which you would not necessarily turn to for inspiration, as the writer details the agony and strife of being overwhelmed or overtaken by enemies, problems, or challenges… although, sometimes we feel that way and are inclined to whisper to the Psalmist: "You too!" Yet even out of the particular Psalms which are about oppression by enemies, there is always a gem buried within that we can lift up to use as an inspiration for the day and a focal point upon which to center our spirits.

The gems mined from the treasure chest of the Psalms skim the surface. Some great ones are missed and will need to be saved for another time. The goal is to provide enough to give you a devotional thought from the Psalms as a way to center your prayer and meditation for the day. If you have ever enjoyed the privilege of watching a potter working with a lump of clay on the potting wheel, you would have witnessed the potter investing a great deal of time and skill to center the clay. If the clay does not begin by being centered, anything the potter creates will be off kilter. So too with your spiritual life. It is worth it to you to invest your best early morning or late evening time by centering your thoughts upon the gems which have come to us though the Psalms.

Notes about this book

Scriptures used in this work come from the New Revised Standard Version, unless otherwise noted.

The Bible consists of the Old Testament and the New Testament. These are also referred to as the Hebrew Scriptures and the Christian Scriptures. In this book, both Hebrew and Christian teachings are interwoven. The gems from the Psalms in this book are viewed through Christian lenses. Jesus of Nazareth, a Jew, would have known the Psalms. They were his prayer book and he often quoted from them. The Apostle Paul, who studied to be a rabbi, also would have been well-versed in the Psalms, which influenced many of his epistles.

I have attempted to use inclusive language wherever possible in the words I have written, although I have not altered the author's reference to God as "he." I recognize that the Divine has no gender and for many it may be just as appropriate and accurate to acknowledge God as Mother or Father. Whichever pronoun is used, consider God as a loving parent.

Some of this work is adapted from other books or eBooks I have written. My website can be found by searching online for *John Zehring books*.

Now, as you engage *Majestic Is Thy Name*, may these Psalms and meditations enrich your faith, your life, and lead you further into your reverence for God and your encounter with the Divine.

John Zehring

ONE

They are like trees planted by streams of water, which yield their fruit in its season, and their leaves do not wither.
1:3

A woman received an invitation to a high society luncheon. She was not sure she wanted to attend, but at the last minute decided to go. The guest of honor was a famous movie actor.

As lunch was winding down, the actor was asked if he would recite something well-known. He came to the podium and asked the guests *What would you like me to recite?* From the back of the room, the woman called out *Will you recite the 23rd Psalm?* The actor strained to see who suggested the psalm. He looked at her and said *Okay. I will agree to recite the 23rd Psalm... if... you will agree to recite it after I finish.* It was an odd request. The guests stared at the woman to await her response. She had to agree, and she did. So, the actor stood at the podium, flashed his gleaming Hollywood smile, made eye contact with every guest in the room, took a deep breath and he began: *THE LORD IS MY SHEPHERD, I SHALL NOT WANT. HE MAKETH ME...* Oh, the way he emphasized the words was magical. His mastery of pause, timing and silence brought listeners to the edge of the seat as they awaited his next word. His deep booming voice reverberated throughout the hall. When he finished, the guests jumped to their feet to reward him with a rousing standing ovation.

Now it was the woman's turn. She came to the podium but made no eye contact. Instead, she closed her eyes and with her frail and somewhat shaky voice, she too recited the 23rd Psalm. When she finished, there was no ovation. The guests were totally silent. You could hear a pin drop. A few appeared to have tears welling up in their eyes. An awkward silence continued.

Sensing the shift in the mood, the actor returned to the podium and said *I think I understand the difference in how you responded to her and how you responded to me. You see, I KNOW the Psalm. But she... she knows the Shepherd.*

7

The Psalms were written by and created for people who desire to know God the Shepherd. Anyone can know about the shepherd. A person could go online and easily look up characteristics which various faiths believe describe the nature of God. But that is not the same as desiring to know God better and to love God more. People who choose to live a God-like life are described by Psalm 1 in beautiful poetic language: *They are like trees planted by streams of water, which yield their fruit in its season, and their leaves do not wither.*

As you prepare to use this book as a guide for your daily devotions, based in the Psalms, may you too endeavor to develop an intimate relationship with God... to come to know the Shepherd.

PRAYER: Loving God, guide me this day to become closer to know, to know you better, to offer you my praise, and to do my best to live a life which is pleasing to you. Amen.

TWO

He who sits in the heavens laughs.
2:4a

A young girl in church school was furiously drawing a picture, switching out one crayon after another. Her teacher came by and asked "Honey, what are you drawing?" Without looking up, the girl answered "I'm drawing a picture of God." The teacher commented "Honey, no one really knows what God looks like." Without pausing from her drawing, the girl replied "They will when I get done!"

If you peruse art books with faces of Jesus created by artists over the centuries, you may notice that they all have one thing in common: he is rarely laughing or even smiling. And yet, the Psalm tells us that He who sits in the heavens laughs. We learn in Genesis that you were created in God's image. If God laughs, so should you. Your inner spirit has a right to laugh and a need to laugh.

Research from the Mayo Clinic provides data about the positive benefits laughter can bring. Mayo staff tell how when you start to laugh, it does not just lighten your load mentally, it actually induces physical changes in your body. Laughter can stimulate many organs. Laughter enhances your intake of oxygen-rich air, stimulates your heart, lungs and muscles, and increases the endorphins that are released by your brain. Laughter cools down your stress response, and it can increase your heart rate and blood pressure. The result? A good, relaxed feeling. Laughter soothes tension and can stimulate circulation and aid muscle relaxation, both of which can help reduce some of the physical symptoms of stress.

Other research has pointed out that laughter lightens anger's heavy load. Nothing diffuses anger or conflict faster than a shared laugh. Looking at the funny side can put problems into perspective and enable you to move on from confrontations without holding onto bitterness or resentment.

9

Laughter may even help you to live longer. A study in Norway found that people with a strong sense of humor outlived those who did not laugh as much. The difference was particularly notable for those battling cancer.

"A cheerful heart is a good medicine, but a downcast spirit dries up the bones," says Proverbs 17:22. And so, celebrate that God laughs and that you were meant to laugh too. Take time to laugh. As needed, laugh at yourself so as not to take yourself too seriously. And as you think about matters of faith, lighten up and recognizes that there is a cheerful, happy, joyful and laughing side to your relationship with God.

PRAYER: Dear God, please keep me from being too serious or becoming too busy to laugh. As I think about you and all you have done and continue to do, let me also see the side of you that laughs. Amen.

THREE

I cry aloud to the Lord, and he answers me from his holy hill. I lie down and sleep; I wake again, for the Lord sustains me.
3:4, 5

Knowing that God has heard the Psalmist's prayer, he is able to sleep. When he awakens, he is refreshed. You too as a person of faith can sleep well, knowing that God has heard your prayer and that God sustains you.

In a Robert Ludlum thriller novel, the hero of the story Jason Bourne is being chased. Then he recognizes a great truth when he says *"Rest is a weapon."* For him, rest becomes as important or perhaps more so than any other weapon for his effective and creative battle against adversity. You too need rest, to face challenges as well as to fully embrace an abundant life.

Allow yourself time to rest. Pushing it to your limits is not in your best interest. Regular times of rest are necessary for your spiritual, physical and emotional health. You will be more effective in your work and creative living when you are rested. Educators advise students to rest before a major test. Studies indicate that rest is more effective than cramming for better exam results. Employers know from experience that employees who are exhausted make more mistakes or stifle their creativity. Anxious? Allow rest to restore you and serve you as a weapon for battling worries or sharpening your effectiveness.

The Psalmist trusts that God hears him, knows what is on his heart, and leads him to lie down in green pastures. Today, allow yourself times away from your busy schedule to take brief vacations of rest. At nightfall, empty your prayers into God's hand, let go, and sleep well.

PRAYER: Dear God, hear all the concerns and worries which trouble me. I place them into your hand. Help me to sleep well tonight so that I may greet the new day well rested. Amen.

11

FOUR

Answer me when I call, O God of my right! You gave me room when I was in distress. Be gracious to me, and hear my prayer.
4:1

The Contemporary English Version translates the Psalm this way: *You are my God and protector. Please answer my prayer. I was in terrible distress, but you set me free. Now have pity and listen as I pray.* The Psalmist tells God that when he was in trouble before, God helped him. Now, it sounds like, troubles return and he need God's help one more time.

Here is a confounding story from the Hebrew scriptures. 2 Samuel 21:19 says *"Then there was another battle with the Philistines at Gob; and Elhanan son of Jaare-oregim, the Bethlehemite, killed Goliath the Gittite, the shaft of whose spear was like a weaver's beam."* This says a man named Elhanan killed Goliath. Of course, 1 Samuel 17 tells how David slew Goliath. So, which was it? It appears we have a… giant… discrepancy.

While biblical scholars appear unable to explain the two slayings of Goliath, the message suggests to us that the giants return. Giant problems or challenges can come back to you. You thought they were dead and gone, but the giants return. You thought Goliath was slain, but here he comes again! You thought you slayed your giants. You thought the problems were faced and resolved. You thought the challenge was over. Just when you think everything's okay, here it comes back again.

What do you do when the giants return? You are already worn down. Your bones are weary. Anxiety strains your body and mind, frustration fills your emotions, and your spirit is exhausted.

The Psalmist tells how God was there for him when he was in distress before. God has been with you before and God was with you when you conquered your giants. God will be with you again. And again. There is no place in the Bible which suggests that God limits the number of times you can turn to God when problems, challenges, difficulties, or giants return. God is gracious to you and will hear your prayer. Again.

PRAYER: Thank you, God, for being with me and helping me when I needed you most in the past. Be with me again as I look ahead to my future to become the best person I can be and to succeed at living the abundant life you desire for me. Amen.

FIVE

But I, through the abundance of your steadfast love, will enter your house
5:7

Who feels good enough to enter the house of the Lord? The Psalmist did, but only because of the abundance of God's steadfast love. In the epistles of Paul, a similar comparison is made to the grace of God. By God's grace, you and I may enter the house of the Lord.

A good synonym for the word *grace* is the word "*anyway*." That means that no matter what you may have done to make a mess of things, no matter how bad a mistake or decision you have made, no matter what behavior or action you might regret or wonder about, God loves you *anyway*. God forgives you *anyway*. God accepts you *anyway*. God showers mercy upon you *anyway*. God pardons you *anyway*. By the abundance of God's love, God gives you the gift of grace so that you may start anew with a fresh slate. Because God loves you anyway, you are welcome into God's presence.

There is nothing – no behavior, thought or act – that falls outside of God's grace. If there is anything you have ever done which you think God might not forgive, you are incorrect and here is why: you cannot limit God. To believe that any action you ever did could fall outside of God's mercy is to limit God. Placing a limit on God's love is impossible.

Sometimes we are not good at accepting gifts, from people or from God. I once went to an expensive concert with a friend. He approached the ticket counter and paid for both of our tickets. I protested. He should not have to pay for me. I wanted to pay for my own admission. He turned to me and said "John, teach me how to accept a gift graciously." A good lesson: could we be like that with God? Perhaps we are not good at accepting God's gift of grace, believing we are not worthy or deserving of it. Perhaps God calls you by name and asks you to accept the gift of grace graciously.

14

PRAYER: Compassionate God, help me to become better at accepting your gift of grace. Knowing that you have forgiven me, help me to forgive myself. I am not worthy to be in your presence, but because of the abundance of steadfast love, you accept me and welcome me. Thank you, God, for your gifts. Amen.

SIX

Be gracious to me, O Lord, for I am languishing; O Lord, heal me, for my bones are shaking with terror.
6:2

The Psalmist is hurting. He uses the most dramatic language to describe his pain, to the point of terror. We do not know if he is speaking metaphorically, referring to emotional pain, or if he is in physical agony. Either way, he feels like he is languishing. He is afraid of dying. We feel badly for him. And yet, are there not moments in our own lives where we are inclined to say to this hero of biblical literature "You too?" Are there not times when we are hurting, emotionally or physically, that we pray for God to be gracious to us because we feel like we are languishing?

Woven throughout the Psalms are the themes of the Psalmist's pain, yet his praise for how God has delivered him, served as his rock and his fortress, and restored his soul. There is a hymn that reminds us that even when we battle stormy weather, God is gracious to us and out of the storm we proclaim "It is well with my soul."

When peace, like a river, upholds me each day,
When sorrows like sea billows roll,
Whatever my lot,
You have taught me to say,
"It is well, it is well with my soul."
It is well, with my soul,
It is well, it is well with my soul.

Hopefully most of our days will be good ones, but when we hurting we know we are not alone, for God is with us and is gracious to us. The writers of the Bible and authors of hymns were humans too and they also experienced times of suffering or pain. Yet they lift our sights to be able to say that "whatever my lot… it is well, it is well, with my soul."

PRAYER: Caring God, be gracious to me and heal me when I am hurting. Increase my faith to know that even in pain or grief, I will praise you and trust without reservations that it is well with my soul. Amen.

SEVEN

*I will give to the Lord the thanks due to his righteousness, and
sing praise to the name of the Lord, the Most High.*
7:17

Early in my life I purchased a small New Testament. When it
arrived, I discovered that it was the New Testament and The
Psalms, symbolizing to me that this book from the Hebrew
scriptures was considered almost on par with the gospels and the
epistles. I suppose I should have questioned why the Psalms?
Why not Genesis, or Exodus, or the Proverbs? My best guess then,
as now, is that the Psalms were given such honor because of how
they praise God. By example, the Psalms encourage us to praise
God.

One of the best ways to praise God is to get a praise hymn stuck in
your mind and center upon it from your morning shower to the
closing thoughts in your mind as you close your eyes at night. Let
this hymn lead you into singing praise to the name of the Lord, the
Most High:

Praise to the Lord,
the Almighty, the King of creation!
O my soul, praise him,
for he is thy health and salvation!
All ye who hear,
Now to his temple draw near;
Join me in glad adoration!

Praise to the Lord!
O let all that is in me adore him!
All that hath life and breath,
come now with praises before him.
Let the Amen,
Sound from his people again;
Gladly for aye we adore him.

PRAYER: Dear Lord, hear my prayer of praise to you. You are my health and salvation. May my words, my thoughts and my actions adore you. Amen.

EIGHT

***O Lord, our Sovereign, how majestic is your name in all the
earth! You have set your glory above the heavens.***
8:1

*O Lord, our Lord, how majestic is thy name in all the earth!
Thou whose glory above the heavens is chanted.* (RSV)

The title of this book comes from the RSV version of the verse…
Majestic is thy name. Most of the time I favor the NRSV, but this
time I like the use of the pronoun *thy*. The Psalmist in most cases
is not speaking about God but is speaking to God. He engages in
an I-Thou relationship with the Divine, as you and I can be led to
do through the inspiration of the Psalms. We too want to tell God,
our God, how majestic is thy name in all the earth!

The word "name" is used frequently in the Bible and especially in
Psalms. It is used more than a thousand times in the Bible. It is a
uniqueness of biblical language, for the word name actually means
the person himself or herself. When you see references to God's
"name," make a substitution in your mind, for the intent is to speak
about God's own being. Substitute God for "name." And so…

"Hallowed be thy name" means to praise God, not to praise the
word by which God is called.

"You shall not take the name of the Lord your God in vain" is not
about cursing. It means to not take God in vain, which would be to
live as though God did not matter.

*"A good name is to be chosen rather than great riches, and favor
is better than silver or gold,"* from Proverbs 22:1, does not refer to
the word by which you are called but to the kind of person you
choose to become.

20

"O LORD, our Lord, how majestic is thy name in all the earth!" It is the Lord who is majestic, not simply the original Hebrew word for God, which was composed the letters YHWH and was pronounced "YahWay." The Psalmist in this verse is really saying "O Lord, our Lord, how majestic are YOU in all the earth!" We share something in common with anyone who proclaims those words, for they and we agree that it is God in whom we believe, trust, follow and praise.

PRAYER: O Lord, my Lord. You are the creator and ruler of the universe and you are majestic to me. Amen.

NINE

I will give thanks to the Lord with my whole heart; I will tell of all your wonderful deeds.
9:1

A good prayer has four parts: praise, thanks, confession and petition (asking). Over the Psalms, all four parts are employed regularly, but this one centers upon thanking. He thanks God with his whole heart.

We might wonder, to whom does he tell of all God's wonderful deeds? Does he stand behind a podium to do so, or go door to door, or perhaps tell his family and friends over a meal? Maybe the one he tells most is himself. He tells himself... reminds himself... of all God's wonderful deeds.

That makes me wonder of I do that. Do you? Do we look back on our lives and recall all the times when we felt God did a wonderful deed? We have prayed hundreds if not thousands of times to ask God for something, for ourselves or for another. Do we look back to say thank you? Do we enumerate for ourselves the wonderful deeds God has done for us or for someone we care about? Perhaps we feel blessed and say so, affirming that "God has blessed me." A fine way to give thanks to God is to say thank you and to tell of God's wonderful deeds in our lives. A hymn of thanksgiving also leads us into an attitude of gratefulness:

Now thank we all our God,
with heart and hands and voices,
who wondrous things has done,
in whom this world rejoices;
who from our mothers' arms
has blessed us on our way
with countless gifts of love,
and still is ours today.

O may this bounteous God
through all our life be near us,
with ever joyful hearts
and blessed peace to cheer us;
and keep us still in grace,
and guide us when perplexed;
and free us from all ills,
in this world and the next.

All praise and thanks to God
the Father now be given;
the Son, and him who reigns
with them in highest heaven;
the one eternal God,
whom earth and heaven adore;
for thus it was, is now,
and shall be evermore.

PRAYER: Gracious God, I thank you with my whole heart for all of your blessings to me. May I take moments to look back and recall how you were with me when I needed you most. Thank you, God. Amen.

TEN

***Why, O Lord, do you stand far off? Why do you hide yourself in
times of trouble?***
10:1

In the previous Psalm the Psalmist just finished thanking God with
his whole heart and telling of God's wonderful deeds. Now it feels
like his on the other end of a see-saw, sensing that God is far away,
especially in times of trouble.

A few things to note about this verse. First, are there not times we
feel this way, that God stands far off? We do not want to appear to
doubt God's power or love, but there may be times we want to say
with the Psalmist "You too?" C. S. Lewis reflected *"Friendship is
born at that moment when one person says to another, 'What! You,
too? I thought I was the only one'."* We become a friend of the
Psalmist when we recognize that sometimes we feel the ways he
describes.

Second, note that the Psalmist is not telling about God but rather,
he is addressing God. He is holding a conversation with God,
asking in a sense "Where are you?" He feels alone, yet never does
he forsake his faith. He still believes, praises and follows God.
Indeed, his faith is strong enough that he does not need to worry
about offending God. He believes in a God who is big enough to
hear us, understand us, and have compassion on us. This suggests
that we too might grow our faith to the point where we can address
God with our questions, trusting that God will not love us any the
less for our asking.

There is a dramatic story about a Nazi prison camp. Two men
were forced to watch as their friend was being led to the gallows,
to be hung. They had lost everything. They had no idea where
their wives were, or their children, or their possessions. All they
had were rags on their bodies and not even shoes on their feet.

As the guards roughly pushed their friend to the gallows and placed the rope around his neck, one man said to the other "Where is God?" His friend answered "God is up there on the gallows with him."

In the worst of times, even when it feels like God stands far off, and even in the valley of the shadow of death, God is with us. We may not recognize God's presence, but that does not mean it is not there. The Psalmist, even after feeling that God hides in times of trouble, returns to the rock-solid core of his belief... "For Thou art with me."

PRAYER: Tender God, when I feel far away from you, guide me to raise up my gaze to see that I am in your presence. Strengthen my faith to know in my heart that you are always with me. Amen.

ELEVEN

Rise up, O Lord; O God, lift up your hand; do not forget the oppressed.
10:12

Throughout the Psalms, the Psalmist experiences an I-Thou relationship with the Divine. Frequently he prays for help as he feels besieged by enemies. Frequently he praises God's majestic name. Frequently he says thank you for the times God delivered him and helped him. It's all about me and God, you might think, and that sounds a little self-centered. Now, as in a number of other Psalms, the Psalmist implores God not to forget the oppressed. He prays here not for the high and mighty, but for those on the margins of society. He asks God not to forget those who have the least. This now makes sense to us, for a faith which is based solely on a person's intimate relationship with God is insufficient. Faith must lead us out of ourselves into a caring for and sharing with the oppressed.

This was the point of one of Jesus' most important parables, in Mathew 25. He tells how God will judge people. It is not what you might expect. It is not about how well people engage in religious practices, master the scriptures or even follow the commandments. No, rather, it is about favoring the oppressed. Jesus' whole point is that what you do for the child, you do for the parent, for God. What you do for the oppressed, you do for God. Consider his parable, as presented in The Message (Matthew 25:34-40):

I was hungry and you fed me,
I was thirsty and you gave me a drink,
I was homeless and you gave me a room,
I was shivering and you gave me clothes,
I was sick and you stopped to visit,
I was in prison and you came to me.'

"Then those 'sheep' are going to say, 'Master, what are you talking about? When did we ever see you hungry and feed you, thirsty and give you a drink? And when did we ever see you sick or in prison and come to you?' Then the King will say, 'I'm telling the solemn truth: Whenever you did one of these things to someone overlooked or ignored, that was me – you did it to me.'

That was me, says God. What you did for the oppressed, you did it to me!

And so, in your prayers, thoughts and actions, do not forget the oppressed.

PRAYER: Dear God, help me to know how to help those who are oppressed. May I radiate your love, care and kindness whenever I encounter someone who is oppressed. Grant that I might pledge to speak for and stand with the oppressed, wherever they might be from. Amen.

TWELVE

For the Lord is righteous; he loves righteous deeds; the upright shall behold his face.
11:7

God loves righteous deeds. God loves people who do things for the right reasons, even if no one else sees or knows about it. It is a great comfort to us to know that our acts of integrity or goodness are known to God even if other people do not know. In that sense, we do the right thing, not to be seen by others, but for God.

The Psalmist's phrase *the upright shall behold his face* reminds of Jesus' beatitude from Matthew 5:8: *Blessed are the pure in heart, for they will see God.* If you were asked the question *"Are you pure in heart?"* would you raise your hand? My first inclination is to think that this is not me. Pure in heart? How many of us ever feel we are pure in heart? Could you imagine the disciples, upon hearing this beatitude, pass around a fleeting glance, perhaps rolling their eyes, thinking "He can't be talking about us"? So, dig a little deeper to uncover more of Jesus' meaning.

The word for *pure* here was what was said about wine which was pure wine, unmixed with water. In Palestine, they did not drink the water and neither would you if you went there today. At meals, they drank wine. But you cannot drink too much wine or you know what happens. So they watered it down. The basic meaning of the word *pure* used in this beatitude is *unmixed* or *unadulterated.* Using this interpretation as an illustration, *pure in heart* refers to those whose motives are unmixed or to those who do things for the right reasons. That is integrity. Sometimes no one else sees or knows when you are doing things for the right reasons, but God sees and knows.

Blessed are you when you do things for the right motives, because when people do things for the right reasons, they see God in a way that others cannot. Have you ever found yourself saying *People see what they want to see?*

28

People see things different ways: A biologist and an artist look at a plant in different ways. A poet and an astronomer do not look at the stars in the same way. When you choose the course of doing things from the right reasons, you climb a little higher and see a little more of God's face – *the upright shall behold his face.*

PRAYER: Dear God, help me to do things for the right reasons, even if no one else knows or sees. May I choose as one of my highest goals to be a good person. May my deeds be pleasing to you. Amen.

THIRTEEN

But I trusted in your steadfast love; my heart shall rejoice in your salvation.
13:5

God's salvation causes the Psalmist's heart to rejoice. For anything to have that effect, we want to know more about it, for it might cause our heart to rejoice too. How might we understand the word *salvation*? In a purely secular sense, it can mean deliverance from difficulties or preservation from bad things happening. That alone could cause a heart to rejoice. It is a common theme for the Psalmist, for he uses the word more than all the books in the Old Testament and more than all the times it is used in the New Testament. Theologically the word is often referred to as deliverance from sin and its consequences, or to rescue from danger or destruction. That too could cause a heart to rejoice.

One translation of the Greek word *sozo*, which is the root word for *saved*, is *to* be *made whole*. That makes sense when we consider that Jesus came that we may be made whole – now, today, in the present moment, on earth as it is in heaven. How can a person be whole without attending to his or her spirit? What is the opposite of being whole? It is fragmented. Sometime is missing from a person who does not have God as a part of his or her life. Paul wrote to the Colossians (1:17) that *"in him all things hold together."* God's salvation helps us to be whole people and in Jesus all things hold together. He helps you to hold your life together. God sent Jesus to make you whole, to save you from being fragmented but never to condemn, as Jesus insisted in John 3. Jesus came to make us whole, to deliver us and to rescue us when we end up being the wrong person in the wrong place at the wrong time. Jesus came to help people who are in the wrong place.

The Apostle Paul affirmed that *"In hope we are saved."* (Romans 8:24). Looking at the word *sozo*, we can paraphrase to say that in hope, we are made whole, delivered, protected and healed. In your hope, you are made whole. But healed?

An enlightened nurse – a woman of faith – explained how illness is the opposite of wholeness. *"Healing occurs,"* she says, *"when we achieve a sense of wholeness and spiritual well-being, even though the illness or disability may not be cured."* Do you see the difference between being cured and being healed? You can achieve a sense of wholeness and spiritual well-being even though the illness or disability may not be cured. How astute to recognize that being healed is not identical with being cured.

The Psalmist recognized that it was God who delivered him from trouble. God saved him because he trusted in God's steadfast love. Let us look to his trust in God for inspiration and know that our God desires us to be whole, spiritually healthy people.

PRAYER: Dear God, help me to trust you more. Thank you for all the times you were with me, helped me, saved me from trouble and strengthened my spirit to face challenges and opportunities. When I think about it and recall your help to me, it makes me want to rejoice. Guide me, O Lord, into a sense of spiritual well-being. Amen.

FOURTEEN

You would confound the plans of the poor, but the Lord is their refuge.
14:6

The pronoun can seem confusing in this verse. It does not make sense that God who is the refuge to the poor would also confound the plans of the poor. The Psalmist often addresses God as *you* or *thou*, so it may be that the pronoun in this verse applies to the evildoers described in the previous verses: *Have they no knowledge, all the evildoers who eat up my people as they eat bread, and do not call upon the Lord? There they shall be in great terror, for God is with the company of the righteous.*

The part which bears no confusion is that the poor find their refuge in the Lord. God is an advocate for the poor. Presumably, God's people should advocate for the poor on God's behalf. The book of Proverbs (14:31) says *"Those who oppress the poor insult their Maker, but those who are kind to the needy honor him."* Proverbs also notes that *"Whoever is kind to the poor lends to the LORD, and will be repaid in full."* (19:17).

Jesus too advocated from the poor. He healed the poor, ate with the poor, and cared for the poor. He lifted up a poor widow who put a mite in the offering as the model for generosity. He preached about bringing good news to the poor: *"The Spirit of the Lord is upon me, because he has anointed me to bring good news to the poor…"* (Luke 4:18a). He encouraged generosity to the poor: *"Be generous. Give to the poor."* (Luke 12:33,34, The Message). The Bible lifts up God as a refuge for the poor.

But could there be a deeper meaning? Consider Jesus' beatitude *"Blessed are the poor in spirit, for theirs is the kingdom of heaven."* (Matthew 5:3). It does not say *poor*, although Luke's version does. I think Matthew's version is more accurate. Sometimes people who are poor feel blessed, even more so than those who are not poor. But it is not consistent with the rest of Jesus' teachings to think he believed poverty was a good thing.

Jesus would never have called *blessed* a condition where people live in slums, do not have enough to eat or where health deteriorates. Christians, in service to God, aim to remove that kind of poverty from God's children.

This says *poor in spirit*. The first thing that might pop into the mind is why does it not say *rich* in spirit? That would appear to make sense. You would think that a person of faith who has cultivated a deep, seasoned walk with God and a maturity of spirit would be rich in spirit and thereby blessed. But Jesus chose the opposite word.

Blessed are those who know they are spiritually poor. To recognize your own spiritual poverty is to know you are dependent upon God to fulfill your spiritual needs. To recognize your spiritual poverty is the realization that *"I do not have enough of what I need... so I'm going to have to trust God... and I know I can."* When the light bulb goes on and a believer recognizes that he or she needs God, the blessing begins.

If you feel like your spirit is not strong enough, good enough, deep enough or rich enough, then you recognize your need for God's help. You own up to your spiritual poverty. When you turn to God, you are blessed. In the gem from the Psalm, poor need not be limited to a socio-economic status, but to anyone who recognizes their own poverty of spirit and therefore turns to God to find refuge. For all who realize that they must trust in and depend upon God, God will be their refuge.

PRAYER: Dear God, lead me to be more generous to those who are in need. As I consider the state of my own spiritual strength, I recognize that it's not so great. I turn to you out of my need. Be Thou my refuge, Compassionate God. Amen.

FIFTEEN

O Lord, who may abide in your tent? Who may dwell on your holy hill? Those who walk blamelessly, and do what is right, and speak the truth from their heart;
15:1, 2

Tell the truth. That is the lesson parents desire to instill in their children. It is the message from the Bible and it is the wisdom from the ages. The Psalmist captures this basic life principle in simple and few words: Do what is right. Speak the truth. In our time, truth has become bent out of shape. If news is reported that is not liked or flattering, it can be labeled as false news. If judges in courts rule against what is desired, they can be labeled as partial to another party. Information about actions which go against what is best for people can be "spun" to sound like just the opposite. People who lie, tell half-truths or spin their interpretation of reality lose the trust of others. Think of a political leader whom you do not trust to tell the truth. Or a business executive. Or a TV ad. Or a family member or friend. Oh, what a world his could be if people spoke the truth.

The Bible's message is for you and me to speak the truth. It is the way of God.

Truthful lips endure forever, but a lying tongue is but for a moment.
Proverbs 12:19

These are the things that you shall do: Speak the truth to one another; render in your gates judgments that are true and make for peace;
Zechariah 8:16

Therefore, having put away falsehood, let each one of you speak the truth with his neighbor, for we are members one of another.
Ephesians 4:25

34

Speaking the truth can be hard. Sometimes little white lies or half truths have advantages. And yet, the wisdom of the ages captures the value and need for us to be people of integrity to speak the truth:

Honesty is the first chapter of the book of wisdom.
Thomas Jefferson

Never be afraid to raise your voice for honesty and truth and compassion against injustice and lying and greed. If people all over the world...would do this, it would change the earth.
William Faulkner

Truth never damages a cause that is just.
Mahatma Gandhi

We learned about honesty and integrity – that the truth matters... that you don't take shortcuts or play by your own set of rules... and success doesn't count unless you earn it fair and square.
Michelle Obama

No legacy is so rich as Honesty.
William Shakespeare

In a time of universal deceit, telling the truth is a revolutionary act.
George Orwell

Who lies for you will lie against you.
Bosnian Proverb

A half truth is a whole lie.
Yiddish Proverb

Truth is such a rare thing, it is delightful to tell it.
Emily Dickinson

The least initial deviation from the truth is multiplied later a thousand fold.
Aristotle

In a room where people unanimously maintain a conspiracy of silence, one word of truth sounds like a pistol shot.
Czesław Miłosz

A lie has speed, but truth has endurance.
Edgar J. Mohn

When you stretch the truth, watch out for the snapback.
Bill Copeland

When you tell a lie, you steal someone's right to the truth.
Khaled Hosseini, The Kite Runner

A lie gets halfway around the world before the truth has a chance to put its pants on.
Winston Churchill

One of the most striking differences between a cat and a lie is that a cat has only nine lives. Mark Twain

PRAYER: Dear God, forgive my past half-truths and lies and lead me in the pathway of honesty. Guide me to choose to tell the truth. I want to be a person of integrity who can be trusted. Amen.

SIXTEEN

You show me the path of life. In your presence there is fullness of joy; in your right hand are pleasures forevermore. (16:11)

In God's presence there is fullness of joy. Ideally, when you go to worship or when you engage in private devotions, your hope is to seek an encounter with the Divine. What you are seeking is nothing short of desiring to find yourself in God's presence.

There may be times when we worship, pray, or pursue our devotions when we do not sense God's presence. Maybe we wonder if we are doing something wrong or not uttering the correct order of words in prayer. God's presence is full of mystery. Sometimes it comes to us when least expected, like a surprise. Because the Psalmist speaks frequently of being in God's presence – and he had no special gift for this that would exclude you from the same experience – then let us consider pathways which men and women have found over the eons to tiptoe into the very presence of the Almighty.

ANTICIPATION and EXPECTATION. Look forward to your next time at worship, or your personal devotions, or even your walk with God in nature. Anticipate that the next time you enter a sanctuary for the worship of God, you will go to actively participate in worship and you will enter with the expectation of some kind of encounter with the Divine. Open your soul to allow God to enter, to speak to you, to move you, to be present with you. Close your eyes to drown out all external sounds to focus upon you entering into the very presence of God. It need not feel like the most earth-shattering experience you have ever had. God's presence can often best be found in the ordinary. By anticipating your worship, you prepare yourself, you open your heart, you engage your readiness and you center upon the most important experience of the worship service, which is for you to find yourself in the presence of the Divine.

INVITATION. Invite God into your soul and treat God as an honored guest. There is a famous painting of Jesus standing at a door titled "The Light of the World" by the English artist William Holman Hunt (1827–1910) representing the figure of Jesus preparing to knock on an unopened door, illustrating Revelation 3:20: *"Listen! I am standing at the door, knocking; if you hear my voice and open the door, I will come in to you and eat with you, and you with me."* According to Hunt: "I painted the picture with what I thought, unworthy though I was, to be by Divine command, and not simply as a good Subject." The door in the painting has no handle. It can be opened only from the inside. Imagine the Son of God himself standing outside your door. There is no latch for him to open the door. He will not push himself in. And so, he knocks, but he will not enter unless invited in. I will stand at your door and knock. The door metaphor contains a powerful message about the nature and character of God. God knocks on a person's door, but if the person will not open the door to extend hospitality, welcome and openness, God will not enter. It is as though the Divine calls out: "The ball is in your court!" Create a mental picture of God standing at your door, knocking. Open it widely to welcome God in.

SEEKING. If you want to discover the presence of God, seek it. In the book of Jeremiah (29:13), God spoke, saying *"You will seek me and find me, when you seek me with all your heart."* To seek is an active verb, not passive. It prompts us to do something, to take action, to go looking and searching. If we wish to share with the Psalmist's experience of being in God's presence, the journey requires our intent to seek it. In the bookstore at a Benedictine Priory, I saw a sign that said *"That which you are seeking is causing you to seek."* The majestic and mysterious wonder of God may be reaching down to touch you and cause you to seek God's presence.

FASTING. Not from food. We usually think of fasting as giving up food. Fasting is not about food, although some people do fast from eating. You can fast from anything. A fast does not have to be for 40 days. It can be for 30 minutes. The purpose of fasting is to seek to know God in a deeper experience. In fasting, you give something up to center your spirit, to be led beside the still waters and to restore your soul.

Here is an idea: fast from noise. Take a half-hour vacation from the screen, from electronics, from anything you can control that makes sound. The purpose of fasting is to seek to know God in a deeper experience. Fast when you can to experience God's presence in your life. Half an hour without some electronic screen? What am I supposed to do? I will suffer from withdraw! Answer: use that brief time to seek to be in the presence of the Divine.

SILENCE. Set aside a few minutes for silence. What? I can't... be... silent. What will I do? Shouldn't I at least be asking for something, for someone else if not for myself? I can't not talk or think or plan or act. Yes. You can. Teach yourself to appreciate silence. Mother Teresa wrote that *"God is the friend of silence. We need to find God and God cannot be found in noise and restlessness. See how nature, the trees, the flowers, the grass grow in perfect silence. See the stars, the moon and the sun, how they move in silence. The more we receive in silent prayer, the more we can give in our active life. Silence gives us a new outlook on everything."* Ironically, research indicates that multi-tasking decreases your effectiveness. And silence gives you a new outlook on everything. Why not choose to go placidly amid the noise and haste, and remember what peace there may be in silence?

CHANGE YOUR VERB. Everyone clamors to know "What's your plan? What are your goals? Where are you heading? What do you want? What are you doing today? Where are you going next?" The verb: to do. The world grabs at you and wants to know what you are to do. It seems to be all about doing. Change your verb from doing to being. To be. Actually, God's name is *to be*: *God said to Moses, "I am who I am." He said further, "Thus you shall say to the Israelites, 'I am has sent me to you.'"* (Exodus 3:14). "I am" is the verb "to be." God is being. Take minute sabbaticals to rest from the world's requirement that you "do" and instead, just "be." When you are engaged in any spiritual practice with the intent of seeking to be in the presence of the Divine, just be. Be yourself, be who you really are, bring all of your being to God and enter into the presence of the Almighty.

PRAYER: Loving God, more than anything, I would like to feel myself in your presence. I seek after you, I open the door of my heart for you to enter, and I want you to be with me. In this day, guide me to walk in your pathways and to sense that you are by my side. Amen.

SEVENTEEN

I call upon you, for you will answer me, O God; incline your ear to me, hear my words. Wondrously show your steadfast love.
17:6, 7

This is another of those wonderful *"you too?"* expressions in the Psalms. We have an inclination that God hears our prayers, but the intensity of our need prompts us to plead... answer me. Incline our ear to me... hear my words. The Psalmist lays bare his feelings about craving God's attention and we feel that way too. Not to sound sac religious, but there are times we want to ask "Are you listening to me, God?"

When Stephen Spielberg produced the movie *"ET"* one of the most amazing features of that movie was that it was filmed from a child's-eye view, about knee-cap high. When the camera looked at adults, it looked up. When the camera looked at a child, it was on the same eye level. The Psalmist asks God to come down to my eye level. In his book of prayers titled <u>Are You Running with Me Jesus</u> Malcolm Boyd is talking to God about being busy and on the run. The prayer goes: *"Where am I running? You know these things I cannot understand. It is not that I need to have you tell me. What counts most is just that somebody knows, and it is you. That helps a lot."*

We know that God hears all of our prayers. We may not receive everything we ask for in the way we desire it, but we trust that God knows what is best for us and will answer us, as God loves and cares for our very best interests.

PRAYER: Dear God, sometimes I feel far from you and I want to holler "Answer me!" Strengthen my faith to know that you care for what is best for me in the long run, that you hear my words and that you appreciate my reaching up to you. Even before I reach up to you, Dear Lord, you have already sensed what is in my heart and you are reaching out to me and calling me to trust and be faithful. Amen.

41

EIGHTEEN

By you I can crush a troop, and by my God I can leap over a wall.
18:29

This gem is about the Psalmist's positive attitude. The Bible's attitude is a can-do attitude. That is how David slew Goliath. He believed he could. He said so in this Psalm and again when he faced Goliath (2 Samuel 22:30): *"By you I can crush a troop, and by my God I can leap over a wall."* This phrase is hyperbole, a dramatic or exaggerated statement to illustrate the point that by your God you can embrace the attitude to leap over walls that appear to block your way.

The Bible encourages a can-do attitude:

"I can do all things through him who strengthens me." (Philippians 4:13)

"If God is for us, who is against us?" (Romans 8:31b)

"With God all things are possible." (Matthew 19:26)

"...all things are possible to the one who believes." (Mark 9:23)

Many figures through history embraced this attitude:

Ralph Waldo Emerson, quoting a Roman general, wrote *"They can conquer who believe they can."*

Henry Ford observed: *"If you think you can or can't, you are right!"*

Jesus' parable of the mustard seed is one of his most beloved parables, perhaps because of its potential to speak to the faith of every person. *"If you have faith the size of a mustard seed, you will say to this mountain, 'Move from here to there,' and it will move; and nothing will be impossible for you'.* (Matthew 17:20b). If you have even the tiniest seed of faith you can move mountains of challenges, problems or opportunities. The mustard seed is the smallest of seeds. You do not need the towering faith of a saint or the mature wisdom of a life tempered by experience. It is enough to come to Jesus with whatever faith you have. The mustard seed illustration invites you to trust that your faith is sufficient for God to give you the attitude to move mountains, leap over walls, and to believe that nothing will be impossible for you.

Over the doorway to a church hangs a sign which says: *"We believe that the power behind us is greater than the task ahead."* That is in the spirit of the Psalmist's teaching about leaping over walls. Adopt that attitude that *"I believe that the power behind me is greater than the task ahead."*

PRAYER: Dear God, please give me a stronger faith to have a positive attitude. Help me to trust in you and to believe in myself. Instill in me a can-do spirit. Amen.

NINETEEN

The heavens are telling the glory of God; and the firmament proclaims his handiwork.
19:1

The heavens tell of God's glory. This is metaphor, of course, but to the Psalmist, everything in creation speaks of the glory of God.

That idea is so profound and mysterious that it requires poets, psalmists and musicians to tell about it. Like the hymn...

This is my Father's world,
And to my listening ears,
All nature sings and round me rings
The music of the spheres.

This is my Father's world.
I rest me in the thought
Of rocks and trees,
Of skies and seas,
His hand the wonders wrought.

Or, consider the Psalm after which this book is titled:
"O Lord, our Lord, how majestic is thy name in all the earth!
Thou whose glory above the heavens is chanted... When I look at
thy heavens, the work of thy fingers, the moon and the stars which
thou hast established; what is man that thou art mindful of him,
and the son of man that thou dost care for him?" (Psalm 8:1, 3, 4, RSV).

Or, consider how God told Job about the creation, adding *"when the morning stars sang together   and all the heavenly beings shouted for joy?"* (Job 38:7), which is interesting, because scientists have found that each star emits a radio signal that identifies it from all other stars. It is like the stars really do sing!

To these majestic and poetic descriptions, the Apostle Paul adds his conviction that not only is God the creator but that God's power and divine nature are understood and seen through God's creation:

"Ever since the creation of the world his eternal power and divine nature, invisible though they are, have been understood and seen through the things he has made." (Romans 1:20).

A plaque read "When God is Lord, everything is sacred." Let us attempt to see through the lenses of the Psalmist to see that everything in the heavens and in the firmament proclaims God's handiwork.

PRAYER: Dear God, teach me to see better so that I may see you in rocks and trees, in stars and in all that you have created. Grant that I may see the beauty, the good and your loving touch in all that you have made which tells of your glory. Amen.

TWENTY

Some take pride in chariots, and some in horses, but our pride is in the name of the Lord our God.
20:7

The horse was a beast of war. When a king came riding up to the gates on a horse, he was bent on war. The colt was a beast of peace. When a king approached the gates on a colt, he came intending to seek peace. It is interesting that when Jesus entered Jerusalem for the last time on what we celebrate as Palm Sunday, he arrived on a colt rather than a horse, for Jesus came as the Prince of Peace.

Psalm 20 is a prayer for victory, petitioning God to be on the Psalmist's side. In any skirmish where adversaries meet, that is the prayer... that God would be on our side. A movie in the 1960's, The Longest Day, portrayed the events of D Day during World War Two from both the Allied and the German point of view. One scene portrayed Americans planning for the battle with a battle planner commenting "I hope God is on our side." Immediately following, a German battle planner commented "I hope God is on our side." The juxtaposition illustrated the illusion that God is on the winning team's side.

Does God take sides? The message from Paul is that God is the Father of all the nations and loves each person on every side. In Romans he wrote *"I have made you the father of many nations."* (4:17). There is a wonderful, newer hymn by Lloyd Stone, sung to the tune Finlandia, which puts to music the same idea as Paul's verse:

This is my song, O God of all the nations,
A song of peace for lands afar and mine.
This is my home, the country where my heart is,
Here are my hopes, my dreams, my holy shrine.
But other hearts in other lands are beating,
With hopes and dreams as true and high as mine.

46

My country's skies are bluer than the ocean,
And sunlight beams on clover leaf and pine.
But other lands have sunlight too, and clover,
And skies are everywhere as blue as mine.
O hear my song, thou God of all the nations,
A song of peace for their land and for mine.

God is the God of all the nations. Not just ours. A nation is fortunate when people love their own land and value their country's beauty and goodness. A citizen can love his or her own land without denying others the same love for their land. When we feel we are the best, we lose connectedness with our brothers and sisters. For God so love the world… and not just a few chosen countries. God's love is global. No fences, boundaries or borders.

The Psalmist, apparently in battle with adversaries, prays for victory and believes in the rightness of his position. We would too in the face of threat. Then the Psalmist adds *"but our pride is in the name of the Lord our God."* Abraham Lincoln, when asked during the Civil War if he thought God was on our side, said: *"Sir, my concern is not whether God is on our side. My great concern is to be on God's side."*

That is what we would want, to follow in the way of the Prince of Peace, and there are many places where the Psalmist desires that too. Let that prayer be ever on our lips:

PRAYER: Dear God, may I always desire to be on your side. When facing threats or battles, may I always seek your will and to represent your values of love, forgiveness, grace and kindness. Amen.

TWENTY-ONE

Your hand will find out all your enemies; your right hand will find out those who hate you. You will make them like a fiery furnace when you appear.
21:8, 9

You do not find poems, edifying stories or beloved hymns inspired by Psalm 21. I try to imagine the Psalmist's mother saying "David, it's not nice to wish for bad things to happen to enemies and hope God sends them to a fiery furnace." The tone of the Psalm sounds unlike the loving, grace-giving, forgiving and merciful God which Jesus taught about. So how can this Psalm be considered a gem? It might make us wonder how it even made it into the Bible.

Therein lies its value. Whether or not the expression is theologically correct, it describes the real, heart-wrenching feeling experienced by the writer. The enemies he talks about are not his own, but are the enemies of God. The writer is speaking not about God but to God: *"Your hand will find out all your enemies..."* The Psalmist craves that there will be some sort of justice, that those who choose to hate God will eventually be found out and punished. He is not wishing this for those who love God or even those who may be indifferent, but rather for those who actively and purposefully hate God. Those are the ones who have self-selected to exclude themselves from God's love.

A woman lost her husband of many decades. They loved each other dearly and experienced life together fully. After his death, she said "I'm mad at God. Why would God allow my husband to die?" She still clung to her faith, still believed in God, and still worshipped, but she had to let her feelings out: I'm mad at God. This is not who the Psalmist is talking about. Indeed, God is big enough to embrace her feelings of pain. Like a loving parent, God still loves her just as much and easily forgives any misunderstanding she may have about the nature of the Divine.

Another person might feel even more strongly, might even say the words "I hate you God for what you have allowed," and still God hears, understands, loves and gives the gift of grace.

That may be the sense of what occurs in Psalm 21. The Psalmist, humanly, expresses his emotions and wants God to punish those who hate God. The lesson from the overwhelming message of the Bible is that even with expressions like that, God still hears, understands, loves and gives grace. That may signal that there may be times when you and I have said things to God which were expressions of our anger or disappointment, and we wonder if God will punish us for that. And it is almost as though God, the Divine Counselor, replies "Let it out. Express what you feel. I will not stop loving you."

PRAYER: O God, I have said things or at least thought things which accused you of not caring enough. I have wished for bad things to happen to others. I have hoped that you would condemn people who have done evil. Forgive me for not understanding your ways. Thank you for forgiving me and loving me anyway. Amen.

TWENTY-TWO

My God, my God, why have you forsaken me? Why are you so far from helping me, from the words of my groaning?
22:1

The Psalmist is not one to hesitate to let his feelings hang out. Now he feels abandoned, no, even stronger, forsaken by God. Deserted. It was not so many Psalms ago that he gave thanks to the Lord, sang praises to the Most High and proclaimed *"How majestic is your name in all the earth!"* In an earlier Psalm (4:8b) he wrote *"...for you alone, O Lord, make me lie down in safety."* Now he feels forsaken. His feelings seem like a yo-yo, up and down, high and low. Perhaps this is one of the charms of the Psalms. People can relate to them because sometimes we feel that way too, wondering *"Why are you so far from helping me, from the words of my groaning?"*

The Psalmist is not shouting these innermost feelings from the rooftops or delivering them in the Temple. Rather, he is directing them to God and to God alone. People are inclined to tell God in private about how they feel in ways that they would never share with another human. We only know about these most intimate thoughts because they come from the Psalmist's own pen.

This gem from the Psalms sounds familiar to Christians because they recognize it as one of Jesus' seven last words from the cross: *And about three o'clock Jesus cried with a loud voice, "Eli, Eli, lema sabachthani?" that is, "My God, my God, why have you forsaken me?"* (Matthew 27:46). Jesus knew this Psalm. This is worthy to take note of: Jesus read and knew the Psalms. On the cross, he was quoting his own Bible. Jesus felt the same way! He used the Psalmist's words to describe his own depths of abandonment. That sounds like a very human cry of rejection. If that is what it was, it assures that God can understand it when you and I do not feel valued, wanted, included, appreciated or needed. God hears when we cry with a sense of abandonment.

It is often the words to a psalm or a hymn that come to mind in troubled times as well as in times of praise for God. Some read the Psalms, love them and internalize them so that the Psalms become their own words. Repeating a Psalm can often express a feeling better than our own words can express. This was the human side of Jesus speaking. He was God, he was man. Now he expresses the depths of despair and feelings of abandonment like we do. Is that not a natural human thing to do?

After a natural disaster, it is not uncommon for the question to be raised: Where was God? How could a loving God allow this to happen? Same with violence on the streets or from wars or hunger, poverty, meanness, poor government leadership, disease or the loss of a loved one – we might question the same way. Did you ever feel that way? We know in our heart of hearts that God is with us and God loves us and loves them but there are times the question haunts: My God, my God, why hast thou forsaken me?

The feelings were temporary for Jesus and for the Psalmist, both of whom devoted their lives and work to the glory of God. In the New Testament, God reassures *"I will never leave you or forsake you."* (Hebrews 13:5). When we feel far away from God or even wondering why God does not help us or hear the words of our groaning, we are in good company. And also like the Psalmist and like Jesus, may we too hold steadfast to our faith, love and devotion to God, knowing in our hearts that God will never leave us nor forsake us.

PRAYER: Loving God, know that I love you and trust in you, even if there are moments when I feel abandoned or forsaken. Thank you for your everlasting love which never lets me go. Amen.

TWENTY-THREE

The Lord is my shepherd, I shall not want.
23:1

Psalm 23 is one of the greatest works of literature ever penned by humankind. If the Psalms were mountains, Psalm 23 is Mount Everest. It is one of humanity's favorites. A woman told me she always thought of it as a funeral Psalm because that is the only time she ever heard it. I make the case that it is an everyday Psalm which you can use to center your faith and to lead you into the presence of the Divine, which I did in my book *Psalm 23: An Everyday Psalm*. There is far too much in the Psalm to cover it all here, so I will focus only on the first verse.

The Lord is my Shepherd

To say *The Lord is my Shepherd* is to utter the most powerful faith statement a person can make. Much as the word *Islam* means *submission*, a person of faith who declares *The Lord is my Shepherd* gives himself or herself over to management by Another.

To recognize that you are the sheep and God is the Shepherd is a choice which goes against every fiber of our independent natures. Are we not inclined to desire to be the master of our fate and captain of our soul? Yet here in five words is a personal faith statement that yields to the will of another. Jesus taught followers to pray *Thy will be done*. A beloved hymn by Adelaide A. Pollard goes *Have Thine own way, Lord, Have Thine own way*. To choose to follow the Shepherd indicates a willingness to be yielded.

There is a difference between saying *The Lord is a shepherd* and *The Lord is my shepherd*. Anyone can acknowledge *The Lord is a shepherd*. It is possible to acknowledge that something exists and yet have no feeling about it. U.S. polls frequently report that more than nine out of ten Americans believe there is a God. But believing that God exists or describing the characteristics of God as they might be found in an encyclopedia is a far cry from describing yourself as one who chooses to be owned by and managed by the Shepherd. This is the difference between knowing about God and knowing God.

This is a Psalm for those who desire to belong to the Shepherd, to be owned by God and to be see God as owner and manager. *We are his people, and the sheep of his pasture.* (Psalm 100:3b). God is not <u>a</u> shepherd. God is <u>my</u> shepherd. Psalm 23 is based upon the Shepherd knowing each sheep individually... knowing you and being known by you because the Lord is your Shepherd. Religion, theology, faith, and life can become complicated. The majesty of Psalm 23 rests upon its simplicity. Perhaps it is enough to declare ever so simply that *The Lord is my Shepherd.*

<u>I shall not want</u>

This verse can be interpreted to mean *"I shall want for nothing."* When the Lord is my shepherd, I shall have everything I need. <u>The Message</u> puts it this way: *"I don't need a thing."*

Look for a moment at what the verse does NOT say. This is not a commandment from the Almighty on high declaring *"Thou shalt not want."* The verse is not telling you that you should not want. That would be unnatural and impractical. We want stuff all the time. Our lives are filled with wanting.

A member of the elite wealthy Forbes 400 was at a dinner party where a woman had a moment alone with the great man. She asked, *"Sir, I am curious. How much does a person need to be happy?"* He knew the answer and without a second's hesitation replied *"Just a little bit more."*

That does not sound greedy... *just a little bit more.* It describes our never-ending wanting. It would seem an unnatural and impossible expectation for the Psalm to suggest we should not want. Our lives are dominated by wanting. Who would dare to tell people who are hungry that they should not want food? Do we not want better lives for our children and grandchildren?

Do we not want to aspire to be the most we can be as people and in our careers? Do we not want to acquire sufficient resources for retirement, health care and the enjoyment of life?

Wanting just a *little bit more* is subtle. It sneaks up on you. It invades your spirit. It changes how you see. At its worst, it can metastasize like spreading cancer throughout the soul and turn into full-blown materialism, even in the best of people.

However, the Psalm does not say *"Do not want."* It is not a commandment or even advice for you from Holy Scripture. Rather, it is a faith statement from one who has chosen to be managed by the Shepherd. WHEN the Lord is my shepherd, the Psalmist writes, THEN I shall want for nothing. I shall have the vital things in life that I need and the most important: a relationship with God.

Might a person think that choosing to follow the Shepherd means giving up a valued part of life? Jesus, who described himself as the Good Shepherd, said that he came that followers *"may have life, and have it abundantly"* (John 10:10). Paul too used the word when he wrote *"God is able to provide you with every blessing in abundance, so that by always having enough of everything, you may share abundantly in every good work"* (2 Corinthians 9:8).

A person who says *"The Lord is my Shepherd, I shall not want"* can discover a newfound way of seeing. Instead of seeing through lenses of scarcity, he or she sees through lenses of abundance. Changing the way you see has potential to change your enjoyment of life. As Wayne Dyer, American philosopher (1940-2015) noted "If you change the way you look at things, the things you look at change." When you choose to see through lenses of abundance, your focus is no longer on what you do not have, what you cannot do, or what is wrong. Now your focus centers upon what you do have, what you can do, and what is right. This does not happen by magic. Rather, what changes is your resolve. You determine that you will see through lenses of abundance.

When suddenly you worry about what you do not have or perhaps about a regret over a past decision, your spirit resolves to look instead at your abundance. This is why it is possible for people of faith who have suffered loss, illness, tragedy or bad things happening to them can still proclaim *"The Lord is my Shepherd, I shall not want."* They have shifted their way of seeing from lenses of scarcity to lenses of abundance. They have transformed their focus into a God-like way of seeing. Make that your choice: determine that you will see through lenses of abundance rather than lenses of scarcity.

PRAYER: This Psalm is my prayer, O God. You are my Shepherd. I give myself over to you to lead me and guide me. I belong to you. With you, I have all that I need. Help me to change my vision to choose to see through lenses of abundance, to see all that I do have and can do. Amen.

TWENTY-FOUR

The earth is the Lord's and all that is in it, the world, and those who live in it;
24:1

With just five words, the Psalmist captured the entire theology of environmental stewardship. In this phrase is the most important apostrophe on the Bible. *Lord's*. Possessive case. The earth belongs to God. God possesses it. God possessed it in the past, possesses it now and will possess the earth in the future. It is God's. Not ours. We are its managers. We manage the earth on behalf of the one who entrusted it to us.

A great synonym for the word *steward* is *manager*. A steward or manager is a person who looks after another's property, finances, or other affairs. The Parable of the Talents in Matthew 25 talks about the owner entrusting to his servants the management of his assets. *Entrusting* is the key word. And so, God entrusts to us the looking after and managing that which belongs, not to us, but to God: the earth. God is the owner and possessor. We are the managers.

Here is an interesting idea: when the earth is the Lord's, nothing is secular. To the person who believes that the earth is the Lord's and that God is creator of all, nothing is secular. Everything is sacred and is treated that way. A Native American leader told how every time the Indian dances, he or she touches the earth twice: one light step gently taps the earth to signify that the ground is holy. Then the Indian steps to the ground in dance with the other foot. Each step begins with a touch. Touch. Step. Touch. Step. In a sacred dance, the Native American touches the earth twice to signify that the earth is sacred and therefore all things are connected. Take another look at how you see God's creation and consider treating the earth as sacred because it belongs to God. In much the same way, every woman and man, every boy and girl is viewed as a unique wonder, never to be repeated in all of history, and should be treated as God's most sacred creation.

The gospel of John (3:16a) says *"For God so loved the world that he gave his only Son…"* The Greek word used in this verse for *world* is *kosmos*. That is where our word *cosmos* comes from. Here the word refers not just to planet earth but to all of God's creation, through time and space. One of the translations of the word for *saved*, from the Greek *sozo*, is "to be made whole." So, the following verse, John 3:17, could be understood to mean: *"Indeed, God did not send the Son into the world to condemn the cosmos, but in order that the cosmos might be made whole through him."* The broadens our understanding of God's love considerably and tells of God's love for all the cosmos.

So, as we consider these powerful five words from Psalm 24, let us pledge to be caretaking stewards of that which belongs to God, let us also love what God so loves, and let us care to make it healthy and whole. We do this for ourselves, for future generations, but most of all, we do it for the One we love, who entrusts it to us.

PRAYER: Grant that we may be good stewards of this beautiful swirling blue-green sphere that you created and which belongs to you. Help us to adopt the attitude that the earth is yours and we will care for it because of our love for you. Then, may we see every inch of land and sea as sacred, because it is created by you and so loved by you. Amen.

TWENTY-FIVE

He leads the humble in what is right, and teaches the humble his way.
25:9

The Psalmist describes two of God's attributes: God leads and God teaches. In a way, these two attributes are the same. The Latin root of the word "to educate" is "to lead." To lead is to educate, and to educate is to lead. Sometimes God leads us by teaching us. God leads the humble in what is right and teaches the humble God's way. The Psalmist is astute to recognize that the humble can be led and taught. On the flip side of the coin, a know-it-all or one who is full of pride cannot be taught and cannot be led, because he or she is not open to God's leading.

Charles Spurgeon said *"Humility is the proper estimate of oneself."* Right on. The humble man or woman does not think too highly of himself or herself. She or he has no need for constant stroking of the ego. While the Psalmist puts it in the positive, the author of Proverbs tells it this way: *"Pride goes before destruction, and a haughty spirit before a fall."* (Proverbs 16:18) and *"When pride comes, then comes disgrace."* (Proverbs 11:2).

The word *pride* illustrates a dichotomy. There is good pride and there is bad pride. Good pride is when you are proud of your child or grandchild, when you feel good about something you did well, or when you are proud of your nation, state or community. How wonderful it feels to hear someone say "I'm proud of you." Good pride represents our self-respect and dignity. Bad pride, on the other hand, is vain, self-centered, conceited and delights in calling attention to itself. Bad pride hogs the spotlight. It is conceited and arrogant. Jane Austen, in <u>Pride and Prejudice</u>, wrote *"Vanity and pride are different things, though the words are often used synonymously. A person may be proud without being vain. Pride relates more to our opinion of ourselves, vanity to what we would have others think of us."* The pride spoken of in Proverbs is the bad pride, the vain and the egotistical.

The pleasure of good pride can morph into bad pride. When another speaks well of you or praises you, it feels good. You like hearing it. Soon you wish you could hear even more of it. When others pay attention to you, you could begin to crave more. Chazz Palminteri, a playwright and screenwriter, said *"Oh, great reviews are the worst. They mislead you more than the bad ones, because they only fuel your ego. Then you only want another one, like potato chips, and the best thing you get is fat and bloated."*

In Galatians 5:23, Paul wrote about self-control as one of the fruits of the spirit. The word he employed for *self-control* means having the ego under control. We all have an ego. We desire to be valued, cherished, appreciated or at least noticed. When we are not, sometimes we call too much attention to ourselves. That backfires. When the ego gets out of control, you cannot do anything and no one thinks highly of you. In fact, they will think more highly of you when your focus shifts to them. When thoughts or prayers are dominated by the first-person singular pronoun, the prescription to this weakness is to invite God's spirit within to help refocus your aim. The fruit of the spirit describe the goals of a person who desires for God's spirit to dwell within. When we see this fruit of self-control weakening or lacking in ourselves, it is a red flag signaling us that we are running short of God's spirit. In response, a person who recognizes this need within will set as his or her life-goals the fruits of the spirit: love, joy, peace, patience, kindness, goodness, faithfulness, gentleness and self-control. Those become the goals of a person who desires to live a God-like life. Self-control leads to humility, which is open to being led by God and taught by God.

The word Paul used for self-control, in Greek, is *praus*. This is the same exact word Jesus used in the beatitudes (Matthew 5:5) when he said *"Blessed are the meek..."* To paraphrase, Blessed are those who have the ego under control. The Greek word for *meek* (*praus*) is not the way we usually think of meek. Meek here has to do with having your ego under control. Self-control, *praus*, brings the ego back into control. It takes a humble person to desire for God's spirit to dwell within.

59

Self-control is a form of humility. Without humility, a person cannot learn, because you cannot teach a know-it-all. Without humility, a person cannot love, because all a narcissist can consider is herself or himself. Without humility, there can be no right relationship to God, who said in Isaiah (57:15) *"I dwell in the high and holy place, and also with the person who is of a contrite and humble spirit..."*

Do not be distracted by the egotism or lack of humility in others. Rather, allow this gem from Psalm 25 to speak to your own growth as a person of faith: *He leads the humble in what is right, and teaches the humble his way.*

As you center yourself upon this gem, consider some wisdom of the ages:

"Humility is not thinking less of yourself, but thinking of yourself less." C.S Lewis

I tell my kids and I tell proteges, always have humility when you create and grace when you succeed, because it's not about you. You are a terminal for a higher power. As soon as you accept that, you can do it forever. Quincy Jones

"The world tells us to seek success, power and money. God tells us to seek humility, service and love." Pope Francis

Humility is the solid foundation of all virtues. Confucius

Do you wish to rise? Begin by descending. You plan a tower that will pierce the clouds? Lay first the foundation of humility. Saint Augustine

"The best of people is the one who humbles himself the more his rank increases." Prophet Muhammad

"Pride makes us artificial and humility makes us real." Thomas Merton

This gem from the Psalmist – *He leads the humble in what is right, and teaches the humble his way* – encourages us to seek God's leading and teaching, which inspires us to consider our own journey into genuine humility.

PRAYER: Leading and teaching God, help me to think of myself less. I welcome your Holy Spirit to dwell within me so that I may pursue the goal of keeping my ego in control. Teaching me and show me that I do not really gain anything by calling attention to myself, but my richest gain is when my words and deeds glorify you. Amen.

TWENTY-SIX

I do not sit with the worthless, nor do I consort with hypocrites;
26:4

Aesop wrote that a person is known by the company he or she keeps. Your parents told you this in childhood. You become known by who you associate with. Birds of a feather flock together. If you associate with bad friends, you will have a bad reputation. If you associate with great friends, you become a better person. You will become known by who you hang around with. Guilt by association. Do not sit with the worthless. Do not consort with hypocrites.

There is a saying in business: *First rate people hire first rate people. Second rate people hire third rate people.* You see the logic: a person might feel threatened by great staff members who draw lots of attention, so the person hires less effective staff members whose work will not threaten or draw the spotlight away from the insecure boss. Visionary leaders hire the best and the brightest to build a winning team and allows them to shine in the spotlight. That too reflects on the leader.

Consider some of the great leaders. Lincoln and Obama were known for building a team of rivals, and so they had a diversity of wise opinions to guide them. Kennedy was known for recruiting the best and the brightest. That is how journalist David Halberstam named it in his 1972 book *The Best and the Brightest*, focusing on policy crafted by academics and intellectuals who were in John F. Kennedy's administration… Kennedy's "whiz kids" who were leaders of industry and academia brought into Kennedy's administration. Compare that to other leaders whose associates seems to push moral or ethical boundaries to their breaking point. What does that say about the leader who recruited them? You are known by the company you keep.

Distance yourself from people who disrespect you, mistreat others, do not tell the truth, are abusive, lie to you, are negative, have no goals, use you, use others, or put you down.

"Whoever walks with the wise becomes wise, but the companion of fools suffers harm," wrote the author of Proverbs (13:20). Humans radiate an invisible energy. When you walk with the wise and the good, they radiate a positive energy which enters your energy field. They give you energy. In the company of fools, they radiate a negative energy, which drains away your energy. We even use the language of polarity when talking about a positive person or a negative person. Attract yourself to positive energy. General Colin Powell captured this so well:

"The less you associate with some people, the more your life will improve. Any time you tolerate mediocrity in others, it increases your mediocrity. An important attribute in successful people is their impatience with negative thinking and negative acting people. As you grow, your associates will change. Some of your friends will not want you to go on. They will want you to stay where they are. Friends that don't help you climb will want you to crawl. Your friends will stretch your vision or choke your dream. Those that don't increase you will eventually decrease you.

Consider this: Never receive counsel from unproductive people. Never discuss your problems with someone incapable of contributing to the solution, because those who never succeed themselves are always first to tell you how. Not everyone has a right to speak into your life. You are certain to get the worst of the bargain when you exchange ideas with the wrong person. Don't follow anyone who's not going anywhere. With some people you spend an evening: with others you invest it. Be careful where you stop to inquire for directions along the road of life. Wise is the person who fortifies his life with the right friendships. If you run with wolves, you will learn how to howl. But, if you associate with eagles, you will learn how to soar to great heights."

Look for ways to associate with those who are true, honorable, just, commendable, and those who strive for excellence. Associate with excellence wherever possible and that is what you will become.

PRAYER: Excellent God, lead me to associate with and sit with others who strive for excellence and who desire to be good people. And lead me away from choosing to be with those who do not tell the truth, who put others down, who mistreat others or who are negative. Allow me to be open to good people inspiring me to become a better person. Amen.

TWENTY-SEVEN

***Wait for the Lord; be strong, and let your heart take courage;
wait for the Lord!***
27:14

The word *wait* is a good substitution word. When you come to the
word *wait* in the Bible, substitute the word *trust*, for that is a good
synonym and helps to explain the word more accurately in our
language. For example, Isaiah (40) wrote *"Those who wait for the
LORD shall renew their strength, they shall mount up with wings
like eagles."* Make the substitution to see that those who trust in
God shall renew their strength. The Contemporary English
Version translates the verse *"Those who trust the Lord will find
new strength."*

The Psalmist uses the word frequently:

"Wait for the LORD; be strong, and let your heart take courage..."
(Psalms 27:14)

"Lord, for what do I wait? My hope is in thee." (Psalms 39:7)

"I wait for the LORD, my soul waits, and in his word I hope."
(Psalms 130:5)

Hope is directly connected to waiting for the Lord, or trusting in
God.

An old Christian hymn reminds us to yield your trust into God's
hand:
Have Thine own way, Lord! Have Thine own way!
Thou art the potter, I am the clay.
Mold me and make me after Thy will,
While I am waiting, yielded and still.

Perhaps there are times when you are waiting… waiting to decide, waiting for something to happen, waiting to be led or guided to a next step. Waiting can feel like living between trapezes! You have let go of one trapeze bar but have not yet caught the other and are hanging in mid-air where there is both adventure and danger. That can be what waiting feels like.

It must have felt like that for Jesus' disciples in the time between Jesus' Ascension and the coming of the Holy Spirit at Pentecost. They were living between trapezes. The disciples wondered what they were supposed to do. Jesus answered that they were supposed to wait: *"While staying with them, he ordered them not to leave Jerusalem, but to WAIT there for the promise of the Father."* (Acts 1:4). Wait there. That is not the answer they hoped for. Waiting is not likely to pop into the forefront of your mind when facing anxiety about a challenge. Just the opposite. It feels like you should be doing something.

Who likes to wait, especially when you are mid-air between trapezes? You want to do something. Humans are naturally inclined to take action, to change, to do… even if it is the wrong thing. Indeed, the New Testament book is not named the Book of WAIT, but the Book of ACTS. Waiting sounds inactive like you do not know what to do, which way to turn or how to respond. Many of us are not good at waiting. We want to see the time-line, the strategic plan, the goal and the expected outcomes. We want to see more of the map. We want a GPS to display a picture of the road to follow and a voice to tell us where to turn. Waiting upon the Lord? When you are living between trapezes in the air with nothing to hang onto, waiting is not what you have in mind. Waiting feels passive, responsive and reactive. Acting feels proactive. And yet, our feelings are not always our best guide, for often our best course of action is to wait… *"Wait for the Lord; be strong, and let your heart take courage; wait for the Lord!"*

When you are between trapezes, indecisive or uncertain about what to do next, God says to you: *Trust me. Have faith. Trust. Wait expectantly. Trust ME.* There is still a vision for the appointed time.

It may seem like it is not coming according to your timetable, but wait for it. When facing an unknown future, remind yourself that waiting and trusting is frequently the best response. Patience is almost always rewarded. In so much of your life you have been taught to take initiative and to act. When between trapezes, learn that it is not completely up to you but to you and God. Live by faith.

PRAYER: Dear God, teach me to be better at waiting for you. I am not good at waiting. I like to take action. I crave to see more of the plan. Help me to learn how to trust you more. Guide me into new adventures of faith. Amen.

TWENTY-EIGHT

The Lord is my strength and my shield; in him my heart trusts; so I am helped, and my heart exults, and with my song I give thanks to him.
28:7

The Psalmist frequently employs battle metaphors. We do not know if he intended them to apply to physical battles or to struggles which we all face, but they fit either way. God is your strength and your shield. The idea of a shield is medieval and bears little resemblance to our 21st century experience, but we understand his metaphor and like the idea of God as the one who gives us strength and shields us from evil.

The Apostle Paul used the metaphor of battle armaments to the fullest in Ephesians (6:13-17):

"Therefore take up the whole armor of God, so that you may be able to withstand on that evil day, and having done everything, to stand firm. Stand therefore, and fasten the belt of truth around your waist, and put on the breastplate of righteousness. As shoes for your feet put on whatever will make you ready to proclaim the gospel of peace. With all of these, take the shield of faith, with which you will be able to quench all the flaming arrows of the evil one. Take the helmet of salvation, and the sword of the Spirit, which is the word of God."

When facing adversaries, whether they be people or whether they be problems and challenges that confront us, Paul affirms the Psalmist's poetic expression that God is your strength and your shield:

Put on the whole armor of God. That is what you need to face difficulties: armor. You have the armor of God to protect you, so that you may be able to stand firm.

Fasten the belt of truth. Others may employ lies, deceit or half-truths, but truth will serve you well and guide you to maintain your integrity no matter what comes your way.

Put on the breastplate of righteousness. Righteousness is well translated as *right relationships.* When you face adversaries coming at you or problems to conquer, nothing is more important than your right relationship with God and your right relationship with others. Like friends. When the odds are against you, you will have some friends… you might be surprised at who they are. They will be your treasure and your breastplate of right relationships.

As shoes for your feet put on whatever will make you ready to proclaim the gospel of peace. In battle with either people or problems, you are called to be a peacemaker. Jesus entered the world as the Prince of Peace. As his followers, we seek to be ambassadors of reconciliation, to bring together those who are apart, and to tell about… to proclaim… that peace is God's way, even if the entire world should favor otherwise.

Take the helmet of salvation. The helmet protects your head, your mind, your eyes, ears and mouth. Under a time of attack by adversaries or adversity, you need your mind to make good choices and decisions, to help frame things the right way, to gain perspective, to know what to do next. God gives you that helmet of salvation, to think and to use your mind when it is needed most.

When you face challenges, difficulties or people who may seem to be against you, turn to God for the extra strength you need, to be your shield, and to gird you up with the whole armor of God.

PRAYER: Almighty God, let me never forget that you are my strength and my shield. When it feels like others are against me or when I face giant problems or challenges, guide me to put on the armor of God so that I may choose the God-like path of love, grace and forgiveness. Use me as your ambassador of peace and help my mind to be at its best when I need it most. Amen.

TWENTY-NINE

The voice of the Lord is over the waters; the God of glory thunders, the Lord, over mighty waters. The voice of the Lord is powerful; the voice of the Lord is full of majesty.
29:3, 4

When the voice of the Lord is referred to, it us usually accompanied by thunder and majesty. Loud. Perhaps like a sonic boom. That is how the Psalmist perceived the voice of God. There are times I wonder if might not be the opposite. Perhaps the voice of the Lord is more like a whisper, the still small voice of God. It seems like that is how Jesus entered the world. Quietly, when God whispered to the world.

It does not need to be loud. Sometimes a whisper says more. Or even silence. Jesus entered the world, not with a shout but with a whisper. When God sent Jesus into the world... when the Word became flesh and dwelt among us... it did not happen with trumpets, the crash of cymbals the roll of tympani, fireworks or strobe lights. He did not do it loud, born in a manger, that night when God whispered to the world.

Do you ever wonder: if Jesus were to return, would there be special effects? Would the earth tremble, the sea roar, or would there be fire in the sky? Would the World Wide Web light up at a trillion points? Would his return make the internet's top five news stories of the hour? Tomorrow, would he be yesterday's news? Or, like the first time, would Jesus enter with a whisper?

Once at a denominational meeting, the keynote speaker was a seminary professor and also a minister. The service was at the end of a long day and he was long. And loud. He was pounding the pulpit, shouting and revving them up. It felt like I ought to be getting more out of it. Maybe it was because I was tired, but I cannot remember a thing he said. It seemed like he was more interested in the sizzle than in the steak.

70

When we got in the car, my young daughter said to me, *"Daddy, why was that man shouting?"* I never forgot her message that night. The speaker was so loud, you could not hear him.

I had a similar experience when I was an invited guest at a church denomination's headquarters, from a Sunday night through Tuesday afternoon. There were sixty of us pastors from across the nation, selected from the most vital and active churches in our denomination. Sunday night, Monday morning, Monday night, and Tuesday night we worshiped in the denomination's Chapel. There were four powerful sermons delivered over the course of 48 hours. Even for a preacher, that's a heavy dose. On the plane home, I was thinking about what they all had in common. In all four cases, the preachers were shouting. The whole twenty-minute message of each one of them was at a volume just below a chain saw. When I returned, all I wanted to do was to whisper. And I remembered my daughter's insight: *"Daddy, why was that man shouting?"* I had trouble hearing them because of how loud they said it. The volume and intensity of their presentations drowned out the message.

I realize that there is a time to be loud, firm, and decisive. For everything there is a season and a time for every matter under heaven, says Ecclesiastes. A time to speak loudly and a time to keep silence.

A teen shared these feelings: *"I know my father loves me, even though he's never actually said it."* She would have been so happy had he only whispered those three words. Are there people in your family who have never told you they loved you? Are there people in your family to whom you have not whispered those words? It would not have to be shouted, would it? It might be barely audible, spoken in the softest whisper, but it would be heard louder than the roar of a jet engine or a shouting preacher.

When God sent Jesus into the world, God did not need to shout. Our lives are bloated on relentless noise. Where is the quiet in your life? What do you miss that is heard only in the silence?

Remember the Desiderata: *"Go placidly amid the noise and haste, and remember what peace there may be in silence. Speak your truth quietly and clearly; and listen to others... Avoid loud and aggressive persons; they are vexations to the spirit."* Constant loudness is a vexation of the spirit.

Mother Teresa wrote that *"God is the friend of silence. We need to find God and God cannot be found in noise and restlessness. See how nature, the trees, the flowers, the grass grow in perfect silence. See the stars, the moon and the sun, how they move in silence. The more we receive in silent prayer, the more we can give in our active life. Silence gives us a new outlook on everything."*

Teach yourself to appreciate silence. Here is the irony: current research indicates that multi-tasking decreases your effectiveness. And silence gives you a new outlook on everything. Why not choose to *"Go placidly amid the noise and haste, and remember what peace there may be in silence?"* Who you are speaks louder than words. Shouting does not mean the message gets heard any better. Shouting does not make the content of the message received more clearly. Ralph Waldo Emerson said *"What you do speaks so loud that I cannot hear what you say."*

People are craving to hear a message of hope, of meaning, of love but the message they need is hardly heard when it is shouted. If that happens, all they are likely to say is *"Why is that person shouting?"* But their need is real. They will listen to what you do. St. Francis said: *"Preach the gospel always. If necessary, use words."* Preach the gospel by your role model, by example, by what you do. Without words, preach the gospel of love. Preach the gospel of kindness. Preach the gospel of gentleness. Preach the gospel of compassion. Preach the gospel of God's peace. Go out into a noisy world as a representative of God's love.

"So we are ambassadors for Christ," wrote the Apostle Paul, since God is making his appeal through us. If it becomes necessary to use words, whisper... so you can be heard.

PRAYER: O God, whose voice has been heard throughout the generations, let me be quiet and still so that I might listen for your voice, whether spoken in thunder or offered to me in a whisper. Guide me to appreciate silence, so that I may gain a new outlook that you wish me to possess. Use me to share your love and grace to others, as a quiet model of love, kindness, gentleness and compassion. Amen.

THIRTY

Weeping may linger for the night, but joy comes with the morning.
30:5b

Isn't it interesting that our worries often feel magnified in the darkness of night? But then, when the early light of morning dawns, a fresh perspective becomes illuminated. You will appreciate that if you have ever tossed and turned the night away in worry or anxiety, only to awaken at dawn to wonder what you worried about so much.

Darkness can stand for aloneness or being left behind. There is fear of the dark. Dark is unknown. You cannot see, you could fall or bump, and who knows what lurks in the dark. Darkness can symbolize evil, threat, danger, hopelessness or dark shadows.

In the 23rd Psalm, the Psalmist comforts us by assuring: *Even though I walk through the darkest valley, I fear no evil.* The King James Version translated the verse *"Yea, though I walk through the valley of the shadow of death..."* While the poetic beauty of the KJV is lovely and often renders this as a psalm read at funerals, the more accurate translation of the NRSV means the valley of dark shadows. We experience valleys of dark shadows all the time, which makes this much more of an everyday psalm than a funeral psalm. The Bible never says there will not be dark valleys. Bad things happen. But the Lord lights your way. Whoever follows me, said Jesus, will never walk in darkness.

Psalm 23 embraces every valley. You face dark shadows in your life: uncertain, sad, or dark times when all is not well. Perhaps moments of dark shadows occur daily. Dark shadows on an x-ray can mean bad news, but not necessarily health problems that cannot be healed. Grief that lingers in the background, open emotional wounds still hurting, or conflict left unresolved can blow like an unexpected wind across moments of the day and remind of dark places that haunt the recesses of our minds.

No one ever wishes for dark valleys, yet how many stories have you known of people who faced difficult times and emerged finer and stronger from their testing? When put to the test, people often discover strength within themselves that they never realize existed. A renewed zest for life can emerge from the valley. When facing future challenges, there can be the affirmation that *"I've faced things like this before, I can face this new problem now."*

While darkness or the unknown can frighten and valleys can hurt, pleasant surprises and even treasures can be found in valleys of dark shadows. There are the treasures of people who stand by you in a time of need. There can be the surprises of new insights that enlighten and enrich your inner being. A valley can change your course and set you on a new direction that turns out to be better in the long run.

In the dark valley, that is when sheep become closest to the shepherd. We too, when facing dark places, find time alone with the Shepherd. That is the place where our loving and trusting relationship grows deeper and richer. Had it not been for the valley, we might have missed the motivation, out of our need, to reach out to the Shepherd to seek a renewed closeness to the One we follow.

In Psalm 23, lift up the word "through." *"Even though I walk through the darkest valley..."* You do not remain stuck in the valley, but will get through it. Eleanor Roosevelt put it succinctly: *"This too shall pass."* The darkness is followed by the light and you will emerge from your valley. The Psalmist is a realist: Weeping may linger for the night. There are times of sadness, fear, aloneness or worry. Because he employs metaphors throughout the psalms, we presume that "night" is a metaphor for the dark times of our lives. Likewise, "morning" is a metaphor for the time which follows the darkness or weeping. When the morning of your life returns again, there is joy. And even though this verse is a metaphor for the rhythms of everyday life, it applies as well to eternal life, knowing that at the end of it all, it is not over but that *"joy comes with the morning."*

PRAYER: Dear God, my Shepherd, when I weep or am afraid in the night times of my life, be with me to comfort and protect. Lead me out of the darkness I face and grant that my eyes may be open to experience the joy that comes with the morning. Amen.

THIRTY-ONE

But I trust in you, O Lord; I say, "You are my God." My times are in your hand;
31:14, 15a

I grew up in a church where a previous pastor, more than a century before me, was responsible for the motto on our nation's money "IN GOD WE TRUST."

His name was Mark R. Watkinson. Watkinson was born in New Jersey in 1824 and became a Baptist minister. Shortly before he was ordained, he served a small church in Ridleyville, Pennsylvania in 1850. The name of the church was the First Particular Baptist Church. Mark Watkinson was ordained in 1851 and stayed at Ridleyville a couple more years before going to serve The First Baptist Church of Richmond, Virginia. Watkinson was in Virginia when the civil war broke out and, in 1861 moved back to the First Particular Baptist Church of Ridleyville as their pastor for a second time.

These were troubling times, the depths of which we can hardly imagine as the country was divided and no one knew how it would turn out. Watkinson felt that the Civil War was going to leave the country with a bad name, "brother fighting brother in a civil war." And so, The Rev. Mark Watkinson wrote to Secretary of the Treasury Salmon P. Chase suggesting that a motto be placed on United States coins which recognize God. Over the years, others wrote similar letters, but according to Treasury Department records, the first appeal and the one that made the difference came in a letter dated November 13, 1861 from The Rev. M. R. Watkinson from Ridleyville, Pennsylvania.

As a result, Secretary Chase instructed James Pollock, Director of the Mint at Philadelphia, to prepare a motto, in a letter dated November 20, 1861: *"Dear Sir: No nation can be strong except in the strength of God, or safe except in His defense. The trust of our people in God should be declared on our national coins. You will cause a device to be prepared without unnecessary delay with a motto expressing in the fewest and tersest words possible this national recognition."*

Congress approved, and the motto IN GOD WE TRUST first appeared on the 1864 two-cent coin just three years after Mark Watkinson wrote his letter from The First Particular Baptist Church of Ridleyville, Pennsylvania. Over time, the motto was placed on all United States coins and in 1957 it was added to our paper money.

Mark Watkinson died in 1878 at the age of 54 and his contribution of motto on U.S. currency was largely forgotten until the 1950's when research uncovered his role. In April 1962 a plaque was placed at Watkinson's Church, now named the Prospect Hill Baptist Church on Lincoln Avenue in Prospect Park, Pennsylvania. I was there that spring day in 1962. That was my church. I spent the first years of my life in Prospect Park, lived a block away from the church, was baptized there, went to church school there, headed up the youth group there, and have preached there.

It's hard to grow up in the shadow of the origin of our currency's motto IN GOD WE TRUST without incorporating that motto into daily thoughts.

One of the greatest prayers of trusting God occurs in this gem: *"I trust in you, O LORD; I say, 'You are my God. My times are in your hand'."* The most beautiful prayers in the Bible are short and this is one of the best. You can pray it about anything, entrusting into God's hand whatever it is that you worry about or the one you are caring about. Substitute that which makes you anxious, the person you want to pray for, or whatever concern is filling your mind.

Turn it over to God: *My son or daughter is in your hand. My health is in your hand. My career is in your hand. This conflict I am facing is in your hand. What I am worrying about is in your hand.* You can make the substitution to place anything into God's hand. It is poetic that the Psalmist chose the word *times*: *MY TIMES are in your hand.*

What does *my times* mean? It could mean your <u>past</u>. Perhaps you cling to regrets, mistakes you are sorry about, or decisions you wish you chose differently. Let it go. There is nothing you can change about your past. It was what it was. Put in into God's hand and allow God to heal open wounds. It could mean your <u>present</u>. Live in the present tense. *THIS is the day that the Lord has made.* Do not long for tomorrow. Rather, rejoice and be glad in this day. Put this day into God's hand and cherish the gifts from God to you in the present moment. It could mean your <u>future</u>. There is a beautiful credo that proclaims *I may not know what my future holds, but I know who holds my future.* Place the uncertainty, worry and the unknown about the future into God's hand.

Your prayers to God need not be long or complicated. It is sufficient to reaffirm that the Lord is your God, that you trust God, and that you place your past, present and future into God's hand.

The next time you hold a coin or paper money in your hand, remembering the motto "In God We Trust," pause for a micro-second, give a little knowing smile, and silently pray this gem: *"I trust in you, O Lord; I say, 'You are my God.' My times are in your hand."*

PRAYER: Faithful God, strengthen my faith, remind me that I can trust you, and grant me the spiritual courage to let go and to place my times, my worries and my concerns into your hand. Amen.

THIRTY-TWO

Happy are those whose transgression is forgiven, whose sin is covered.
32:1

COMPANION VERSE: *Then I acknowledged my sin to you, and I did not hide my iniquity; I said, "I will confess my transgressions to the Lord," and you forgave the guilt of my sin.* (32:5)

There are four parts to a good prayer: PRAISE, CONFESSION, THANKSGIVING and PETITION. We rarely have trouble with the petition part, asking God for something, either for ourselves or for another. In many cases, our prayers are dominated by asking. If we use the Lord's Prayer as a model for our prayers, we too might begin with praise: "Hallowed be thy name." If you have read this far in this book, you are well acquainted with how much of the Psalms are in praise to God. We are also pretty good at thanking God for our many blessings. We know from whom our blessings flow. From God. Then the fourth part, confession. At that, we are not always so good and often omit or gloss over the confessing of our transgressions.

It has been my tradition, as a pastor, to celebrate communion on the first Sunday of every month and on that Sunday, a Prayer of Confession was substituted for the usual Invocation. Once when I began a pastorate with a new congregation, I carried this tradition with me. That congregation did not like it. "We don't like confessing our sins," said one member, hinting that perhaps the members of that church did not really think they committed any. Yet without confessing our transgressions to the Lord, our prayers are incomplete. For that matter, the practice of communion is basically about the forgiveness of our sins, but confession precedes forgiveness.

The Psalmist begins this gem *"Happy are those whose transgression is forgiven."* Happy. If a person feels no need of confession because of his or her blindness to their transgressions to the Lord, then there can be no resulting feeling of happiness. On the other hand, when a person knows full well that he or she has transgressed to the Lord and then she or he experiences the cleansing freshness of God's evergreen grace and forgiveness. That feels so good and makes for a sense of being happy. Forgiveness. Grace. A new beginning. A chance to start over. Past mistakes and transgressions are forgiven. Ah, what a great feeling which can only be described as happiness.

And so, may your prayers include the four parts of praise, confession, thanksgiving and petition, and may your deep and personal prayer of confession lead you to know the joy of God's grace and the happiness that comes from knowing that you are forgiven.

PRAYER: Gracious God, hear now my prayer of confession for my transgressions and sins. I am sorry and want to try harder to live a life pleasing to you. Please forgive me, God, and let me start anew. In love, I pray. Amen.

THIRTY-THREE

He loves righteousness and justice; the earth is full of the
steadfast love of the Lord.
33:5

This gem from Psalm 33 lifts up two of the most important words
in the Bible: *righteousness* and *justice.*

RIGHTEOUSNESS
The word *righteousness* is one of the most-used and least-
understood words in the Bible. *Righteousness* is well-translated as
right relationships. That is much more than right moral behavior.
Who would ever be good enough to require you to adhere to some
code of their interpretation of correct moral behavior?
Righteousness does not mean being goody good. Jesus said
(Matthew 6:33, KJV) *"Seek ye first the kingdom of God, and his*
righteousness." Right moral behavior alone is not worthy of being
first in God's book, but seeking to be in the right relationship with
God and with God's children is most certainly worth seeking first
in your life. To Jesus, religion was about right relationships. The
theme of the entire New Testament is right relationships. Seek
first to see every woman and man, every girl and boy as a unique
wonder, never to be repeated in all of human history, and to treat
each one as God's most sacred creation.

Defining *righteousness* in terms of moral behavior can lead to a
legalistic view of faith and life, which is contrary to the intended
meaning of the word. An old real estate axiom proposes that the
three most important rules of real estate are location, location, and
location. Same for God's word: the three most important
messages from the Bible are relationships, relationships, and
relationships. Look behind every great teaching to discover it is
ultimately about having the right relationship with God or having
the right relationship with God's children. All God's children. No
exceptions. The word *righteousness* is a good substitution word.
Whenever you come to the word in your reading of the Bible or
hearing it read, substitute in your mind the term *right relationships*
to see if that does not make much more sense.

In the Sermon on the Mount, Jesus taught *"Blessed are those who hunger and thirst for righteousness, for they will be filled."* (Matthew 5:6). What is blessed about hungering and thirsting for right behavior? Perhaps you have witnessed moralists who misunderstood the teaching. What a sad pursuit of faith they have experienced. But, by this beatitude, a person who hungers and thirsts for right relationships will be filled and they will be blessed.

Why bother? Why should you make the pursuit of right relationships your highest goal? The Psalmist answers that in the 23rd Psalm, verse 3b: *"He leadeth me in the paths of righteousness for his name's sake."* For his name's sake. For God's sake. It is because of our love for God and desire to please God that we seek to be in right relationships with others, even when that goes against our natural inclination. You might guess that those who are not people of faith would have little or no interest in making right relationships a high priority, other than for pragmatic reasons. But those who follow the Shepherd do things for him, for his name's sake.

"For thy name's sake" means a thing is done for God. That is why a follower of the Shepherd would bother to desire the right relationship with others. Like sheep who butt up against one another, we too experience conflict in our relationships. People might hurt you, insult you, injure you, undermine you, or be mean, nasty or unkind to you. You are not inclined to want to be in relationship with those people. You do not like them. They can make you angry, and anger is one of the unhealthiest diseases of the soul. How do you get out of that messy situation? The Shepherd leads you in the paths of right relationships. You would not care to choose to seek the right relationships with those people except for the only reason that could change your direction: for God's sake. For God, you will do it. But you need some help, some guidance, and some shepherding to get there. For those who choose to follow, the Shepherd leads in paths of right relationships.

JUSTICE

The second word in this gem from Psalm 33 is *justice*. As love is the central ethical idea of the New Testament, so justice is of the Old Testament. In the Old Testament, justice was the standard by which penalties are assigned for breaking the obligations of the society. You break the rules, here's what happens. In the Old Testament, justice was thought to be handed out by God: *"Vengeance is mine, I will repay, says the Lord."* (Romans 12:19 quoting Deuteronomy)

Justice was used in the Old Testament as the system by which wrongdoing was punished. The earliest system of human justice is rooted in Babylonian law and known as *lex talionis*, which is the eye-for-an-eye law. This law was quoted in Exodus 21, which is the chapter immediately following the Ten Commandments: *"If any harm follows, then you shall give life for life, eye for eye, tooth for tooth, hand for hand, foot for foot, burn for burn, wound for wound, stripe for stripe."*

In the best case, justice is used in the Old Testament for how people are treated, especially widows, orphans, resident aliens (also called "sojourners" or "strangers"), wage earners, the poor, prisoners, slaves, and the sick (Job 29:12-17; Psalm 146:7-9; Malachi. 3:5). Each of these groups has needs which keep its members from being able to participate fully in life. Justice involves meeting those needs. The forces which deprive people of what is basic for life are condemned as oppression (Micah 2:2; Ecclesiastes 4:1). To do justice is to correct that abuse and to meet those needs. Isaiah (1:17) admonished readers to *"learn to do good; seek justice, rescue the oppressed, defend the orphan, plead for the widow."*

To do justice is to open our eyes to those in need, to those hurting from unfair treatment, to those suffering from unfairness, and to be led to stand with and to speak for those who are oppressed. Martin Luther King, Jr., said *"Injustice anywhere is a threat to justice everywhere."*

Stand with and speak for those who are being bullied – on the playground, at work or even in a global setting – for people of faith embrace all women and men, girls and boys as sisters and brothers regardless of where they were born or how they look.

Justice calls people of faith to speak for those whose voice is powerless and to advocate for those on the margins of society – those with the least. Mahatma Gandhi said, *"A nation's greatness is measured by how it treats its weakest members."* Justice calls people of faith to care for those who are hungry, naked, in prison, discriminated against, and oppressed.

Justice calls Christians to favor those who are oppressed or bullied. Should the oppressed become freed and become oppressors, justice calls followers of the Shepherd to favor the new oppressed.

To do justice is about how we treat people. That is the same for both Testaments... not just how we treat people, but especially those who are hurting, who are discriminated against, or those who are oppressed.

God loves righteousness and justice, says the Psalm. If we love God, we will love what God loves. We will then join God as people who care for those in need and those suffering from unfairness. As God's agents for justice on earth, we will try our best to stand with and to speak for those who are oppressed, for those whose voice is powerless and for those on the margins of society.

PRAYER: God of all peoples, lead me out of preoccupation with myself to love what you love so that I too may come to love right relationships and justice. When I think about it, this really is what religion is all about: being in a right relationship with you and then, with your help, trying my best to be in right relationship with others. Use me, O God, as your ambassador for justice and open my eyes to be inclusive of all of your people, even those very different from me. Amen.

THIRTY-FOUR

O magnify the Lord with me, and let us exalt his name together.
34:3

COMPANION VERSE: *I will bless the Lord at all times; his praise shall continually be in my mouth.* (34:1)

It is difficult to consider this gem from the Psalms – *"O magnify the Lord with me"* – without thinking of the Magnificat of Mary, mother of Jesus. Consider what we know about Mary. We know that at Jesus birth, Mary was likely a teen-ager, probably in her mid-teens. In most states today, she would not be old enough to drive. During biblical times, a woman became engaged shortly after reaching puberty, at twelve to fifteen years of age.

Early Christian writings indicate that Mary was the child of elderly parents, Joachim and Anna, in Jerusalem. We have no hint anywhere that Jesus ever knew his grandparents on his mother's side.

We know that Mary was betrothed to Joseph, which, in Jewish tradition, is the one-year period between engagement and marriage where the couple was known as husband and wife, although they did not enjoy the privileges of marriage. Betrothal could not be terminated except by divorce.

Mary had seven children that we know about. Jesus was the first, the oldest. The gospels tell us that Mary had four other sons named James, Joses, Judas, and Simon. Five boys in the family. According to the gospel of John, (7:4,5), Jesus' brothers did not believe in him during his lifetime. The gospels also tell that Jesus had *sisters*... plural... but we do not know how many or their names. So, Mary and Joseph needed at least nine chairs around their table.

Since women tend to outlive men and because there is no mention of Mary's husband Joseph following the story of Jesus found in the Temple at age twelve, it is probable that Joseph died and that Jesus because the carpenter of Nazareth to provide for his family, until he was age thirty. They were talking about Jesus, not Joseph, when they asked *"Is not this the carpenter, the son of Mary and brother of James and Joses and Judas and Simon, and are not his sisters here with us?"* (Mark 6:3a). Mary would have become a widow in her late thirties or forties.

Ninety percent of what we know about Mary are in the events surrounding Jesus' birth. One of the most famous sayings from Mary in the Bible is known as The Magnificat. When Mary, pregnant with Jesus, went to stay with her cousin Elizabeth for three months, she walked in the door and Elizabeth blurted out: *"Blessed are you among women..."* Somehow, Elizabeth knew. Mary responded with one of the most beautiful phrases in the Bible, The Magnificat: *"My soul magnifies the Lord, and my spirit rejoices in God my Savior..."* (Luke 1:46, 47).

Use this historic saying as your own to center yourself spiritually. Close your eyes, draw near to the presence of the Divine, and pray: *"My soul magnifies the Lord, and my spirit rejoices in God my Savior..."* So many times, our prayers focus upon our own needs, our prayers for others or asking God for something. Instead, simply magnify God. As the Psalmist wrote: *"O magnify the Lord with me, and let us exalt his name together."*

Novelist Sidney Sheldon told the story of a famous concert pianist. As the pianist's star began to rise, he started to drink too freely of the ovations heaped upon him by his audience. The conductor of the orchestra saw this. Once, during a standing ovation for the pianist, the conductor walked onto stage and held the musical score over the head of the pianist. He did this to demonstrate that it was Bach that they applauded, not just the pianist. It was the MUSIC that was great, more so than the PERFORMER. It's the music, not the musician. It's the song, not the singer. It's the message, not the messenger... and Mary knew that! Magnify the Lord, she might have insisted, not me.

87

The word used was "*megaluno*." This is where the term "*mega*" comes from -- like mega-ton, mega-phone, or mega-bomb. The word means to make great, to declare magnificence, to extol or to enlarge – like a magnifying glass.

Mary could have said *"I make great the name of God"* but instead she coined a poetic phrase you can use to center your spiritual life: "My soul MAGNIFIES the Lord."

PRAYER: O God, whom I love and follow, my soul magnifies You! My spirit rejoices in You, O God, my savior. May my thoughts, words and deeds magnify Your holy name! Amen.

THIRTY-FIVE

Let ruin come on them unawares. And let the net that they hid ensnare them; let them fall in it – to their ruin.
35:8

Shadenfreude is a German word for delight in another person's misfortune, the malicious enjoyment at the misfortunes of others, or finding joy in other people's misery. It is that feeling that we hope they fall flat on their face. May they get what's coming to them. Let them be caught. Let them suffer. What do we wish for nasty people? Let them get what's coming to them! When someone has insulted you, made you look stupid, has led you to feel devalued, or has betrayed you, you do not exactly feel like telling them to have a nice day. In fact, if justice were to be fulfilled, you sort of hope they get back some of what they gave… an eye for an eye, a tooth for a tooth. Shadenfreude secretly wishes bad things to happen to those who have been nasty, unfriendly, who have gossiped, spread rumors, or spoken lowly of another. "HA!" jeers Shadenfreude. "They got what they deserved."

The whole of Psalm 35 is a glaring example of Shadenfreude. The Psalmist wishes ruin for his enemies. He wants bad things to happen to them. But how could this be God's way? Why did this make it into the Bible? Shadenfreude stands in stark contrast to the way Jesus taught about love and grace. This is a prime example of why the Bible should never be taken literally. It was not meant to be taken literally. Psalm 35 reflects the inner feelings of the Psalmist. He is human. His wish for ruin upon those whom he dislikes is no different from similar feelings which creep into your mind and mine from time to time. We can get so upset at those whose behavior is adversarial that we wish them nothing but the worst. May bad things happen to them, we secretly wish, even though we know that is not a Godlike attitude. And so, this Psalm is a gem in that it mirrors the real feelings of people who wrote the Bible – feelings which are similar to ones we experience.

They too experience the kind of reactions we can feel. We can relate to them even though we know their attitudes stand in contrast to *agape*.

The Apostle Paul wrote to the Romans (12:21) *"Do not be overcome by evil, but overcome evil with good."* His teaching pairs well with another of his most beloved writings: *"Love does not rejoice at wrong, but rejoices in the right."* (I Corinthians 13:6, RSV). The Psalmist, of course, did not have the benefit of the teachings of Jesus or Paul. For him, the code of *lex talionis* was the norm – an eye for an eye and a tooth for a tooth. Jesus stood the world on its ear when he proposed a new way. In the Sermon on the Mount, Jesus taught *"You have heard that it was said, 'An eye for an eye and a tooth for a tooth.' But I say to you, Do not resist an evildoer. But if anyone strikes you on the right cheek, turn the other also; and if anyone wants to sue you and take your coat, give your cloak as well; and if anyone forces you to go one mile, go also the second mile. Give to everyone who begs from you, and do not refuse anyone who wants to borrow from you."* (Matthew 5:38-42).

Jesus here quoted *lex talionis* and then added a line – do not resist an evildoer. Then, Jesus' new way changed everything about how people of faith are to respond: the second mile. If anyone forces you to go one mile, go also the second. Do more than expected. Forevermore, people who follow Jesus became known not for the revenge they extracted or the retaliation they desired but for their grace, forgiveness, love and for doing more than expected: they walk the second mile. Why would you do more than expected? Because Jesus asks you to. You do it for him.

When the spirit of God dwells within, we desire to do more than expected. We go beyond lex talionis. Retaliation or shadenfreude may be a natural instinct, but our spirits propel us to the Christian ethic of turning the other cheek and walking the second mile. Why? Because of our love for Jesus and our desire to become more like God in our attitude and behavior. Jesus asks those who choose to follow to love. There are numerous Greek words for *love* in the Bible but the one Jesus used was *agape*.

90

One of the best meanings of *agape* means to desire that which is truly in the other's highest and best interests. Love does more than is expected.

Shadenfreude, cathartic as it might feel, is an opposite of the highest and best of what we want to be. Shadenfreude is the opposite of *agape*. Agape, the Bible's word for love, is the God-like wish and hope that what is best for the other is what happens. This has sometimes been referred to as Christian love. Bible scholar William Barclay wrote that *"agape means that no matter what that person does to us, no matter how he or she treats us, no matter if she or he insults us or injures us or grieves us, we will never allow any bitterness against him or her to invade our hearts, but will regard her or him with that unconquerable benevolence and goodwill which will seek nothing but his or her highest good."*

And so, as Paul advised the Corinthians, love does not rejoice at wrong, but rejoices in the right. Shadenfreude rejoices at wrong. Agape rejoices in the right.

Agape is patient.
Agape is kind.
Agape is not envious or boastful or arrogant.
Agape is not rude.
Agape does not insist on its own way.
Agape is not resentful.

Paul counseled the Romans, who like the Psalmist, were facing very real threats from enemies: *No, 'if your enemies are hungry, feed them; if they are thirsty, give them something to drink; for by doing this you will heap burning coals on their heads.'* This is extreme language, a metaphor which we hope is true. This is another example of walking the second mile and doing more than expected. It is the magnanimous act of meeting meanness and ill will with kindness. We wonder if the enemies will "get it." And yet, we suspect that those truly bent upon evil have their minds closed to this kind of response and may actually view it as weakness or stupidity on our part.

And so, they may persecute us anyway. Even then, Christians hold fast to their integrity and their representation as God's people, for the glory of God.

"Do not be overcome by evil, but overcome evil with good," wrote Paul in this startling verse. It reminds of perhaps the most Christian verse in the New Testament, a teaching not found in other world religions and unique to Jesus: *love your enemies.*

"You have heard that it was said, 'You shall love your neighbor and hate your enemy.' But I say to you, Love your enemies and pray for those who persecute you, so that you may be children of your Father in heaven; for he makes his sun rise on the evil and on the good, and sends rain on the righteous and on the unrighteous. For if you love those who love you, what reward do you have? Do not even the tax collectors do the same? And if you greet only your brothers and sisters, what more are you doing than others? Do not even the Gentiles do the same? Be perfect, therefore, as your heavenly Father is perfect." (Matthew 5:43-48)

In this, Jesus stands alone. To encourage followers to love their enemies is rare among major world religions. Others may encourage kindness or mercy to your adversaries, but love? This may be the most Christian expression in the Bible.

If someone were to ask you to make a list of your enemies, would you have a long list? For some, it is difficult to think of even one or two people to name as an enemy. There may be some people whom you wouldn't mind if they took a long walk of a short pier, but enemies? Adversaries? Once more, here is extreme Christianity: to desire truly that which is in the highest and best interest of all... extended to the ones you like least. It does not actually say that you have to like your enemies, invite them out to lunch, feel warm affection for them, enjoy being in their company, or add them to your Facebook page. In the classic simplicity of Jesus, it simply says to love them. THAT does not come naturally. To follow this teaching will require a change of the heart and a determination of the will to wish for enemies that which is in their highest and best interests.

Pray for those who persecute you. Extreme Christianity continues. Who would ever be inclined to pray for an enemy, except the person who loves Jesus and desires to obey his commandments? To pray for the highest and best interest of an enemy is a high expression of love. This shows a love which flows out of the person praying because of the love flowing into them from God. It is hard to hate a person when you are praying for them.

Underneath Jesus' teaching is a word which means even more than to pray. The word *pray for* which Jesus used is a translation from the Greek word *eulogeo*, which *means to speak well of.* Perhaps this is more difficult than praying for an enemy, for what Jesus is actually asking his followers to do is to speak well of their enemies. That is where the word *eulogize* comes from, like when a person is eulogized at his or her funeral. He or she is spoken well of.

That, said Jesus, is how disciples are to treat those who persecute you, those who are nasty to you, mean to you, who embarrass you, who undermine you, threaten you or who give you a bad day: you are to speak well of them, even when you might prefer bad things to happen to them to teach them a lesson. No. You are instructed to speak well of them. Eulogize them. Why? *So that you may be children of your Father in heaven.* Because this is God-like behavior. Choose God-like thoughts and actions, for God's glory.

Jesus' taught...
to love your enemies,
to turn the other cheek,
to walk the second mile,
to not resist an evildoer, and
to speak well of those who persecute you.

Paul taught...
to rejoice in the right,
to leave vengeance to God,
to feed and give nourishment to your enemies, and, most dramatically
to overcome evil with good.

This is the way of God. This is the way of peace. It is not the world's way. It is not the way of aggressively ambitious nations. But, if a critical mass of people desires to choose a God-like way and pledge to overcome evil with good, it is possible to usher in the Kingdom of God.

What shall we do then with a Psalm filled with the raw crudeness of shadenfreude? All we can do is to put it into context and to recognize that human thought has evolved over the centuries. The Psalmist expressed how he felt. He had real enemies and wished for their ruin. The values taught by Jesus and Paul had not yet come. Now we know more about God's way. And yet, like the Psalmist, we can regress into inappropriate attitudes and values. All we can pray is that God will guide us and lead us into true faithfulness to the love, forgiveness and grace that is God-like behavior.

PRAYER: Dear God, when I catch myself secretly harboring wishes for bad things to happen to people whom I don't like, gently shake me by the shoulders and turn me around to face the beautiful light of your way of love, forgiveness and grace. Forgive me for my ill wishes for others. Teach me more and more about how to love and speak well of others, even my enemies. Amen.

THIRTY-SIX

For with you is the fountain of life; in your light we see light.
36:9

In this gem, the Psalmist is not talking about God. Rather, he is talking to God: *For with you is the fountain of life.* This image of God as a fountain is a popular concept in the Hebrew scriptures. In Jeremiah (2:13), the Lord declares: *"my people have committed two evils: they have forsaken me, the fountain of living waters, and hewed out cisterns for themselves, broken cisterns, that can hold no water."* God's self-image, by this verse, is as a fountain of living waters.

God is the source, the fountain for your nourishment. You need God to be sustained, to quench your thirst, and to be whole. Without God, a person cannot be whole. When God was forsaken by his people, they created a life for themselves without drinking from God's living water... *broken cisterns that can hold no water.* A cistern is like a flower pot. If a pot is cracked it will not hold water, which renders it useless. A broken cistern that cannot hold water is useless. Useless is not something you want to be.

Jesus, who would have known the verse from Jeremiah, uses the phrase to describe the living water that he gives. He was speaking to the Samaritan women at the well. He asks her for a drink of water. She notices he has no bucket, which means he needs her to share hers. He tells her *"If you knew the gift of God, and who it is that is saying to you, 'Give me a drink,' you would have asked him, and he would have given you living water... Everyone who drinks of this water will be thirsty again, but those who drink of the water that I will give them will never be thirsty. The water that I will give will become in them a spring of water gushing up to eternal life."* (From John 4).

Jesus uses metaphor and symbolic language here to point to a deeper truth, for whatever he meant by the living water, we see that he gives it to those who ask, it quenches thirst, and it becomes in the receiver *a spring of water gushing up to eternal life.*

That certainly sounds like it is worth asking for and pursuing. It sounds like Jesus gives, to those who ask, the Spirit of God within. His gift transforms the person into one who is fulfilled, content, and whose thirst is satisfied. How do you get this water? Jesus' reply to the woman at the well: ask for it.

Many who search for the fountain of life look in the wrong places. They pursue a quest which they hope will lead to contentment, satisfaction, happiness or inner peace. But the wells of the world will not refresh. They are, ultimately, broken cisterns that will hold no water. When you desire the nourishment that only God provides, allow the Psalmist's wisdom to guide you to the source of living water, for with you, O God, is the fountain of life.

PRAYER: Hear my earnest prayer, O God, Fountain of Life. I invite you to place your Holy Spirit within me and allow me to drink from the living water that you give. When I thirst for something which I do not possess, guide me to look in the right place to be sustained, nourished and refreshed at your fountain. Amen.

THIRTY-SEVEN

Refrain from anger, and forsake wrath. Do not fret—it leads only to evil.
37:8

Refrain from anger. The Psalmist provides wise, simple and brief advice. Anger is dangerous to your spiritual and your physical health. Put a "D" in front of the word to see that it becomes "Danger."

An Amish farmer perceptively stated: *"The acid of anger eats the container that holds it."* This is anger which will not forget, which refuses to be calmed, or which seeks revenge. Anger can destroy you from the inside out. You do it to yourself. Your anger has the potential to make your own life a living hell. Anger is dangerous to your spirit and to the quality of your life... not to mention the impact it has on others. Anger is an acid which eats the container that holds it.

The book of Proverbs says about anger *"Fools show their anger at once, but the prudent ignore an insult."* (Proverbs 12:16). Anger begets anger. But the prudent, wisely advises Proverbs, ignore an insult. The internal gyroscope of the prudent keeps them upright and balanced even when insulted, for they know that ignoring an insult can keep them out of trouble. It is possible that the one hurling the insult may recognize his or her hurt and later feel bad about it. Perhaps onlookers will sympathize with the one being insulted, root for the underdog, and admire the Prudent's maturity by not retaliating like for like. Onlookers may also think that the one doing the insulting is mean, unkind or thoughtless.

But alas, we are human. When attacked, initial impulse is to strike back. That is why we must turn to God for internal strength of spirit when strength is needed to "let it go." The book of James (1:19, 20) offers similar wisdom: *"Be quick to listen, slow to speak, slow to anger; for your anger does not produce God's righteousness."*

Bambi's mother in the Disney film framed it so even the youngest child could grasp it: *"If you can't say something nice, don't say anything at all."* This is common sense, from Bambi's mother to Solomon's wisdom to the pen of James: It is the tongue which gets you into trouble. Be quick to listen, slow to speak, slow to anger.

James wrote that anger does not produce God's righteousness. We saw from Psalm 33 that *righteousness* is well-translated as "right relationships." And so, to paraphrase James, *"...your anger does not produce right relationships."* When we are angry, we are not fit to desire the right relationship with God or with God's children.

Those who cause anger may be doing so out of their own anxiety, insecurity or need. Responding to their anxiety with a quick, anxious or angry response only creates a vicious cycle which spirals out of control. The antidote for the unhealthy behavior of anger and a hot-temper is to provide a non-anxious presence. When others about you are anxious, you bring healing when you remain calm and do not let anxiety show. Your non-anxious presence is like when anxious, scared or nervous sheep sense they are in the presence of their Shepherd. The Shepherd, leaning on his staff, radiates a non-anxious presence, which signals that all is well. Then, the sheep settle down. They lie down in green pastures and experience calm rest. Your non-anxious presence has the potential to disarm conflict.

And so, advises the Psalmist, refrain from anger. No good comes from it, and harm from your anger can easily spill over into the lives of others.

PRAYER: Patient God, when I get angry, help me to calm down, put things in perspective, and seek your counsel. Place your spirit within me so that my eyes may behold your non-anxious presence. When others around me become angry, steady me so that I may remain calm and become your agent for healing. Amen.

THIRTY-EIGHT

I confess my iniquity; I am sorry for my sin.
38:18

One of the earliest teachings of ancient Greek philosophy is captured in two words: Know thyself. The phrase was later expounded upon by the philosopher Socrates who taught that "The unexamined life is not worth living." Here now in Psalm 38 is a model for knowing yourself. The Psalmist knows his faults, his sin and his shortcomings. He knows the evil within him. That is one of the hardest things for anyone to acknowledge.

On a TV show, the main characters in the workplace were required to complete a self-assessment in preparation for their annual employment evaluations. One of the beloved characters left blank the box that asked for a self-assessment of weaknesses and areas that needed improvement. When his supervisor asked him why he left it blank, he ever-so-humbly responded that he couldn't think of any. Perhaps we are not so different. Who wants to go around thinking about their weaknesses or faults? Would it not be healthier for us to dwell upon our strengths and our gifts? And yet, knowing of our faults, our sin and even the evil within us is a part of the examined life and of knowing ourselves.

For this, the Psalmist should be commended and serve as an example to us. He not only confesses his iniquity, but adds that he is sorry for his sin. He is speaking to God, who is God of mercy. God's heart longs to give the gift of grace. God will give the Psalmist grace, but saying "I am sorry" precedes forgiveness.

Do you think there might be anything in the Psalmist's past that God might not forgive? Do you ever wonder if there is anything you have said or done that God might not forgive? There is nothing – no behavior, thought or act – that falls outside of God's grace. If there is anything you have ever done which you think God might not forgive, you are incorrect and here is why: you cannot limit God.

To believe that any action you ever did could fall outside of God's mercy is to limit God and placing a limit on God's love is impossible.

This gem from the Psalms illustrates the natural order of confessing and receiving forgiveness. First comes the "I'm sorry" and then comes the gift of grace: forgiveness.

American Quaker poet John Greenleaf Whittier puts to verse a hymn which captures the Psalmist's sentiment:
Dear Lord and Father of mankind,
Forgive our foolish ways;
Reclothe us in our rightful mind,
In purer lives Thy service find,
In deeper rev'rence, praise.

PRAYER: Loving God, help me to know myself better, warts and all, and to come to you to say I am sorry for my sins. I ask for your forgiveness and thank you with all my heart for your gift of grace to me. Amen.

THIRTY-NINE

*"Lord, let me know my end, and what is the measure of my days;
let me know how fleeting my life is.*
39:4

This is a prayer not likely to be answered. God's time is God's
alone. No one knows when their end will be, or how it will occur.
The Psalmist has encouraged readers to live in the present. Just a
few chapters ago he entrusted his past, present and future into
God's hand when he wrote *"My times are in your hand."*
(31:15a). Later, in one of his most beautiful works of literature, he
declares *"This is the day that the Lord has made; let us rejoice and
be glad in it."* (118:24). This day. Rejoice in be glad in the
present. Live not in the past nor the future, but in the present. No
one could have said it better than the Psalmist.

Henry Wadsworth Longfellow wrote in <u>*A Psalm of Life*</u>:
Trust no future, howe'er pleasant!
Let the dead past bury its dead!
Act, act in the living present!
Heart within and God 'oerhead!

So, perhaps the Psalmist is curious. He knows where his
preoccupation should be: in the present. And yet, he wonders
about the measure of his days. When will he die? How will he
die? Many people have said that they are not so much afraid of
death but of how and when they might die. Then, when he prays
"Let me know how fleeting my life is," perhaps that is not such a
bad prayer. Life is fleeting. The older we get, the faster time
seems to go. To recognize that leads to cherishing every moment
and valuing every new day.

A successful actress was giving a commencement address when
she told about her one year-old daughter: "Our daughter is one
year old. She lives absolutely and truthfully moment to moment.
She's not interested in the movie that may or may not be made.
She could care less about the deal that may or may not fall through,
or the part that may or may not be offered.

She is interested in lunch, a beautiful flower, a tiny speck on the rug, the wind in high branches, a bird flying across the setting sun. She has taught me that after all the compulsion, ambition and anxiety that the little moments are the sum of our lives, not the huge, earth-shattering events. Life is now. The emotional moments are more vital to our souls than the practical, have-to-do-this-now chores."

To those worried about the quality of their life tomorrow, Jesus comforted them (Matthew 6:34) when he taught *"Do not worry about tomorrow, for tomorrow will bring worries of its own. Today's trouble is enough for today."* And so, live in the present.

Perhaps like the Psalmist in his curiosity, the thought crosses our mind about our end times. We do well to recognize the preciousness and fleeting nature of our life, but nothing should distract us from living in the precious present, for as the Psalmist encourages "THIS is the day which the Lord has made." Rejoice and be glad in it!

PRAYER: Eternal God, sometimes I wonder about how fleeting my life is. Reassure me of your everlasting love and faithfulness, and redirect my attention to rejoice and be glad in the precious present. Amen.

FORTY

I delight to do your will, O my God; your law is within my heart.
40:8

The person who prays these words is very close to the Kingdom of God. This desire must be very pleasing to God. It is a prayer of trust, of love and of obedience. That does not mean that the person who prays this prayer never falls away from this desire, as the Psalmist seems to do often with his "Where are you God?" or "Why are you so far away from helping me?" But the internal spiritual gyroscope steadies us on course again, keeps us upright and returns us to the highest commitment we can make, which is to pray *"I delight to do your will, O my God; your law is within my heart."*

When you study world religions and come to the Muslim faith, you discover that the word *Islam* means *submission*. Islam encourages a complete submission to Allah. When you examine the Sermon on the Mount, the same could be said of Christianity: Jesus encourages complete submission to the God's will: *"Thy will be done."* That is part of what we know as the Lord's Prayer, found in Jesus' Sermon on the Mount in Matthew: *"Thy kingdom come, Thy will be done in earth, as it is in heaven."* (Matthew 6:10)

Pray that phrase with trepidation and the utmost of holiness because when you say these words, you are inviting God to have God's will with you... to put God's will above your own will. It is a prayer of yielding. The one who prays these words is volunteering to submit to God's will, to yield to God's desire, and to trust that God knows and wants what is best for you. There is a Hebrew literary device contained in this phrase known as a parallelism. A parallelism is where two phrases side by side have parallel meanings. They both mean about the same thing. In other words. One phrase amplifies, clarifies or illuminates the other. This is significant because Jesus spoke more about God's kingdom than almost any other topic. More than half of his parables begin with the phrase "The Kingdom of God is like..."

The odd thing is, he never came right out and said what he meant by the Kingdom. Here in this phrase is a clear understanding, for the parallel phrases help us to understand that *"thy kingdom come"* means approximately the same thing as *"thy will be done."* God's kingdom exists wherever and whenever God's will is done – right here and now as well as in heaven. When you and I say this prayer and tell God we want God's will to be done above our own will, we enter God's kingdom.

PRAYER: O Lord my God, may I make the prayer of the Psalmist my prayer: I delight to do your will. Strengthen my faith so I can have courage to yield to you and trust that you know about and care for what is best for me. May Thy will be done in my life, Dear God. Amen.

FORTY-ONE

But you have upheld me because of my integrity, and set me in your presence forever.
41:12

You would hope that anyone who prays for God's will to be done, as the Psalmist did in the previous chapter, would aim high at being a woman or man of integrity. You would wish that all people of faith could be counted upon to choose integrity as a life goal.

The Bible is filled with encouragement for you and me to walk in the way of integrity. Proverbs (10:9) declares *"Whoever walks in integrity walks securely, but whoever follows perverse ways will be found out."* People of integrity desire to have a good name: *"A good name is to be chosen rather than great riches."* (Proverbs 22:1). Your name is your greatest treasure. Your integrity gives value and brings trust to your word.

The Apostle Paul wrote in Romans 12: *"Love one another with mutual affection; outdo one another in showing honor."* A good self-query to ask is "Are my words and actions honorable?" Honor is a sister to integrity. There is a story about J. C. Penney, who founded a chain of department stores. Penney who became dismayed when it was alleged that some Penney executives were involved in kick-back schemes with some of the company's contractors. Penney quoted Shakespeare's *Othello: "Good name in man and woman, dear my Lord, is the immediate jewel of their souls: Who steals my purse steals trash; 'tis something, nothing; 'Twas mine, 'tis his, and has been slave to thousands. But he that filches from me my good name robs me of that which not enriches him, and makes me poor indeed."* (Act III, Scene 3, line 155).

C. S. Lewis wrote *"Integrity is doing the right thing, even when no one is watching."* That is true integrity. Even if no one else notices, God does. God knows of your good works and you doing the right thing. It is likely that eventually, others will find out about your good works.

105

Then, there is another who counts: you. You know when you have chosen the right thing to do, and you are rewarded by knowing that you have chosen a good name and walked in the way of integrity. When you lay your head down upon the pillow to sleep, you can sleep well and be pleased with your choice.

The Psalmist, talking with God, prays *"you have upheld me because of my integrity."* Be people of integrity and honor, Paul implored the Romans. That is also the wisdom of the ages:

"Real integrity is doing the right thing, knowing that nobody's going to know whether you did it or not."
Oprah Winfrey

"The supreme quality for leadership is unquestionably integrity. Without it, no real success is possible, no matter whether it is on a section gang, a football field, in an army, or in an office."
Dwight D. Eisenhower

"We learned about honesty and integrity – that the truth matters... that you don't take shortcuts or play by your own set of rules... and success doesn't count unless you earn it fair and square."
Michelle Obama

"Moral authority comes from following universal and timeless principles like honesty, integrity, treating people with respect."
Stephen Covey

"Whoever is careless with the truth in small matters cannot be trusted with important matters." Albert Einstein

"Ability without honor is useless." Marcus Tullius Cicero

PRAYER: Steadfast God, set me in your presence and uphold me as I try as hard as I can to be a person of integrity, honor and a good name. Forgive me when I fail, help me to forgive myself, and then guide me to move on with renewed commitment to holding high my aim of integrity. Amen.

FORTY-TWO

Why are you cast down, O my soul, and why are you disquieted within me? Hope in God; for I shall again praise him, my help and my God.
42:11

The word *"cast"* in this verse is a shepherd's term. Since David the shepherd boy, who slew Goliath and became King of Israel, is believed to have authored some of the Psalms, it fits that he would use the language of shepherds as a metaphor to describe the disquieted state of his soul.

Sheep, especially fat ones, have a tendency to roll over on their back and then they cannot get up again. They will flail their legs in vain and in time will die if they cannot get right side up. In shepherd's language, this is known as being *cast*. A sheep that gets stuck upside down is a cast sheep. Did you ever have a pet turtle? Same thing happens to turtles: they can get stuck upside down and they cannot right themselves. So, in the case of sheep, the Shepherd must remain on the watch for sheep which have become cast. When they find one, they turn it back on its legs and then the sheep is off and running again. Note that a cast sheep cannot right itself. The sheep requires the help of the shepherd to get back on its feet.

In Psalm 42, this behavior of sheep is applied to us as people: *Why art thou cast down, O my soul? And why art thou disquieted in me?* There is a feeling we know. It suggests that our souls get stuck upside down and no matter how we flail about, we cannot right ourselves. We require the Shepherd to turn our soul back on its legs and then we are off and running again. We can become like fat sheep, bloated on desires to acquire, to please or to achieve. Perhaps we have run away from something, or maybe the open wound of a conflicted relationship hurts deeply. And so, our souls become cast down and disquieted. If you have felt cast down, discouraged or disquieted, Psalm 42 is a Psalm for you.

The Psalmist, feeling stuck upside down, also knows the pathway to help. He concludes this Psalm *"Hope in God; for I shall again praise him, my help and my God."* God is your help when your soul is cast and your heart is disquieted.

PRAYER: Faithful God, I recognize this feeling of a disquieted spirit. Something within me is stirring but I know not what it is or why. When my spirit is faint and my soul is weak, you know my way, you get me back on my feet and you are truly my help whom I praise. Amen.

FORTY-THREE

O send out your light and your truth; let them lead me; let them bring me to your holy hill and to your dwelling.
43:3

The Psalmist loves the hills and high places, and feels closest to God in the hills. Later, in Psalm 121, he proclaims *"I lift up my eyes to the hills - from where will my help come?"* The first thing to note is that the Psalmist WANTS to be where God is, in God's presence. As he also said in Psalm 23 *"and I shall dwell in the house of the Lord my whole life long."*

Notice the difference between the beautifully poetic King James Version and the modern and more accurately translated New Revised Standard Version. The KJV uses the phrase *"in the house of the Lord forever"* whereas the NRSV uses *"my whole life long."* This is a significant difference, because the King James might lead the reader to assume that this speaks of eternal life. It does not. There are many places in the Bible which refer to eternal life, but the actual translation of this verse is about living in the present, for your whole life long. In the present.

The *"house of the Lord"* is a metaphor. It does not refer to a physical place, such as the Temple. It does not refer to the synagogue or to the worship meetinghouse. God is found in those places, but the metaphor actually is interpreted as *"the place where God is."*

Now, of course, God is everywhere. God is omnipotent, omnipresent, and omniscient – all powerful, all present, and all knowing. The *house of the Lord* refers not to a physical location where God resides but rather to that state of being when you become more aware that you are in the Shepherd's presence. God is always there, but we are not always tuned-in to God the Shepherd's presence.

To say *I will dwell in the house of the Lord forever* is a personal pledge and a declaration that I will choose to live my days aware of being in God's presence. That, in Psalm 43, is the author's heart felt longing. He wants to be there.

Polls tell about the high percentage of Americans who say they believe in God. And yet, a substantial part of those do not participate in a community of faith, do not engage in spiritual practices like prayer or reading the Bible, and most would find it a foreign concept to declare that they put God first in their lives. It is not for us to judge another, but it appears that these folks are not on the same page as the Psalmist who truly wants to be led to God's Holy Hill and into God's presence. He wants to be there.

A second thing to note is the Psalmist's recommendation for how to get to God's Holy Hill: *"O send out your light and your truth; let them lead me."* He needs to be led into God's presence and the pathway to that destination is God's light and God's truth. God's light illuminates the way for us to see clearly the pathway into God's presence. That pathway perhaps best begins with the kind of desire that the Psalmist has – to want to be in God's presence. Those who want to seek an encounter with the Divine are likely to be more receptive to God's light shining in the darkness.

How do we know God's truth? Again, it may be the "wanting" to be brought to God's holy hill and to God's presence that creates a receptiveness and readiness to be open to God's truth. And so, what is most remarkable about this gem from Psalm 43 is to view the heart and soul-felt desire to be led into God's presence. While we might not possess the eloquence or the spiritual depth of the ones who wrote this book of the Bible, we are led by their example and role model. The Psalmist, like us, can feel cast down and disquieted in his souls. The Psalmist, like us, can feel far away from God sometimes and wonder why God does not act in the way he wishes God would act. But then, we take our inspiration from the Psalmist to recognize that the pathway into God's holy hill and presence begins with the first step, and that is to want to be there.

PRAYER: Eternal God, I feel an inkling of a leading to want to be in your presence. Light the pathway for me, help me to recognize your truth, and lead me to dwell where you are. Amen.

FORTY-FOUR

In God we have boasted continually, and we will give thanks to your name forever.
44:8

Psalm 44 is titled "National Lament and Prayer for Help." It is a dreary Psalm, even blaming God for bad things happening. This is not a Psalm you would normally turn to for inspiration or encouragement. And yet, in the midst of bad times, the Psalmist pledges to give thanks to God forever.

"In God," he writes, *"we have boasted continually."* Boasting seems like an unusual choice of words. Normally we think of a self-centered person boasting or bragging about himself or herself. It is often the unusual choice of words that makes for interesting literature. In the Bible, boasting is most often condemned as an act of arrogance or weakness. And yet, there are a few examples in the letters of Paul where he uses the word *boast* in the positive way, which is what the Psalmist did. For example:

"We boast in our hope of sharing the glory of God."
Romans 5:2b

"...we even boast in God through our Lord Jesus Christ, through whom we have now received reconciliation."
Romans 5:11

"Let the one who boasts, boast in the Lord."
1 Corinthians 1:31

"May I never boast of anything except the cross of our Lord Jesus Christ, by which the world has been crucified to me, and I to the world."
Galatians 6:14

This normally negative word switches polarity when it is about God that we boast. Isaac Watts reflected on this word in his classic hymn *When I Survey The Wondrous Cross*:
Forbid it, Lord, that I should boast,
Save in the death of Christ, my God;
All the vain things that charm me most
I sacrifice them to his blood.

This gem from Psalm 44 reminds us of two things: First, in the midst of bad things happening, continue to give thanks to God. That may actually be the time when it means the most. Second, boast not about yourself but about God. Give God the credit.

PRAYER: Eternal God, I give thanks to you forever, in good times and bad. When bad things happen which I do not understand, I thank you for all the good things I have had and still have in my life. Help me to have self-control over my mouth so that I do not boast about myself, but rather, let me give credit, praise and glory to you. Amen.

FORTY-FIVE

Your throne, O God, endures forever and ever. Your royal scepter is a scepter of equity; you love righteousness and hate wickedness.
45:6, 7a

King David, who wrote or influenced Psalms, would have a familiar acquaintance with the kingly life. Psalm 45 likens God to a King who sits on a royal throne. Archeological finds have discovered images of Kings in the most ancient of civilizations holding the ornamental staff or wand, the scepter, as a symbol of royal power.

Perhaps because the King was considered the most powerful of people, God was called King and given attributes that are practiced by kings. One characteristic ascribed to God is omnipotence, which means all powerful. God has all the power. So throughout biblical history, humans have wondered "What kind of king is God? How does God rule?" In the Bible, you could find human guesses about God's ruling, ranging from a God of wrath and punishment to a God of grace and love.

Comedienne Gracie Allen said "Never place a period where God has placed a comma." In other words, God is still speaking. What we know about God continues to evolve. We do well never to place a period about what is revealed about God, for what is known about God has grown since the time of the Psalmist. Jesus revealed much about what God is like and about how God rules. For Jesus, God rules with love, forgiveness, mercy, and the gift of grace. That was not fully known in the days of the Psalmist, so consider his interpretation of God's rule: he rules with equity, loves righteousness and hates wickedness.

Equity is the rule of evenhandedness, fairness, impartiality and justice. All are treated the same. One group or one kind of person is not given preference. All are treated fairly and equally.

Righteousness and wickedness are subject to a wide range of interpretation, which changes over time. Often, we think of righteousness as applying to behavior. There is a story of the Tillbury sisters who attended church in rural Maine. One Sunday, during the days of the Christian Temperance Union, a guest preacher was their worship leader. He began "Today we are going to condemn the evils of cussing!" he shouted. From their pew, the Tillbury sisters muttered "Amen. Amen." The preacher continued, "And today, we are going to condemn the evils of tobacco!" Again, the Tillbury sisters answered "Amen. Amen." On a roll, the preacher went on "And today, we're going to condemn the evils of alcohol!" The Tillbury sisters looked at each other and one said "Now he's meddling!"

By whose standards shall we interpret righteousness? In graduate school, my wife and I invited another couple whom we met to come over for dinner and perhaps a game of cards. They responded that their church denomination did not allow them to play cards. They owned, however, a deck of cards that was different from normal playing cards, and that was ok to use. They nicknamed them "Christian cards." By their interpretation, our cards were unrighteous but theirs were allowable!

In my teen years, I enjoyed dancing. Every Friday night, kids from all the schools gathered at a school where records were played, soda and snacks were available, and boys and girls enjoyed dancing to the newest popular songs. It was great fun and part of the social development of young people. In high school, I took public transportation a couple times a week into a Philadelphia TV studio where I danced on a program named "Dick Clark's American Bandstand." Rock and Roll music was a cherished part of teen culture then and we danced and danced. Then I met a woman who told me that her church denomination did not permit dancing. Why? The best she could answer was that it might lead to promiscuous behavior. In that faith, dancing was considered unrighteous.

Do you see how righteousness is usually thought of as some kind of good or bad behavior, depending upon who you talk to? But who is good enough to dare tell you or me what we should or should not do? And it changes over time. Some of the people in history who condemned dancing, playing cards or alcohol had no trouble embracing the evil practice of slavery. Or not allowing women to even speak in church. Or of punishing their children with a strap, a board or worse.

The key to understanding this Psalm and one of the most important words in the Bible is: It is not about behavior. It is not about behavior! The word *"righteousness,"* as we have seen from Psalm 33, is well-translated as "right relationships." That is what God loves, values and judges: right relationships. Your right relationship with God. God cherishes your right relationship with God's children, no exceptions, for every woman and man, every girl and boy is a unique wonder, never to be repeated in all of history, and should be treated as God's most sacred creation.

Like the Psalmist, we as people of faith affirm that God is our ruler, that God's throne endures forever, and that God loves right relationships most of all.

PRAYER: Dear God, I thank you for ruling with fairness and equity. Help me to grow up from old interpretations of righteous behavior so that I understand that you want me to pursue right relationships more than anything else. In some ways, that is harder to do than simply abstaining from some behavior. Help me to look at every person I encounter as one of your beloved children. And even when I don't feel like it, guide me to pursue the right relationship with each person with whom I come into contact. Amen.

FORTY-SIX

God is our refuge and strength, a very present help in trouble. Therefore we will not fear, though the earth should change, though the mountains shake in the heart of the sea; though its waters roar and foam, though the mountains tremble with its tumult.
46:1-3

COMPANION VERSE
"Be still, and know that I am God! I am exalted among the nations, I am exalted in the earth."
46:10

When my mother died, I received a sympathy card with only this verse on the cover: *God is our refuge and strength, a very present help in trouble.* I cherished every card, prayer and good wish, but this one towered above the others and I'll never forget how much it meant to me at that moment. Psalm 46:1 is one of the most beautiful, comforting and beloved verses in the book of Psalms. This is a mountain peak of the Psalmist's writings. It reassures that God gives you strength beyond your own, God helps you, and God is your refuge when you need a safe harbor in which to shelter. Anytime you feel the need for help or for extra strength, this is your verse.

I was meeting with a senior high church youth group when I had the opportunity to ask them what they believed about God. Their responses varied, but most replied that God helped people when they were in trouble. That is right on target with the theology of the Psalmist. But, I persisted, what do you believe about God for times when you are not in trouble? Like these teens, are we not most inclined to call upon God when we need help? But then, when trouble has passed, it feels like God is needed less. What if we came to God in prayer equally in the good times as well as the bad? In the worst of times, God is your refuge, strength, and very present help. In the best of times, God is still present and that is when we do well to offer God our praise and our thanks.

God is present all of the time, whether or not we are aware. God speaks through the Psalmist in verse 10: *Be still, and know that I am God!* That sounds passive to the ears of people who are always wanting to do something. But the verb "to do" is not called for here. Listen to God whisper to you "Be still." Just BE. Still. And know. You do not always have to do or to act. Let your soul relax in the company and presence of God and meditate upon how God is God, and God is in control.

When Moses stood before God in the burning bush at Mt. Sinai and God told Moses that God was sending Moses to deliver his people from Egypt, listen to the text, from Exodus 3 (13, 14): *Then Moses said to God, "If I come to the people of Israel and say to them, 'The God of your fathers has sent me to you,' and they ask me, 'What is his name?' what shall I say to them?" God said to Moses, "I AM WHO I AM." And he said, "Say this to the people of Israel, 'I AM has sent me to you.'"*

The verb *TO BE* – *"being:* - is God's name. *"I AM has sent me to you."* Now God says
Be still, and know that I am God! Invest more time in being rather than doing. Be still. Know. Know God. Tarry in the presence of the One who is *"our refuge and strength, a very present help in trouble."*

Consider the verses which follow this gem: *"Therefore we will not fear, though the earth should change, though the mountains shake in the heart of the sea; though its waters roar and foam, though the mountains tremble with its tumult."* Sometimes the earth does change and the mountains shake, with disastrous consequences. There are earthquakes, hurricanes, tornados, tsunamis, floods, droughts and every manner of natural disaster. With the greatest of irony, these incidents are referred to by insurance companies as "Acts of God." But God does not cause bad things to happen to the creation which God created and loves. In the same way, our loving God would not cause bad things to happen to you. God does not cause your life to feel like an earthquake in order to teach you a lesson, to test your strength, or to temp you. That is not God's way.

118

Be comforted, though, that when your personal ground shakes or you feel flooded and overwhelmed, God is with you in your time of need. "For Thou art with me," assured the Psalmist in Psalm 23.

When you feel in the need of added inner strength or are facing troubles, may this verse come to you: *God is our refuge and strength, a very present help in trouble.*

PRAYER: Exalted God, thank you for being there for me when I need you most, especially in times of difficulty or when I am feeling weak. May I equally seek to be in your presence when things are going well and when I feel strong. Slow me down from always feeling the need to do something, when what may be most called for is for me to simply be still, and know that you are God. Amen.

FORTY-SEVEN

For God is the king of all the earth; sing praises with a psalm.
God is king over the nations; God sits on his holy throne.
47:7, 8

The Psalmist stretches to find the highest compliment he can pay
to God and in his time, that would be to liken God to a king. Later,
Jesus of Nazareth would devote the bulk of his three years of
ministry to teaching about the Kingdom of God. Perhaps in
another time or culture, God might be likened instead to a
president, a sovereign, a monarch, or whatever other titles might be
used for a ruler who governs a nation. It is almost as though
human language fails us to find superlatives worthy enough to
describe God. So. the Psalmist uses the highest office he can think
of: King. He tells how God is king of all the earth. The hymn
<u>Fairest Lord Jesus</u> uses this same idea as it begins *"Fairest Lord*
Jesus, Ruler of all nature..." Many hymns build upon the idea of
God as a king, like:
O worship the King,
All glorious above,
O gratefully sing
His power and his love;
Our Shield and Defender,
The Ancient of Days,
Pavilioned in splendor,
And girded with praise.

It is interesting to wonder how the earth was thought about when
the Psalmist praised God as king of all the earth. In that day, the
earth was believed to be flat. If you sailed off too far, you could
sail off the map and fall off the earth. In that day, the earth was
believed to be the center of the universe. Everything, the planets
and the stars and the sun, was thought to revolve around the earth.
The Psalmist proclaimed that *"The earth is the Lord's"* and *"God*
is the king of all the earth."

The word *earth* is used more times in the Psalms than in any other book of the Bible. Jesus used the word too and also used the word *world,* as when he taught *"For God so loved the world..."* (John 3:16). Underlying that translation, the Greek word for *world* is *cosmos.* That is interesting because we know the cosmos as the entire universe and everything in it, including our planet. Now our praise expands to the idea that God is the creator and lover of all creation... King of the Universe. In the old days, it was not uncommon for Sunday Schools to personalize this verse, substituting the student's name: For God so loved Donna, or, For God so loved Billy. That is true and brings home the verse, but is closer to the idea that the planet, stars and sun revolve around us. We do well to embrace the idea that God loves the cosmos, and if we love God, we will love what God loves.

If the Psalmist were re-writing this gem today, he might update it a bit, something like... *For God is the king of all the cosmos; sing praises with a psalm. God is king over the universe.*

The messages to us: See the whole and not just yourself. So love what God so loves. Care enough to save the cosmos, and do what you can to leave it better than you found it. It is God's. Possessive case. God created it and not only rules it, but loves it. Therefore, let us sing praises to God with a psalm.

PRAYER: O God, Creator and Sustainer of the Cosmos, I praise you with the highest and best words I can think of. Keep me from having too small a concept of you and help me realize that you are big enough to love everything in the universe and still know and love me too. Loving God, "Thee will I cherish, Thee will I honor, Thou, my soul's glory, joy, and crown." Amen.

FORTY-EIGHT

We ponder your steadfast love, O God.
48:9a

The most profound verses in the Bible are often short and simple. Winston Churchill said *"Short words are best and the old words when short are best of all."* Here in old words which are short, the Psalmist ponders God's steadfast love.

The Hebrew word for *love* means *giving*. To love is to give and to give is to love. The one who loves gives of himself or herself to another. Giving establishes a connection between the giver and the receiver. Without giving, no relationship can be enduring. The Hebrew word also means a longing for. The one who gives longs for the other, with fondness and affection. Ponder how God longs for you.

It is a worthy spiritual discipline for us to emulate the model of the Psalmist, to spend some time pondering the gift of God's steadfast love. How does a person feel when receiving a gift? Usually gratitude is the feeling. Our pondering is interwoven with our gratitude to God for loving us.

The Rabbis teach of a young boy who once asked his Rabbi why man was created with two eyes. The Rabbi responded, "With the left eye you should look at yourself, and see where you need to improve yourself. And with the right eye, you should look at others lovingly, always seeking out their best qualities." So, if we truly want to be loving, the first thing we need to do is to examine ourselves to determine where we can make improvements. Then, we attempt to look at others through God-like lenses, seeing in them goodness, loveliness, and their best qualities.

According to Judaism, humans can have several forms of love toward the God of the universe. One is called Eternal Love. This type of love is awakened when one considers God's greatness, in the sense that the entire universe is as nothing when compared with God. It is also the title of a Jewish prayer often spoken in the evenings. Another form of love is called Abundant Love. This love for God is deeply rooted in the Jewish soul and is unwavering. It is also the title of a morning prayer expressing thanks to God for God's love. Jesus would have known and recited these prayers. All people of faith do well to adopt these practices, spending a few moments each day pondering God's steadfast and abundant gift of love.

The prophet Isaiah (43:4) tells of God speaking and saying *"You are precious in my sight, and honored, and I love you."* It is overwhelming to consider that God knows me, sees me as precious, loves me and holds me in the palm of God's hand. Hear those Divine words spoken to you and ponder how that makes you feel, for *"You are precious in my sight, and honored, and I love you."*

PRAYER: Giving God, I ponder your love for me and cherish that you see me as precious, even knowing my inner thoughts. Thank you, God, for loving me anyway. May I attempt to begin and end each day contemplating about your great love for me. Help me to understand that you love all others that way as well. May I look at others and see the best in them too. Anyway. Amen.

FORTY-NINE

Truly, no ransom avails for one's life, there is no price one can give to God for it.
49:7

I remember a friend saying that he was happy just to be alive and grateful to God for the gift of life. At the time, I took life for granted. So, I'm alive. Of course I am. The Psalmist, like my friend, felt that there is no price a person can give to God for his or her life. In other words, do not take life for granted.

The verse reminds of Jesus' parable from Luke 12:
"The land of a rich man produced abundantly. And he thought to himself, 'What should I do, for I have no place to store my crops?' Then he said, 'I will do this: I will pull down my barns and build larger ones, and there I will store all my grain and my goods. And I will say to my soul, Soul, you have ample goods laid up for many years; relax, eat, drink, be merry.' But God said to him, 'You fool! This very night your life is being demanded of you. And the things you have prepared, whose will they be?' So it is with those who store up treasures for themselves but are not rich toward God."

The last sentence compels us to think about the value of our lives:
So it is with those who store up treasures for themselves but are not rich toward God.

Rich toward God. We can understand the message about materialism. We can comprehend the danger of wanting just a little bit more. But does our wanting just a little bit more grab both sides of our head and turn our vision away from our cup running over to wanting more? What would it be like to consider the questions: "Am I rich toward God? How? Why would I want to be? How can I become richer toward God?"

Those are the questions Jesus' parable leaves us pondering. Is there an answer? Ask ten people of faith how to become richer toward God and you might receive ten different answers or interpretations.

And yet, are not these the most important questions a person of faith can ask: How can I become richer toward God?

Perhaps poet Rainer Maria Rilke in his work *Letters to a Young Poet* provides a clue:
Try to love the questions themselves as if they were locked rooms or books written in a very foreign language. Don't search for the answers, which could not be given to you now, because you would not be able to live them. And the point is, to live everything. Live the questions now. Perhaps then, someday far in the future, you will gradually, without even noticing it, live your way into the answer.

Jesus' parable goes deeper than merely warning about the danger of materialism. It haunts us to consider how can we become richer toward God... to ask and continue to ask the question about our own spiritual direction. Love the questions and perhaps someday you will live your way into the answer.

For the Psalmist, his answer is an affirmation that there is no price one can give to God for the value of one's life.

PRAYER: Creating God, forgive me for when I take my life for granted and forget to embrace life as a gift from you. Help me to place in second place all my wants so that I may focus first on becoming rich toward you. Amen.

FIFTY

I will not accept a bull from your house, or goats from your folds.
50:9

Dr. Bruce Metzger, who was my teacher of New Testament at
Princeton Theological Seminary, was also the chair of the
committee which produced the New Revised Standard Version of
the Bible. He told about the work of the committee, the reasons
for some of its translations, and even some humorous illustrations
such as this verse. In the previous version, the Revised Standard
Version (he was on that committee too), the verse read as follows:
"I will accept no bull from your house." Consider the humor that
floated around the translators as they teased about God telling a
person who might be trying to inflate their own goodness "Cut the
bull! I will accept no bull from your house." Or from a person
piling high excuses as he or she attempts to justify to God his or
her behavior, with the Divine responding "That sounds like a pile
of bull."

Now of course that is not the intent of this verse, even though it
sounds like it to our contemporary ears. "No bull." However, in
an ironic way, that may not be far off, for what God is saying is
that God does not what a pile of sacrifices or religious practices.
The prophet Hosea (6:6) tells of God saying to those who see
faithfulness as animal sacrifices *"For I desire steadfast love and
not sacrifice, the knowledge of God rather than burnt offerings."*
No bull. Faithfulness to God, then, had deteriorated into placing
religious practices as the pathway into God's presence. No, says
God. It is not about the practices, for what God desires is not the
practices but steadfast love. The message could not be clearer and
sounds a warning for those of us today who desire to seek an
encounter with the Divine: it's not about practices, but rather,
steadfast love for God.

126

Amos (5:21, 24) put it even more strongly as he tells of God speaking: *"I hate, I despise your festivals, and I take no delight in your solemn assemblies."* But *"Let justice roll down like waters, and righteousness like an ever-flowing stream."* Justice then was interpreted as how you treat people. And *righteousness* is well-translated as right relationships. To God, how you treat people and seeking the right relationships with others is what God wants, much more than religious practices. No bull.

Isaiah encountered the same legalism when religion was interpreted as conforming to rites and rituals. He put it bluntly: *"Such fasting as you do today will not make your voice heard on high."* (Isaiah 58:4). Something different is needed... a different understanding of faithfulness. So what is needed? Isaiah answers in the form of a question (verses 7, 9): *"Is it not... to loose the bonds of injustice... to let the oppressed go free, and to break every yoke? Is it not to share your bread with the hungry, and bring the homeless poor into your house; when you see the naked, to cover them... Then you shall call, and the LORD will answer."* To Isaiah, true faithfulness to God leads to service, especially to those on the margin and to those with the least.

There is a non-Canonical Gospel of the Nazarenes which tells of a man who said to Jesus "I've kept the commandments." Jesus responded: *"How can you say, I have fulfilled the law and the prophets, when it is written in the law: You shall love your neighbor as yourself; and look: many of your neighbors are covered with filth, dying of hunger, and your house is full of many good things, none of which is given to them?"*

And so, we learn from this Psalm, from the prophets and from Jesus what God values. What counts is the steadfast love of God and actively doing something to help those in need. That is true religion. Not sacrifices. Not religious practices. No bull!

127

PRAYER: Dear God, forgive me when my sincere attempts to know you and please you are found more in my religious practices than they are in loving you and loving your beloved children by doing something to help them. Lead me to opportunities to help another and to work for justice. Clear my head to know when and how to act, and give me a gentle push when I need it to put my faithfulness into action. Amen.

FIFTY-ONE

Create in me a clean heart, O God, and put a new and right spirit within me.
51:10

Workers in the helping professions tell how a person who recognizes his or her problem and who wants to find help is far more likely to discover healing and wholeness than the one who is blind to his or her problem and therefore sees no need for help. Apply that observation to this gem from Psalm 51. Who is most likely to seek from God a clean heart and a new spirit? The one who recognizes his or her need. Those are the ones who pray this prayer: *Create in me a clean heart, O God, and put a new and right spirit within me.*

God, who created and continues to create, makes new. God can change people, implant within them a new spirit, renew them and restore their soul. Four of the most important words in the Bible come from the Psalmist: *"He restores my soul."* (Psalm 23:3). Consider the role your sole plays in the total makeup of you. You have many dimensions: you have a physical nature, a social nature, an emotional nature, an intellectual nature and many others, but you also possess a spiritual nature. If your spirit is crushed and broken, it does not matter how great the other pieces and parts of you are functioning. On the other hand, if your spirit is strong and healthy, you can endure or adapt to anything – no matter what you might be missing in other parts of your life.

You have witnessed news stories about people who have suffered from every kind of handicap or loss and yet they still display a positive attitude about life. It is more than just enduring. When your soul is restored you can thrive. When your spirit is in balance, you embrace *life abundantly*, as Jesus called it. You experience *life that is life indeed*, as Paul called it. Is not that the kind of life you desire? When that kind of life is absent, the soul needs help.

Is not your spiritual nature the most important part of all that defines you as a person? Paul wrote about how we have an inner nature and an outer nature. No matter what happens to the outer nature, the inner nature is renewed every day. In his second letter to the Corinthians (chapter four), he called the inner nature our *"treasure in earthen vessels"* or *"treasure in clay jars."* (2 Corinthians 4:7). Look at all the bad things that could happen to the outer nature even while the inner nature stays good: *"We are afflicted in every way, but not crushed; perplexed, but not driven to despair; persecuted, but not forsaken; struck down, but not destroyed..."*

Paul then explains the chemistry of how this happens: *"So we do not lose heart. Though our outer nature is wasting away, our inner nature is being renewed every day."* That may be one of the most hopeful sentences in the Bible: no matter what happens to you on the outside, your inner nature is being renewed by God every day. The Psalmist, in Psalm 23, put it in four words: *He restoreth my soul.*

You have substantial strength within you, more than you realize until it is tested. When inner strength seems to wane, God gives you back what you had before. God REstores your soul to newness. What you once possessed is renewed and infused into your spiritual veins again. Energy is regained for the journey.

Look at all the words about God that begin with *"re"*:
Rebuild
Renew
Restore
Repair
Refresh
Reshape
Rekindle
Revive
Recreate

The Bible overflows with testimony of how God restores and renews:

"When my spirit is faint, you know my way." (Psalm 142:3a)

"Be renewed in the spirit of your minds, and put on the new nature, created after the likeness of God..." (Ephesians 4:22-24)

"He will renew you in his love." (Zephaniah 3:17)

"Anyone who belongs to Christ is a new person. The past is forgotten, and everything is new." (2 Corinthians 5:17, CEV)

And, the gem from Psalm 51: *"Create in me a clean heart, O God, and put a new and right spirit within me."* One of the things this gem tells us is that our Creator God can change the polarity of a person's spirit. God has the power to change negativity to positivity. This verse from Psalm 51 provides the words to ask for this change. Ezekiel (36:26, 27a) phrased it as God's answer: *"A new heart I will give you, and a new spirit I will put within you; and I will remove from your body the heart of stone and give you a heart of flesh. I will put my spirit within you..."*

Paul reduced the polarity of a person's spirit to the simplest of words: *yes* and *no.* He wrote (2 Corinthians 1:19, 20a): *For the Son of God... was not "Yes and No" but in him it is always "Yes." For in him every one of God's promises is a "Yes."*

YES is one of the best words in the English language. Can you remember some of your favorite times hearing that word?
YES, I got accepted.
YES, they made a good offer on the house.
YES, said your parent, we are going to the beach.
YES, reported the doctor, everything's okay.
YES, answers the mechanic, I fixed it for you.
YES, comes the answer from the employer: you've got the job.
YES, says one of your employees: I already took care of that.
YES, she whispers, I will marry you.
YES, announces your child: I'm coming home to visit.

YES, explains your financial advisor, you can retire.
YES you can!
YES is a word you like to hear. It's got to be a favorite word.

YES people give you energy. They radiate positivity. They generate positive energy. They lift up and stimulate creativity, hope, and optimism. They have a CAN DO attitude. It is all in the polarity. From them, you are most likely to hear that wonderful word YES.

A YES attitude expects the best and sets in motion forces which cause the best to materialize. An ad in a business journal described the polarity this way:

The winner is always a part of the answer.
The loser is always a part of the problem.

The winner always has a program.
The loser always has an excuse.

The winner says "let me do it for you."
The loser says "that's not my job."

The winner sees an answer for every problem.
The loser sees a problem in every answer.

The winner sees a green near every sand trap.
The loser sees two or three sand traps near every green.

The winner says, "It may be difficult but it's possible."
The loser says "it may be possible but it's too difficult."

YES people make it happen.
They believe they can do it. They believe you can do it.
They know, as the bumper sticker says, that *"Attitudes are the real disability."*
Their credo is: *If you believe you can or cannot, you are correct!*
Their motto is: *"They can conquer who believe they can."*

Their verse is (Mark 9:23) *"All things are possible for the one who believes."*

YES people know they cannot please everyone so they do not drain their energy trying. A successful entertainer said *"I do not know the key to success, but the key to failure is trying to please everybody."*

YES people are not afraid to fail. Ben Franklin said: *"The person who does things makes many mistakes, but he never makes the biggest mistake of all: doing nothing."*

YES people know a secret which Psychologist William James said was the greatest discovery in HIS life: *"My greatest discovery is that a human being can alter his or her life by altering his his or her attitude."* YES people know that you can choose your attitude, change your polarity, and direct your energy.

Former Senator Mark Hatfield was visiting Mother Theresa and asked her if she became angry at the causes that lead to suffering. She answered: *"Why should I expend energy in anger that I can expend in love?"* YES people choose how to expend their energy.

Can you change polarity? If you feel that you are simply not hard-wired that way and tend to be on the negative side, can you change the direction of energy from negative to positive? You cannot change someone else. You cannot change your spouse's polarity. You cannot change your son's polarity. You cannot change your sister's polarity. You cannot do anything about the polarity of the person on a committee with you. But can you change your own polarity if you want to?

The Bible says yes, that God can change your polarity. God can put a new spirit within you and give you a heart of flesh. Then you will know that the power behind you is greater than the task ahead.

PRAYER: O God, who created me and who continues to re-create me, I make this prayer my own. *Create in me a clean heart, O God, and put a new and right spirit within me.* Where negativity resides within my spirit, I ask you to alter my attitude and change my polarity to renew my direction to the positive. Give me faith and self-confidence to believe that with you, all things are possible. Amen.

FIFTY-TWO

I will thank you forever, because of what you have done. In the presence of the faithful I will proclaim your name, for it is good. 52:9

The Psalms remind us over and over again to thank God. We are grateful to be reminded. Like the Psalmist, let us never tire of saying "thank you" for what God has done.

Notice the tense: done. Past tense. Sometimes it feels like we are always looking forward and wanting just a little bit more. It is almost as though a person asks "What are you going to do for me next, God?" The Psalmists gratitude overflows for what God has already done. Isn't that enough?

Few verses in the Bible express gratitude to God more than Psalm 23 (5c, KJV): *"My cup runneth over."* Cup is a metaphor for your life, for all that you are and all that you have. You have heard how a pessimist says *My cup is half empty* and an optimist says *My cup is half full.* A person of faith says *My cup runneth over.* These are the most powerful four words of gratitude ever written.

In other versions, the verse employs the highest superlative to describe God's blessings:

My cup overflows. (New Revised Standard Version)

You honor me as your guest, and you fill my cup until it overflows. (Contemporary English Version)

My cup brims with blessing. (The Message)

My cup runneth over describes an attitude of gratitude. It could almost sound like the speaker considers himself or herself wealthy. But wealth is not an amount. It never was and never will be. Wealth is an attitude. Some of the wealthiest people in the world feel poor and some of the poorest feel wealthy.

135

What makes the difference? Answer: Adopting the attitude of *My cup runneth over*. You never see a grateful person who is an unhappy person. Grateful people learn to be content. The Apostle Paul (Philippians 4:11) worked on this to the point where he could proclaim *"For I have learned to be content with whatever I have."*

Consider the word *content*. Is not contentment the desired goal behind all of our striving to acquire or achieve? *If only...* then I might be content. In Philippians, the Apostle unveils the secret to being content: it is learned behavior. It comes from saying *thank you*. It comes from praising God from whom all blessings flow. It comes from cultivating the attitude *My cup runneth over*.

We become content by saying *thank you*. Thank others frequently. Watch for opportunities to thank another. Say *thank you* to God. Rather than beginning your prayers with petitions and asking, begin by thanking. Wake up each morning and go to bed each evening with these words on your lips: *My cup runneth over*.

Program your routine so that every morning when your toes touch the floor, you begin your day by proclaiming *My cup runneth over*. It is easy to say it on the good days. Say it especially on your worst days. As you practice this, you will discover yourself pledging to see through lenses of abundance rather than through lenses of scarcity. If you change how you see things, you will change your attitude and that will transform your spirit.

Once after I preached about the topic of thanksgiving, a saintly older woman named Dottie was coming out of the sanctuary and she said to me ever so sincerely *"I'm working on my gratitude."* Her comment surprised me because I knew her to be one of the kindest, gentlest humans I have ever encountered. Dottie radiated a life of being thankful. She said *thank you* to everyone. I considered Dottie a model of gratitude. And yet, she said she was still working on it! Her comment shook me by the shoulders to remind me that gratitude not something you either have or do not have. Gratitude is not infused into your DNA. Gratitude is something to be worked on, day by day. Dottie was right and may her words inspire you too as you work on your gratitude.

May this gem from Psalm 52 inspire you to say "thank you" in prayer at every opportunity: *I will thank you forever, because of what you have done. In the presence of the faithful I will proclaim your name, for it is good.*

PRAYER: Giving God, I thank you forever because of what you have done for me in my life. My cup runneth over. Whenever I feel like I do not have enough of what I want, guide me to see through lenses of abundance for what you have already done in my life. Amen.

FIFTY-THREE

God looks down from heaven on humankind to see if there are any who are wise, who seek after God.
53:2

The comma in this verse is important because it sets up a parallelism: those who are wise are the ones who seek after God. And, those who seek after God are the ones who are wise.

The book of Proverbs (9:10a) notes that *"The fear of the LORD is the beginning of wisdom."* The word *fear* is an ancient word with a beautiful meaning. It does not mean being scared or afraid. A loving, compassionate God would not wish for believers to be afraid of God. The true meaning is "to revere." That makes sense. Revering God is the beginning of wisdom. In Proverbs, wisdom does not mean academic intelligence, content knowledge or the kind of wisdom that we associate with wise old sages. Rather, wisdom in the Bible is always intensely practical, not theoretical. Wisdom, in the Old Testament, is more like common sense or attitude. In many ways, the biblical meaning of wisdom is the art of being successful at life – understanding what about life is truly most important and worthwhile.

This gem from the Psalms encourages us to seek after God. The word *seek* is found throughout the Bible. One of the most important verses from Jesus' Sermon on the Mount is *"Seek ye first the Kingdom of God and his righteousness."* (Matthew 6:33, KJV). That is what Jesus considered of first importance, so much so that he used the word *first* to make clear this priority. If a person is a Christian, his or her first and highest aim is to seek after God.

In the Sermon on the Mount, Jesus again used the word *search* in his classic verse *"Ask, and it will be given you; search, and you will find; knock, and the door will be opened for you."* (Matthew 7:7). Knock, and the door will be opened for you. Ask. Seek. Knock. These verbs are imperatives. Imperatives are verb forms that tell you to do something. In Greek there are two kinds of imperative:

The AORIST IMPERATIVE issues one definite command. *Shut the door behind you* would be an aorist imperative. *Do it now.* An aorist imperative is a command to do something once and to do it in response to the person telling you to do it. If, for example, I said *Stand up*, that means *Stand up right now.* If you enter my car and I ask you to please fasten your seat belt, it means do it now.

The PRESENT IMPERATIVE issues a command that a person should always do something or should keep on doing something. For example, *Always shut doors behind you*, would be a present imperative. Or, *Always lock your car doors.* That is a present imperative. Do it now and keep on doing it. If I suggest that you should wear a seat belt, it means you should do so every time you enter any car.

In his teaching about asking, seeking and knocking, Jesus used the PRESENT IMPERATIVE mood of the verb. What he meant is not so much to *ask*, *seek*, and *knock*, but to:
Keep on asking. Do not ask once and then stop.
Keep on seeking. Do not seek once and then give up.
Keep on knocking and knocking and knocking.
Keep on keeping on.

This is an important lesson to help us understand the imperative to *"seek after God."* It means that your seeking is a work in progress, a continuous journey. You do not seek after God once and done. Rather, keep on seeking your entire life.

In the book of Jeremiah, God spoke and said *"When you search for me, you will find me, if you seek me with all your heart"* (Jeremiah 29:13). You are wise to search for God, to keep on in your seeking after God, and to draw near to God. Then, says God from Jeremiah, you will find me, if you seek me with all your heart.

PRAYER: Spirit of the Living God, be my guide as I seek after you. Lead me and help me to know how to seek after you. Encourage me to continue my seeking every day, as I draw nearer to you and as I seek to know you better and love you more. Amen.

FIFTY-FOUR

Hear my prayer, O God; give ear to the words of my mouth.
54:2

A journalist was assigned to cover the Jerusalem bureau. He rented an apartment overlooking the Wailing Wall, also known as the Western Wall. Whenever he looked at the wall, he saw an old Jewish man praying vigorously. The journalist wondered whether there might be a story there, so he went down to the wall, introduced himself and said: "You come every day to the wall. What are you praying for?" The old man replied: "In the morning I pray for world peace, then I pray for the brotherhood of man. I go home, have a cup of tea, and I come back to the wall to pray for the eradication of illness and disease from the earth."

The journalist was taken by the old man's sincerity and persistence. "How long have you been coming to the wall to pray for these things?" The old man replied: "Maybe twenty, twenty-five years." The journalist asked: "How does it feel to come and pray every day for over twenty years for these things?" "How does it feel?" the old man replied. "How does it feel? It feels like I'm talking to a wall!"

Do you ever feel like you are praying to a wall? You do not know what to say, what to ask... sometimes it feels even like you completely forget how to pray. Or, maybe you get prayed-out. Then we see Paul in Romans 8 observing *"For we do not know how to pray as we ought."* And we want to say "You too!"

In Romans 8 26, Paul writes: *"Likewise the Spirit helps us in our weakness; for we do not know how to pray as we ought, but that very Spirit intercedes with sighs too deep for words."* This is an amazing function of the Spirit. Paul tells us that the Spirit intercedes for you with sighs too deep for words. The Spirit hears what you mean. The Spirit knows your feelings, yearnings and thoughts, and carries them to God.

This is a great relief, for it tells that you do not have to know the right words to say in prayer because God can hear your heart. You can stumble and mumble, trying to tell God what you're feeling and God hears you, because the Spirit intercedes for you.

A Japanese woman who spoke little English came to see me in my office. I could hardly understand her and she could hardly understand me. We were not communicating. A young woman who grew up in Japan and spoke Japanese fluently was sitting outside the office and overheard our labored conversation. She poked her head in the doorway, excused herself for interrupting, and asked if we would like her to intercede for us. She did, and we were able to communicate well with each other, thanks to our helper who interceded.

Paul tells of an amazing gift from the Spirit, for we want to communicate with God and we want to try to tell God what is on our mind and in our heart, but often words fail us. That is not a problem, for the Spirit carries our words to God's ears. Consider how some versions of the Bible tell about Romans 8:26:

Contemporary English Version (CEV)
In certain ways we are weak, but the Spirit is here to help us. For example, when we don't know what to pray for, the Spirit prays for us in ways that cannot be put into words. All of our thoughts are known to God. He can understand what is in the mind of the Spirit, as the Spirit prays for God's people.

Phillips
The Spirit of God not only maintains this hope within us, but helps us in our present limitations. For example, we do not know how to pray worthily as sons of God, but his Spirit within us is actually praying for us in those agonizing longings which never find words. And God who knows the heart's secrets understands, of course, the Spirit's intention as he prays for those who love God.

The Message

Meanwhile, the moment we get tired in the waiting, God's Spirit is right alongside helping us along. If we don't know how or what to pray, it doesn't matter. He does our praying in and for us, making prayer out of our wordless sighs, our aching groans. He knows us far better than we know ourselves, knows our pregnant condition, and keeps us present before God. That's why we can be so sure that every detail in our lives of love for God is worked into something good.

It is interesting that Paul says *"we do not know how to pray as we ought."* Was that not the purpose of Jesus teaching the disciples the Lord's Prayer, when they asked *"Lord, teach us to pray"*? And yet, we understand what Paul means because we too feel that we do not know how to pray as we ought. We thirst for an encounter with the Divine. We desire to be in touch and to remain in communication with God. We long to have a sense that God hears our prayers.

Here is a question about prayer: Should we pray specifically or generically? That is, should we specify the outcomes we would like, telling God exactly what we want? Or, should we entrust our concerns and needs into God's hand, trusting that God knows far better than we ourselves what is in our highest and best interest? When praying for ourselves or for another, we would like to tell God precisely what we want to happen. For example, if praying for another's illness, we pray for them to regain health. That specifies an outcome. On the other hand, is it not sufficient to pray for God's will to be done in their lives? *"Faith is not belief without proof, but trust without reservations,"* said Quaker philosopher D. Elton Trueblood. A generic prayer trusts in God to do what is best for us or for the person about whom we are praying.

Should you pray for a specific outcome or should you pray for God's will to be done? Jesus did both. The night before he was crucified, in the garden, he did both: he prayed for a specific outcome and he prayed for God's will to be done, in the same sentence.

Mathew (26:39) wrote that Jesus he threw himself on the ground and prayed, *"My Father, if it is possible, let this cup pass from me; yet not what I want but what you want."* The word *"cup"* stands for his destiny... the cross. Do you hear what Jesus is asking? If it is possible... let me not have to go through with the crucifixion. No one wants to die at age thirty-three. That is a specific request. But then he prayed for God's will: *"Yet not what I want but what you want."* That is the ultimate prayer of trust and yielding to God's will. The KJV translates it this way: *And He went a little farther, and fell on His face and prayed, saying, "O My Father, if it be possible, let this cup pass from me; nevertheless, not as I will, but as Thou wilt."* That is the most important *"nevertheless"* in the Bible. It is worthy to be included in every one of our prayers. Pray for what you desire, but add the prayer of complete trust without reservations: *"Nevertheless."*

This is Jesus' example for how to pray: pray for the specific outcome you think is best, but trust that God cares about the best possible outcome. *"Nevertheless, not as I will, but as Thou wilt."* That prayer will always be answered.

When praying for another person and you are unsure of what to say, it can be sufficient to say *"I pray for the best possible outcome for the person I name before you"* or *"I lift up in prayer..."* That prayer is just as powerful and received by God as one where words may be more precise or technical. The prayer of your heart will be carried by the Spirit to God's hears and God will hear you.

The Psalmist wrote *Hear my prayer, O God; give ear to the words of my mouth.* Now of course God is always hearing and listening. It is not as though God leaves when you say "amen" and connects to listen when you begin "Dear God." God is always there, always present and always listening. So why ask God to do something... to give ear to the words of my mouth... when we know full well God is already doing it? Because we want to pray deeply and even though our request to God is redundant, it signals that we really want God to hear our prayer.

PRAYER: Loving God, hear our sighs, our hurts, our longings, and our hopes. Bring wholeness, hope and healing to those for whom we pray. May your will be done in their lives. Amen.

FIFTY-FIVE

It is not enemies who taunt me – I could bear that; it is not adversaries who deal insolently with me – I could hide from them. But it is you, my equal, my companion, my familiar friend, with whom I kept pleasant company;
55:12-14a

COMPANION VERSE: *My companion laid hands on a friend and violated a covenant with me with speech smoother than butter, but with a heart set on war; with words that were softer than oil, but in fact were drawn swords.*
55:20, 21

This Psalm stings deeply. It is about betrayal. The Psalmist can face enemies. He can go up against problems. If this were written by David, he battled the giant Goliath. But betrayal is one of the hardest feelings to handle. Not only that, it hurts even more when the betrayal comes from someone who was trusted, perhaps even loved: *It is not enemies who taunt me – I could bear that; it is not adversaries who deal insolently with me – I could hide from them. But it is you, my equal, my companion, my familiar friend, with whom I kept pleasant company.*

There are a million different ways the Last Supper could be remembered, but only one begins the entrance into the celebration of it ever since: *"...on the night when he was betrayed..."* (1 Corinthians 11:23). Betrayal by a trusted companion cuts so deeply that no matter what else may be forgotten, the betrayal lingers like an open wound. *My companion laid hands on a friend and violated a covenant with me with speech smoother than butter, but with a heart set on war; with words that were softer than oil, but in fact were drawn swords.*

If you have ever been betrayed, you know how hard it is. You may try as hard as you can to forgive and if you can, it releases you from much of the anger, woundedness, and wondering how it could have been otherwise.

But forgetting seems near impossible. It stings so deeply that the betrayal is something akin to post traumatic stress that lingers. It is understandable if you have difficulty forgetting. Even the recorders of the holy supper could not forget... *"on the night when he was betrayed."*

These verses have become the banner Psalm for those who are victims of abuse. Around the world, at least one in every three women has been beaten, coerced into sex or otherwise abused during her lifetime. Far more will be emotionally abused. Domestic abuse does not care about how much education you have, how well raised you were, how much money you've got, how successful you've been, what kind of person you are, where you live or where you go to church. You have neighbors, friends, fellow church members and perhaps relatives who have suffered from or who are now experiencing some form of abuse or being controlled by another – a form of betrayal – but it is a quiet suffering. Many are not inclined to talk about it and some believe it is their own fault, often because that is what the abuser tells them.

Sometimes the Bible is taken out of context to justify domestic violence. Perhaps they quote Ephesians 5:22-24 about wives being subject to their husbands: *"Wives, be subject to your husbands as you are to the Lord. For the husband is the head of the wife just as Christ is the head of the church, the body of which he is the Savior. Just as the church is subject to Christ, so also wives ought to be, in everything, to their husbands."* That passage applies to a different context of another age, much like the verses in the following chapter which implore slaves to *"obey your earthly masters with fear and trembling."* These verses were written when everyone believed that the sun and planets revolved around us. Since that time, our understanding of our physical world has changed, as has our social world's understanding that women are not subservient, people of color cannot be considered as property, gay people are not a mistake, and one person may not control another because of gender, race, sexual orientation, or any other reason.

Abuse is not your fault, it is not God's will, and it is not punishment. Sometimes an abused person may see their suffering as just punishment for a past deed. Or, they may see their abuse as God's will, as a part of God's plan for their life, or God's way of teaching them a lesson. Abuse does not occur because God is mad at you. God, who sheds the gift of grace over all, does not cause bad things to happen to people. All people are God's beloved children. A loving Parent would never consider abuse as a way to punish or teach a lesson. God does not work like that. The loving and compassionate God wants for you that which is best in your life.

Abuse is not your fault. Abuse does not happen to you because you did something bad. Do not blame yourself. Being abused is not a failure of your character or your faith. Even if you care for the person who hurts you, they are the one doing wrong. Not you. Abuse is not because you are to blame, even if someone tells you that you are. Abuse is not a consequence of poor choices, being stupid, a bad attitude, or not being able to get your act together.

You have rights: You have a right to a home without constant conflict. You have a right to be you and to be free. You have a right to life, liberty, and the pursuit of happiness. You have a right to your own privacy. You have a right to your dignity and your reputation. You have a right to say *no*. You have the right to be safe, physically and emotionally.

Jesus brought the world a new way of seeing love. The New Testament word for love is *agape*, which can mean to desire that which is in the highest and best interest of the other. If someone hurts another, whether by hitting or by controlling them emotionally, that is not seeking what is truly best for the person. There is no way that behavior can be described as love. That is abuse. It is violence, even if someone does not hit you physically. It is a violation of covenant between two people.

Being abused certainly fits the sentiment of Psalm 55. It is betrayal. But so is betrayal by a friend, family member, co-worker, committee member, neighbor or anyone who you thought you could trust. Bullying is betrayal. Gossip is betrayal, whether in the parking lot or on social media. Passive aggressive betrayal is betrayal, as when a staff member sounds like part of the team, officially, but behind the scenes spreads poison. Anyone who has been betrayed hears Psalm 55 and is inclined to say "You too?" *I am distraught... My heart is in anguish within me... Fear and trembling come upon me... And I say, "O that I had wings like a dove! I would fly away and be at rest; I would hurry to find a shelter for myself..." It is not enemies who taunt me – I could bear that; it is not adversaries... I could hide from them. But it is YOU, my equal, my companion, my familiar friend, with whom I kept pleasant company. My companion laid hands on a friend and violated a covenant with me with speech smoother than butter, but with a heart set on war; with words that were softer than oil, but in fact were drawn swords.*

When betrayed, a few suggestions:

First, find someone with whom you can speak confidentially and let it out. Tell about how you feel about being betrayed. The best thing for you is to surround yourself with the support of caring people who will understand and listen.

Second, seek help. If you have been or are being abused, do not hang in there with the false hope that things will get better. Find a women's resource center or other helping agency to seek their guidance. Call the National Domestic Violence hotline. Help is available 24/7 at 1-800-799-SAFE (7233). Your safety is their priority. Emotional abuse counts as Domestic Violence. Please go to their website thehotline.org or search for *"The National Domestic Violence Hotline."* You can speak with a person, by phone or by internet live chat. They will help you make confidential contact which cannot be traced. Take action, because it will not likely improve even though you are told by the abuser that he or she will try harder not to do it again. If you do not know where to turn, ask your pastor.

148

Call the local police station and ask if they can recommend resources. Turn to the YMCA, talk to your doctor, look online for help. Search for *women's resource center, domestic violence, domestic violence help, domestic abuse, social service agencies, hotlines, community resources,* and similar terms. Add your zip code to the search term to find neighboring resources. The worst thing is to do nothing.

Third, give yourself patience, kindness, tenderness and time. Perhaps you have been raised to forgive anyone who has done wrong. Understand that betrayal is one of the hardest situations for forgiving and forgetting. Eventually you may get to the point where you can forgive, but it may be that forgetting will not be possible even as much as you try or say you want to forget it. Take comfort that the Psalmist could not forget his being betrayed. The Apostle Paul, who was the first to write about the Last Supper, could not forget how his Lord Jesus Christ was betrayed. If you just cannot forgive or forget at this time, give yourself the gift of grace. God gives you grace. If God can give you grace, then give yourself grace too. You are not letting God down when you need to have grace for being unable to forgive or forget. In time, perhaps it might come.

Fourth, do not give up on your faith. Trust that God is with you in your worst of times. To the abused, it can appear like there is no hope, no way out. It is a dark time. The literal translation of the phrase in Psalm 23:4 is *"the valley of dark shadows."* For people who are abused, that may be the most comforting message in the Bible. In the valley, you are not alone: *"Yea, though I walk through the valley of dark shadows, I will fear no evil. For thou art with me."* Some of God's sheep suffer abuse. God leaves the flock to go and be with them in their darkest shadows of brokenness, for they need the compassionate touch of the Shepherd so very much.

PRAYER: O Dear God, what shall I do about the hurt feelings I have? It feels like I should be a bigger person. It feels like I should just forgive and forget. But it's not working for me. O God of compassion, understanding, and grace, be with me as I struggle with the feelings I hold. Help me to know how to proceed. And, Dear Lord, I also pray for another whom I know is going through a difficult time because of being abused or betrayed by another. May they feel your presence close by and look to you for guidance. Amen.

FIFTY-SIX

Be gracious to me, O God, for people trample on me; all day long foes oppress me;
56:1

Do you, like the Psalmist, ever feel like people are trampling on you? How wonderful if you can enjoy a day when your creativity overflows freely and you are launched to do your best work or enjoy your finest moments. But some days, it is not so good. Some days, you feel trampled upon and then you are restrained from doing your best and most creative work.

When others trample on you, perhaps you want to strike back in kind. That may be a natural instinct, but you cannot. Roman Emperor Marcus Aurelius encouraged Christians to live this way:
Today you will meet all kinds of unpleasant people.
They will hurt you, and injure you, and insult you.
But you cannot live like that.
You know better, for you are a person
in whom the spirit of God dwells.

You cannot live like that. Sometimes we would like to live like that, but we cannot because God's spirit of love dwells within and love always seeks that which is in the highest and best interest of another. When the spirit of God dwells within us, instead of retaliating, we are more inclined to pursue the aims of kindness, gentleness, peacefulness, grace, and seeking the highest and best interest of the other. That is how we can live, by the grace of God.

Paul named these high aims the fruit of the spirit (Galatians 5:22, 23). When they trample upon us, how then shall we live? We shall live as people in whom the spirit of God dwells and aim at these qualities:

LOVE. *Agape* can mean to truly desire that which is in the highest and best interest of the other. It does not mean you have to like them, enjoy their company, desire to be with them, or invite them over for dinner. It means to desire their highest and best interest.

Even your enemies, said Jesus. For people you do not like, you might prefer them to get back what they deserve. But when the Spirit dwells within, it changes your goal to desire what is best for them.

JOY. Jesus said *"These things have I spoken unto you, that my joy might remain in you, and that your joy might be full"* (John 15:11). Examine his word *remain*. Unlike happiness which might happen or not, his joy remains in you. Jesus abides with you. What is the likely diagnosis if a person does not experience joy? Answer: more of God's Spirit is needed.

PEACE. This word essentially refers to inner peace. It is translated *"to set at one again,"* as when everything is whole, good and reset to start anew. It is like the hymn that reminds *"It is well, it is well, with my soul."* There are no self-help books or courses that lead to that kind of peace. It comes to you by gift. Jesus said *Peace I leave with you; my peace I give to you. I do not give to you as the world gives. Do not let your hearts be troubled, and do not let them be afraid.* (John 14:27). This is the kind of peace where your heart is not troubled nor afraid.

PATIENCE. This word refers to patience with people. It is like when you are trying to teach another and he or she says *Be patient with me.* It is patience that waits for people, cuts them some slack, forgives their mistakes, gives them grace and believes the best in them. Patience with others is related to grace. You cannot earn it, demand it or earn it. It is a gift. When you give grace to another, it is not easy grace. It can cost you. Yet when the Spirit dwells within you, you become more conscious of the grace you have received and therefore want to turn around and extend grace to others.

KINDNESS. The Dali Lama said: *Kindness is my religion.* We suspect there is more to his religion than one word, but we understand what he meant. If another is not kind, who cares what is their religion? It does not seem to do them much good. If another is kind, we are inclined to see the Spirit's inner light radiating from within.

The prophet Micah (6:8) said that kindness is one of the three things God requires: to do justice, to love kindness and to walk humbly with your God. What to do when others trample upon you? Respond with kindness.

GOODNESS. A person of achievements was asked *"What do you want your legacy to be? How do you want to be remembered?"* His answer surprised. He responded: *"I just want to be a good person."* Of all the goals to which we aspire, maybe it is enough just to want to be good... a good person. Perhaps that is the summit to which we should aspire. A person in whom the Spirit dwells will choose *being a good person* as a life goal.

FAITHFULNESS. Faithfulness is what God wants most from you. What God desires is for you to be God's faithful child... to love, to obey and to follow. Perhaps that is why Jesus asked his followers to become like children. Mother Theresa said: *"God does not call you to be successful. God calls you to be faithful."* Set faithfulness as your goal and declare your intent to be a faithful child of God.

GENTLENESS. Gandhi said: *"Gentleness is an attribute of the strong. Only the strong can be gentle."* In our harsh world, gentleness is in short supply. People who trample upon others lack gentleness, which is a sign that they lack strength and lack God's spirit. Let us pray for the Spirit to dwell within so that we might grow strong enough to be gentle.

SELF-CONTROL. This word means having the ego under control. We all have an ego and desire to be valued, cherished, appreciated or at least noticed. When we are not, sometimes we call too much attention to ourselves. That backfires. When the ego gets out of control, you cannot do anything and no one thinks highly of you. In fact, they will think more highly of you when your focus shifts to them. When your thoughts or prayers are dominated by the first-person singular pronoun, invite God's spirit within to help you refocus your aim.

"O God," prayed the Psalmist, *"be gracious to me, for people trample on me."* Marcus Aurelius hit the nail on the head: *But you cannot live like that. You know better, for you are a person in whom the spirit of God dwells.* When it happens to you, God will be gracious to you and when the spirit of God dwells within you, your aims become love, joy, peace, patience, kindness, goodness, faithfulness, gentleness and self-control.

PRAYER: O God, be gracious to me when I am hurt by another or feel trampled upon. I welcome your spirit to dwell in me so that I can tower above the behavior of those who hurt me to live as one in whom your spirit is present and active. Amen.

FIFTY-SEVEN

For your steadfast love is as high as the heavens; your
faithfulness extends to the clouds.
57:10

Again and again, the Psalmist praises God… which reminds us to
do the same. Sometimes we are in a hurry to tell God what we
want that we forget to begin with praise. The Psalmist reminds us
that God is worthy of our praise and he lifts up God's steadfast
love and faithfulness.

His praise of God's faithfulness reminds of the hymn "Great is Thy
Faithfulness":
Great is thy faithfulness, Great is thy faithfulness!
Morning by morning new mercies I see.
All I have needed Thy hand hath provided,
Great is Thy faithfulness, Lord, unto me.

The inspiration for this hymn came from an unlikely source, from
Lamentations (3:17, 22, 23): *"My soul is bereft of peace, I have*
forgotten what happiness is… but this I call to mind, and therefore
I have hope: The steadfast love of the Lord never ceases, his
mercies never come to an end; they are new every morning; great
is thy faithfulness."

It is out of feeling bereft of peace that the praise of God's steadfast
love and faithfulness are lifted up, both in Lamentations and in the
Psalm. The steadfast love of the Lord never ceases… Great is thy
faithfulness.

Have you ever felt bereft of peace? Did you ever experience a
dark time when you feel like you forget what happiness is? We
know that faith should provide strength, hope and resilience. We
know that in our head but our gut can feel otherwise. Darkness
threatens. The Bible understands the depths of human pain.
Lamentations is a book in the Old Testament named for grieving.
Down times. Dark times. End times. Sad times.

You might expect a hopelessness about it, but out of the valley emerges light. From this writing about valleys arises a bright light of hope:

My soul is bereft of peace, I have forgotten what happiness is... You can't get much lower than that. This is a verse for when you feel terrible.

but this I call to mind, and therefore I have hope... Whatever comes next, we are anxious to hear because this hope sounds like it is going to lead somewhere good, perhaps to a source for the inner light.

The steadfast love of the Lord never ceases... This is it! At first blush, it appears understated until you think about it. In your darkest valleys, what could you want more than to know that the steadfast love of God is there for you... *For Thou art with me.*

His mercies never come to an end... If I were writing this verse, I would have chosen a different word, like His *blessings* never come to an end, His *care* never comes to an end, His *surprises* never come to an end or His *gifts* never come to an end. But *mercies*? The Hebrew word for mercies comes from a root word meaning to have compassion and, even more deeply, *to fondle*. That provides an interesting image, that God's love and compassion for you is so great that God fondles you with affection much like a loving grandmother cannot refrain from hugging and touching with affection the beloved grandchild. That is a source of inner light.

They are new every morning... What would it be like to waken every morning and wonder what new mercies God is going to give you today? People are always asking *What's new?* Here is *what's new*: If there are eyes to see, his mercies to you... God's blessings, God's gifts, God's surprises... are new every morning and proclaim that, for you, the best is yet to come. Imagine growing in faith to the point where on the worst of days you hold fast to the hope that the best is yet to come.

After considering this source of hope, the writer sums it up with *Great is your faithfulness*. May that also be the response of those who desire to know God better and to love God more, a shout and a prayer of praise for God's steadfast love and faithfulness.

PRAYER: Steadfast God, hear the praise of my heart for you. I am grateful for your steadfast love. I am thankful to know that your faithfulness to me is constant and always present. When I am feeling low or when I forget what happiness is, give me eyes to see that you shower new mercies, blessings, gifts and surprises upon me with every new morning. Great is thy faithfulness! Amen.

FIFTY-EIGHT

Do you indeed decree what is right, you gods? Do you judge people fairly?
58:1

False gods. Do they decree what is right? Do false gods judge people fairly? Perhaps the mind conjures up images of golden calves, sacrificing animals in a cave, or worshiping statues, the sun, the devil or gods other than the Creator of the earth. Jeremiah (7:9) wrote *"Will you steal, murder, commit adultery, swear falsely, make offerings to Baal, and go after other gods that you have not known..."* The Psalmist (40:4) also lamented how people chase after false gods: *"Happy are those who make the Lord their trust, who do not turn to the proud, to those who go astray after false gods."*

If the Psalmist were writing today, he might define in a more contemporary way the false gods people worship. What do you see that people make into gods? Materialism? Quality of life? We joking use this phrase, but what is America's *real religion*? Education? Sports? Wall Street? Friends? Community? TV? The TV in the living room even looks like an altar, doesn't it? Twenty-eight hours a week is spent in front of the flat screen. Where do people spend their quality time? What claims their pocketbook's heart? Look around and what do you see people doing? Their necks are bent downward gazing into a little plastic thing that glows in their hand, like an entire civilization lost in virtual reality while cemented to a cell phone. The message of the prophets and of Jesus of Nazareth was that God wants to be first in your life: *"Seek ye first the kingdom of God..."* (Matthew 6:33, KJV). Never did Jesus say you should not enjoy other things, but put God first and other things second. He might look a person in the eyes and ask "What is your real religion?"

Choosing what to put first, gods or God, has been a challenge going back to beginning times. Joshua was one who stated the dilemma poignantly. Joshua was born in Egypt and was Moses' general and servant.

The Lord selected Joshua to be Moses' successor before Moses died. Joshua was a respected military leader, political leader, and a spiritual leader. He was quiet and unassuming, but was a battlefield genius in the areas of careful planning, strategy, and execution.

Moses led the Israelites out of Egypt, across the Red Sea, to the mountain where Yahweh gave the law. They wandered around the desert for forty years, and then to the doorstep of the Promised Land. Finally, Moses climbed a mountain and looked over to the land of milk and honey... the Promised Land. He could see it, but would never set foot on it, for atop that mountain, Moses died. It was Joshua, not Moses, who led the Israelites to the Promised Land of Canaan. Joshua led the Israelites to freedom and to the land where they would settle.

This was an ancient land. There were cities long before the Israelites occupied Canaan. There were ancient trade routes and main highways, and they converged at a city called Shechem.

Why is it that it seems to be the good times and not the bad times when people fall away from God? So intense can be their focus on other things, like the quality of life, that they forget God. That happened at Shechem. No longer was Yahweh their God. Perhaps they paid lip-service to Yahweh, but their real god was something else.

Is that different from today? We too have other gods in our lives. Perhaps we are not so different from the Israelites at Shechem. We fall away from Yahweh and focus on other gods.

Shechem was a turning point. That is where we hear Joshua's call to faithfulness to God rather than to other gods. He sounds like a teacher making a careful and persuasive argument: "*Now therefore revere the LORD, and serve him in sincerity and in faithfulness; put away the gods which your fathers served... and serve the LORD. And if you be unwilling to serve the LORD, choose this day whom you will serve. As for me and my house, we will serve the LORD.*" (Joshua 24:14-15).

159

The Psalmist writes as though addressing the false gods themselves: *Do you indeed decree what is right, you gods? Do you judge people fairly?*

Joshua addresses not the gods but those to whom the choice is faced: *Choose this day whom you will serve.*

Even people of steadfast faithfulness can become attracted to other gods or make something else their real religion. It is hard to keep God in first place. We need God's help to do what God asks us to do, and we will fail. Thank God for God's gift of grace, for God forgives our failures and continues to call us to grow in our faithfulness – a work in progress for all of us.

PRAYER: Loving God, may I try my best to revere you and to serve you in sincerity and in faithfulness. There are so many other things that claim my attention and attract my interest. I have to confess that there are long periods of time when I do not even think of you at all. I can easily make other things my god. Please forgive me and help keep me on track to be your faithful child. Amen.

FIFTY-NINE

O my strength, I will sing praises to you, for you, O God, are my fortress, the God who shows me steadfast love.
59:17

For you, O God, are my fortress. When troubles rain down upon us or conflict stirs our heart or our stomach, we need a fortress. In times of difficulty, the Psalmist praises God for being his fortress.

His psalm reminds of the great hymn *A Mighty Fortress Is Our God,* by Martin Luther. Luther was born in Germany in 1483. In 1517, Luther nailed his ninety-five theses to the door of the Cathedral of Wittenberg, Germany, an act that started the Protestant Reformation. One of the important parts of the Reformation Movement was congregational singing. Luther had strong convictions about the use and power of sacred music. He said, *"If anyone despises music, as all fanatics do, for him I have no liking; for music is a gift and grace of God, not an invention of people. Thus it drives out the devil and makes people cheerful. Then one forgets all wrath, impurity and other devises."* Luther was also known to say *"I wish to compose sacred hymns so that the Word of God may dwell among the people also by means of songs."*

One of those songs, *A Mighty Fortress*, echoes the Psalmist's sentiment and proclaims that God is your fortress, God is your helper, and God is on your side. Even among a flood of ills and difficulties, God remains your aid and your fortress. When you feel troubled, this is your song:

A mighty fortress is our God, a bulwark never failing;
Our helper He, amid the flood of mortal ills prevailing:
For still our ancient foe doth seek to work us woe;
His craft and pow'r are great, and, armed with cruel hate,
On earth is not his equal.

And though this world,
    with devils filled, should threaten to undo us,
We will not fear, for God hath willed His truth
    to triumph through us;
The Prince of Darkness grim, we tremble not for him;
His rage we can endure, for lo, his doom is sure,
One little word shall fell him.

That word above all earthly pow'rs, no thanks to them, abideth;
The Spirit and the gifts are ours through Him Who with us sideth;
Let goods and kindred go, this mortal life also;
The body they may kill: God's truth abideth still,
His kingdom is forever.

PRAYER: O God, my strength, thank you for being my fortress and my help when I am troubled. When I do not know where else to turn or what else to do, remind me to find shelter in you, my fortress. Amen.

SIXTY

O grant us help against the foe, for human help is worthless.
60:11

You have more strength within than you might realize. When it is tested, God renews and restores those who are open to God's leading to draw upon their inner strength. As the Psalmist reminds constantly, you also have access to strength beyond your own, from God. The Psalmist's writing about God's help in time of need reminds of the great verses from Isaiah: *"Those who wait for the LORD shall renew their strength, they shall mount up with wings like eagles, they shall run and not be weary, they shall walk and not faint."*

Look at the whole of this verse's paragraph from Isaiah 40:28-30:

Have you not known? Have you not heard? The LORD is the everlasting God, the Creator of the ends of the earth. He does not faint or grow weary; his understanding is unsearchable. He gives power to the faint, and strengthens the powerless. Even youths will faint and be weary, and the young will fall exhausted; but those who wait for the LORD shall renew their strength, they shall mount up with wings like eagles, they shall run and not be weary, they shall walk and not faint.

Here is another variation of the verses, from The Message:
Don't you know anything? Haven't you been listening? GOD doesn't come and go. God lasts. He's Creator of all you can see or imagine. He doesn't get tired out, doesn't pause to catch his breath. And he knows everything, inside and out. He energizes those who get tired, gives fresh strength to dropouts. For even young people tire and drop out, young folk in their prime stumble and fall. But those who wait upon GOD get fresh strength. They spread their wings and soar like eagles, they run and don't get tired, they walk and don't lag behind.

Wait for the Lord. The word *wait* in the Bible is a good substitution word. When you come to the word *wait*, substitute the word *trust*. The Contemporary English Version translates the verse *Those who trust the Lord will find new strength.* To *mount up with wings like eagles* is a metaphor for strength that comes from trusting in God.

The sentiment from Isaiah and the Psalmist is similar: To those who trust in God, God will renew your strength, energize you, and help you against the problems and foes you battle.

PRAYER: O God, my Creator, I pray that you would energize me, renew my strength, and help me deal with problems effectively so that I may mount up with wings like an eagle. Amen.

SIXTY-ONE

Let me abide in your tent forever, find refuge under the shelter of your wings.
61:4

This is a beautiful prayer. Let me abide in your tent forever. The word for tent basically means where God is present. It can also be used as house, palace, court, tent, abiding place or habitation. The Psalmist is basically asking to abide in God's presence.
Sometimes in our faith we feel like we should be doing something, asking for something, or pursuing some active spiritual discipline. For the Psalmist, the most pleasurable aim is for he and God to be together. Let me be in your presence. When you think about it, isn't that what you want most from a beloved family member – just to be together and abide in one another's presence?

The verse is similar to another he wrote in Psalm 23:6, translated in the NRSV as *"...and I shall dwell in the house of the Lord my whole life long."*

The Psalm embraces the use of metaphor throughout and the *"house of the Lord"* is also metaphor. It does not refer to a physical place, such as the Temple. It does not refer to the synagogue or to the worship meetinghouse. God is found in those places, but the metaphor is interpreted as *"the place where God is."*

Now, of course, God is everywhere. God is omnipotent, omnipresent, and omniscient – all powerful, all present, and all knowing. The *house of the Lord* refers not to a physical location where God resides but rather to that state of being when you become more aware that you are in the Shepherd's presence. The desired state for the person of faith is to become aware of being in God's presence. God is always there, but we are not always tuned-in to the Shepherd's presence.

To say *I will dwell in the house of the Lord forever* is a personal pledge and a declaration that I choose to live my days aware of being in God's presence.

This does not preclude the idea that God's presence extends into the future. People of faith believe that the best is yet to come, even after death. Jesus assured Nicodemus in John 3 that *"God so loved the world that he gave his only Son, so that everyone who believes in him may not perish but may have eternal life... God did not send the Son into the world to condemn the world, but in order that the world might be saved through him."*

Later in the same Gospel (12:32) he proclaimed: *"I, when I am lifted up from the earth, will draw all people to myself."* Jesus took it for granted that after death, the best was yet to come. There were plenty of times Jesus corrected a misunderstanding about matters of the faith (Mark 12:24-27 is a good example) but consider what Jesus did NOT say: he never said *"Now listen folks, it's not like that. When you die you just turn back to dust."* He did not say that, because he believed that there was life with God after death. *In my Father's house are many mansions: if it were not so, I would have told you* (John 142, KJV).

The beloved Scottish New Testament scholar William Barclay, after a career of interpreting and teaching about the Bible, wrote a summary of his life and beliefs which he titled <u>Spiritual Autobiography</u>. He wrote: *I believe in the life to come, not because of the proofs of the philosophers, but because the whole teaching of the New Testament is based on the assumption that there is life after death.*

Psalm 23 is well used and provides comfort at funerals or when people walk the final steps through the valley of the shadow of death, but the actual meaning encourages us to live in the present for THIS IS THE DAY that the Lord has made. Rejoice and be glad in it. Psalm 23 is an everyday Psalm.

Now, in this gem from Psalm 61, the Psalmist again asks God to allow him to abide in God's presence and focus his attention on being in the tent, house, or abiding place all the days of his life, unto forever.

PRAYER: Almighty, All Knowing and All Present God: May I too ask to abide in your presence? Slow me down from always having to do something, so that you and I can just be together, abide together and I can be more aware of your presence in my life. Help me to live more in the moment and to rejoice and be glad in this day you have made. Amen.

SIXTY-TWO

For God alone my soul waits in silence, for my hope is from him.
62:5

My hope is from God, affirms the Psalmist. Hope.

There is an Irish musician named Enya who sings lilting and
hauntingly soothing songs. Consider a few lines from her song
Only If:
If you really want to, you can hear me say,
only if you want to, will you find a way,
if you really want to, you can seize the day,
only if you want to, will you fly away.

If you really want to, you can seize the day. Seize is a word that
grabs. Seize the day. *Carpe Diem*, in Latin. Seize is also a word
used with the word "hope" by the book of Hebrews: Seize the
hope. "SEIZE the hope" is not passive. You must seize it to
possess it. You must reach out, grab it, grasp it, capture it, and
catch it.

Can you seize hope? Enya and the Bible would agree: only if you
want to, will you find a way. Seize the day suggests live for today.
Seize the hope suggests that you live in the present, but also that
you trust that God will be with you tomorrow because *"I do not
know what my future holds, but I know who holds my future."*

The Bible's metaphor for hope is an anchor: *"Hope... a sure and
steadfast anchor of the soul"* (from Hebrews 6:19). The anchor of
hope increases your holding power, even in rough seas. An anchor
holds firm and, as Hebrews encourages, provides you with hope
which is a *sure and steadfast anchor of the soul*. When your soul
trusts in your holding power, strength is renewed.

The anchor was a secret symbol in the Catacombs in Rome. The
Catacombs were underground cemeteries that date back to the
earliest days of Christianity when it was not safe to be a Christian.

Because Christians were hunted down, the Catacombs were the only safe place Christians could gather to worship. Christians were not allowed to meet above ground, but Roman law considered burial places to be sacrosanct, so the catacombs became the one safe place of refuge for Christians to gather. Then, the Romans started to hunt them down in the Catacombs, so the Christians destroyed the old entrances and built new secret entrances. Perhaps it was like trying to find your car in an underground parking garage with multiple levels. Imagine having to find your way to secret passages through levels of dark, underground cemeteries. And so, secret symbols marked the way.

Symbols were needed that could stand for two different things. Those who believed would see one thing, and those who did not would see another. This is known in Latin as *Crux Dissimulata* (as in *dissimilar*) where the symbol was intended to conceal the real meaning from spies and informers.

One of the secret symbols found on the walls of the Catacombs was the anchor. There are many types of anchors: mushroom, plow, and fluke. The secret symbol was the kedge anchor, which is often the kind you see hanging from historic tall-masted schooners.

At the bottom of the kedge anchor's *shank* is a rounded bar called the *crown*. Each end of the crown has a pointed end, like a barb, called the *fluke*. Near the top of the shank is an arm or a bar named the *stock* which puts the anchor in a better position to get a bite of the bottom. A ring at the top allows the anchor to be tied by rope or chain. If the anchor did not have the ring or the crown, what would it look like? A cross! And so, Christians in the catacombs would look at the anchor and see the cross of Jesus Christ. Those who did not believe would see only a kedge anchor. It was a secret symbol. Those who were not Christians would not know that the anchor was the symbol for hope from the book of Hebrews which assures that hope is *a sure and steadfast anchor of the soul.*

The purpose of an anchor is to dig in and hook the bottom. An anchor must hook into something. It is not just a heavy weight. If it could not dig in, the anchor would simply drag across the bottom. It digs in, hooks the bottom, and holds on. That is holding power. Your faith gives you holding power.

The rope or the line which ties the anchor to the boat is called the *rode*. Boaters have a special name for everything. The important fact about the rode is that it must be long enough. If it is too short, that is, if you drop the anchor straight down from the bow of the boat, it cannot grab and will not dig in and hold. You have to let out more rode so the anchor can get a good grip. It is a matter of angle. If the rope is long enough, the anchor will hold just about anything even in the most severe weather. Even a small anchor can hold vast and immeasurable amounts of weight if you let out enough rode.

If your faith does not seem to be helping you in the face of difficulty, what is needed is to let out a little more rode because with enough rode, you have the fortitude to endure anything... to hang in there.

Consider three lessons about the holding power of anchors and the holding power of your trust in God to renew your strength.

First, believe in your own holding power. Believe the rope will not break. A little anchor which is not much more than a small piece of metal attached to a thin rope does not seem like it could hold the weigh. But it can. Boaters trust the great value of their watercraft to that little anchor. Perhaps you have heard the description that a boat is a hole in the water surrounded by wood into which you pour money. Boaters have invested dearly in their boats yet they believe the anchor will hold firm. Believe in the strength you have to hold on.

There is a story about a Pastor named Martin Neimoller who survived the horrors of Dachau which was one of the Nazi's worst concentration camps. For three years he was kept in solitary confinement.

170

Years later he was asked this question by an interviewer: *"How could you stand it without losing your sanity?"* Neimoller answered confidently *"A person does not realize how much he can stand until he is put to the test. You can stand far more than you think you can."* You are much stronger than you think you are. You have deep reserves of holding power within you and you also have the added power of strength given to you by God. Believe in the strength you have to hold on.

Second, let out a little more rode. Increase your patience. If your anchor is not holding well, it may be that you have not given it enough rode… enough line so that the anchor can get sufficient angle to dig in and hold on. It is like the saying *"When you come to the end of your rope, make a knot and hang on."* If it feels like your anchor is not holding, give it some more rope. In nautical language, let out a little more rode so it will grab and hold. That means… let out a little more patience. God's time is not your time. That is another way of viewing the phrase *waiting for the Lord*. Patience is almost always rewarded. The Psalmist embraced the idea of waiting… trusting in God:

"Wait for the LORD; be strong, and let your heart take courage..." (Psalms 27:14)

"Lord, for what do I wait? My hope is in thee." (Psalms 39:7)

"I wait for the LORD, my soul waits, and in his word I hope." (Psalms 130:5)

Third, let the anchor do the work. I sat on the bow of my little sailboat holding the anchor's rope, the rode. The rope twisted around my hand, pulling with all its might, cutting of the circulation to my hand until I tied the rope to the cleat of the boat. Then, I could lean back, rest, and let the anchor do the work. I could let go and let the anchor hold the boat. Let go.

171

Letting go does not come easy. To *Let go and let God* takes a lifetime of practice to learn that you can trust. Tie on your anchor of hope and let go. Let the anchor do the work. Entrust your need into God's hands. Paul says: *"Hope does not disappoint us, because God's love has been poured into your heart through the Holy Spirit which has been given to you."* Trust in the Holy Spirit who comforts you, who advocates on your behalf, and who blows through you like a fresh wind to give you power beyond your own to cope with life and to thrive. That is hope that you can trust which will not disappoint you.

My hope is from God, wrote the Psalmist. God is his anchor which holds steadfast even in the roughest of seas.

If you really want to, you can hear me say,
only if you want to, will you find a way...

Find a way to seize the hope set before you, the sure and steadfast anchor of your soul. Trust in God to help you increase your holding power.

PRAYER: Dear God, my soul trusts in you and I know that my hope comes from you. When I am in rough seas, lead me to trust you more, to believe in myself, to have confidence in my holding power, and to know that my hope in you will not disappoint, because your love has been poured into my heart through the Holy Spirit. Amen.

SIXTY-THREE

O God, you are my God, I seek you, my soul thirsts for you; my flesh faints for you, as in a dry and weary land where there is no water. My soul thirsts for God, for the living God.
63:1,2

Imagine this scenario. A man longs for God and he prays *O God, you are my God, I seek you, my soul thirsts for you; my flesh faints for you, as in a dry and weary land where there is no water. My soul thirsts for God, for the living God.* And so, he also longs for a community of others who also thirsts for God and desires to seek him.

He looks forward to going to church. He anticipates the worship service. He expects the music, liturgy, message, fellowship and even the sanctuary itself to guide him into an encounter with the Divine. That is what he thirsts for – An encounter with the Divine. When he arrives, he is warmly greeted. As he waits for the service to begin, he reviews the bulletin and reads the meditation, the liturgical parts and looks to see which hymns will be sung. Then the service begins. First comes ten minutes of announcements. It is a busy church and it seems like everyone needs some time to tell about their committee or board, some with skits or humor. He then hears how the church is falling short to meet its budget and there is not enough money. Cuts in program and staff are threatened. He listens while the nominating committee representative tells how not enough people can be found for all the openings, suggesting that they are really hard up. There are pitches for more people to teach in the church school and sing in the choir. A negative tone prevails.

Finally, some opening music draws listeners into a worshipful mood. The first hymn, more than 300 years old, is unsingable. The organ is too loud. The man wishes the music was more upbeat, contemporary and included instruments other than the organ. It seems to him that the church worships the organ almost as much as it does the altar. Then comes what seems to be the highpoint, the sermon.

The preacher jokes about how he wrote the sermon late Saturday night. He thinks about all the professions where the practitioner must plan and prepare well in advance, and wonders why this preacher waits until the last minute. It feels and sounds unprepared. The preacher rambles on, using long sentences, many polysyllabic words, and employs illustrations from the 18th and 19th centuries. The preacher gazes out the window as he speaks. You can tell when people are not really listening.

Next comes the anthem. No choir members make eye contact, smile, or groove with the music. They appear to be God's frozen chosen. He wonders if they are singing their faith or just singing notes. The service moves on to the Pastoral Prayer. Here the words are well-organized, warmly heart-felt, and flow poetically. He sees that the preacher is reading the prayer and suspects that someone else wrote it, perhaps coming from a book of prayers. It is beautiful, but it does not feel like the one reading the prayer is actually praying.

He arrived anticipating an encounter with the Divine. His inner spirit is praying *O God, you are my God, I seek you, my soul thirsts for you.* He is seeking, but does not seem to be finding. He remains thirsty. This scenario is exaggerated to illustrate the point that there are people who are truly thirsty and seeking the presence of God and what they find is more about the organizational life and historic practices of the institutional church. Therein lies the challenge and the opportunity for those of us who are engaged in the life of the church. We must become worshipper-centered rather than church-centered. We must learn to give heightened attention to the here-and-now needs of those who long for God and adapt our practices and attitudes to meet those needs.

How many people do you know that would identify with this psalm? How many would say that they thirst for God? How many who attend a worship service would use these words to describe this as their reason for attending? Perhaps there are more than we think.

In Psalm 42 (1) the Psalmist expressed this same sentiment in beautifully poetic terms: *"As a deer longs for flowing streams, so my soul longs for you, O God."* (Psalm 42:1). Where does a person turn when he or she longs for God? Some turn to a community of faith, or to being outside in God's creation. Some turn to spiritual disciplines like prayer, meditation, conversations with other people of faith, listening to music, experiencing art, or reading the Bible or spiritually uplifting books. Others turn to service, volunteering, or helping another to lift a burden. The person who thirsts and longs to be in God's presence is more likely to be satisfied than one whose interest is passive.

Compare this idea of a soul longing for God with your love for another, like a spouse or partner, a child or grandchild, or a special friend. Your soul longs for them. Your heart thirsts to be in touch with them. You want to be with them, to laugh and to experience life together. They are the ones you think about when you awaken and they are in your thoughts as you close your eyes to sleep. Picture their face and an involuntary smile and a warm feeling fills you. Think of people in your past or present who feel that way about you. Perhaps you were never fully aware of how much you meant to them, how frequently they thought about you or pictured your face in their mind. Their soul longed for you and thirsted to be in your presence. Name those people in silence and offer a prayer of thanks for how much they cared about you.

Consider again the word *righteousness*. It makes so much sense when we apply the translation of *right relationships*. Think about what should be the right relationship you have with others. Ponder about what should be your right relationship with God. Jesus taught (Matthew 5:6) *"Blessed are those who hunger and thirst for righteousness, for they will be filled."* When your soul thirsts for the right relationship with God, it will not be in vain. You will be filled. Jesus also taught (John 6:35) *"I am the bread of life. Whoever comes to me will never be hungry, and whoever believes in me will never be thirsty."* And so, when you pray the Psalmist's prayer of longing for God, to be in God's presence and to encounter the Divine, your thirst will be quenched.

175

PRAYER: *O God, you are my God, I seek you, my soul thirsts for you; my flesh faints for you, as in a dry and weary land where there is no water. My soul thirsts for God, for the living God.* O God, lead me into your presence and satisfy my thirst for you. Sharpen my senses to a heightened awareness of you in each place I go and in each person I encounter. Amen.

SIXTY-FOUR

Let the righteous rejoice in the Lord and take refuge in him. Let all the upright in heart glory.
64:10

Glorify God. Give God the glory. Let all the upright in heart glory.

Perhaps one of Apostle Paul's best verses about glory is *"So, whether you eat or drink, or whatever you do, do everything for the glory of God."* (1 Corinthians 10:31). Could there be a more fitting goal for the Christian than to do all to the glory of God?

Quakers have a spiritual practice known as *"queries."* Queries are questions that members ask themselves as a measure of self-evaluation and self-examination. They query themselves about how they are doing in their walk with God. There is no judgment, no reprisal for failing to do their best, or no discipline for failing. Indeed, this is self-discipline at its highest and best. The point is to ask yourself questions as a reminder to adjust your life in response to the question.

Borrowing from the practice of queries, consider questions we as people of faith might ask ourselves: Do my words glorify God? Do my choices glorify God? Do I intend each day to live my life to the glory of God? When problems or difficulties come my way, can I use them to the glory of God? How can I better adopt as my life goal to do all to the glory of God?

If Socrates would enter the room, we should rise and do him honor, said Napoleon Bonaparte. *But if Jesus Christ came into the room, we should fall down on our knees and worship Him.* That would be a symbol of giving him glory.

Paul, in Philippians 2, writes poetically about the only one to whom you would ever bow down: *Therefore God also highly exalted him and gave him the name that is above every name, so that at the name of Jesus every knee should bend, in heaven and on earth and under the earth, and every tongue should confess that Jesus Christ is Lord, to the glory of God the Father.*

Is that so? Would you bow down to him?

In the earliest days of the Christian church, a person had to make a confession in order to become a member. It was the simplest of all confessions, only four words: *Jesus Christ is Lord.* In those days, the word *Lord* meant a master or owner. Followers of The Way were essentially confessing that Jesus Christ owns me and has a right to possess me totally. Would that be your confession, that Jesus Christ owns you?

Perhaps we should have stayed with that simple four-word confession. Ever since, people tried to define what it meant and argued and quarreled about it, calling one another heretics and fools. And all the while, it is enough for the woman or man of faith to say simply *Jesus Christ is Lord.* My Lord.

In the Sermon on the Mount, Jesus taught: *Let your light shine before others, so that they may see your good works and give glory to your Father in heaven.* There is that phrase again: give glory to God. A college teacher raised the question *What is the purpose of life?* Most of us work on that question for a long time, as I suspect the teacher did. Here was his answer: *The purpose of life is to glorify God.* I have been thinking about that for decades and I am still working on it and wondering if I would phrase it the same way, but I am getting closer to thinking that he was right.

Sometimes people say that it is not a matter of what you believe but of how you live. How you live is important and is a reflection of what you believe. For Paul, how a person lives does not go far enough, for to Paul, *at the name of Jesus every knee should bend... and every tongue should confess that Jesus Christ is Lord, to the glory of God the Father.*

PRAYER: Almighty God, may my words, my thoughts and my actions glorify you. May I set out each morning to give glory to you with my life. And whatever may come my way, good or bad, may I use it to your glory. Amen.

SIXTY-FIVE

By awesome deeds you answer us with deliverance, O God of our salvation; you are the hope of all the ends of the earth and of the farthest seas. By your strength you established the mountains; you are girded with might. You silence the roaring of the seas, the roaring of their waves, the tumult of the peoples.
65:5-7

The roaring seas! Even the seas praise God:

Let the heavens be glad, and let the earth rejoice; let the sea roar, and all that fills it. (Psalm 96)

God is our refuge and strength, a very present help in trouble. Therefore, we will not fear, though the earth should change, though the mountains shake in the heart of the sea; though its waters roar and foam... (Psalm 46)

Let them give glory to the LORD, and declare his praise in the coastlands. (Isaiah 42:12)

I was raised by my parents to go down to the seashore, where I fell in love with the sea. Later in life, it became my passion to create a place for my family to be by the coastlands on the margin of the continent and we built a simple cabin by the sea, in Maine. Anyone who lives by the sea is aware of the sea's mighty power. Sometimes it is placid and invites us to kayak out on a sunny and clear day to fully embrace its beauty. Other times, especially with storms, it rages and declares its powers over human control or taming. Anywhere you touch the sea, you become aware of its inter-connectedness, for every ocean is connected to ever other. What you do to the one, you do to all. The sea claims many lives each year. Those who abide by its side are aware of its power and might. Three-quarters of this planet is sea and when it is at its greatest might, it roars. But then, says the Psalmist, God is even more powerful and silences is roar. *"Let the sea roar, and all that fills it; the world and those who live in it."* (Psalm 98:7).

180

There is a modern hymn titled _God of the Sparrow, God of the Whale_ which captures the sentiment of this Psalm: _"God of the sparrow, God of the whale, God of the swirling stars. How does the creature say Awe, How does the creature say Praise."_

I went whale watching in Maine. The captain of the whale watching boat turned off the engine and waited. First, we saw the blow and then in the distance watched a 60-foot finback whale surface. Next came the playful and curious humpback whales. They floated under the boat and surfaced next to us. It was beautiful to see their blow from the spout. It stinks to have it blow in your face when they are that close.

One humpback surfaced and kept watching us. Then he did something unique to humpbacks: he spyhopped. Spyhopping is whale behavior when the whale rises and holds position partially out of the water, often exposing its entire rostrum and head. It is like standing on its tail. Spyhopping is similar to a human treading water. Spyhopping is controlled and slow, and can last for minutes at a time if the whale is sufficiently inquisitive about whatever or whomever it is viewing.

For hour after hour, in the midst of the whales' feeding grounds in the Gulf of Maine, we watched in awe. In awe. How does the creature say _awe_? It was one of the most spiritual experiences in my life to witness these magnificent, giant creations. And God said, _"Let the waters bring forth swarms of living creatures... So God created the great sea monsters and every living creature that moves, of every kind, with which the waters swarm.... And God saw that it was good."_ (Genesis 1:20, 21)

And God saw that it was good. Everything that God created, creates, and will create is good. Creation has God's fingerprints on it and God's DNA in it. Albert Schweitzer developed his philosophy which he named "a reverence for life."

He wrote: *"The person who has become a thinking being feels a compulsion to give to every will to live the same reverence for life that he gives to his own...."* I felt that for the whale... giving to the whale the will to live and the same reverence for life that I give to my own.

The seas are so mighty, deep and powerful. And yet, they serve as a metaphor for how God is even more mighty, powerful and worthy to be praised. God has the power to silence the roaring seas. To God be the glory. Amen.

PRAYER: Almighty God, whose hand stills the sea and calms the roar of oceans, by your awesome deeds you answer the world with deliverance. Even in my own small corner of the world, you deliver me too. I praise you, God, and thank you for delivering me from difficulties when I have needed you the most. Amen.

SIXTY-SIX

For you, O God, have tested us; you have tried us as silver is tried.
66:10

Which do you think is more accurate? That God tests you? Or, that it is not God who tests you, but God is with you in times of testing? If you turn to the many human views represented by those who wrote the Bible, you could find verses to support either position. As we consider this question, let us frame the arguments with the perspective that God is like a loving parent. What would a wise and loving parent do?

There was something of a glacial shift in theology between the testaments as the tectonic plates ground together and brought forth earth-shattering changes. In the Old Testament, there was the sense of this psalm that God caused everything to happen, including making bad things happen to good people and testing people for some reason. Perhaps, as the psalm explains, the testing is designed to test our strength, as silver is tested and tried. In the New Testament, there is more the sense that people are tested and tried, but the testing is not caused by God. However, the New Testament is clear that God is with you when you face times of testing.

The Epistle of James (1:13-14) says *"No one, when tempted, should say, "I am being tempted by God"; for God cannot be tempted by evil and he himself tempts no one."* This is New Testament theology with a message we need to hear: God does not cause bad things to happen to you. Further, bad things that happen to you are not caused by God to test you or to teach you a lesson.

The word *to temp* which James used means something different from our use of *temptation*, as though we were being seduced into sin. The word means *to test*. The Greek word James chose means to put to the proof, to examine, to verify – much the way steel must be tested before it can be used to build a bridge or a student must be examined to certify that the student has mastered a subject.

We all face tests and many of them make us better and stronger people. You do not want to buy a car that has not been tested. You do not want to fly in a plane which has not been tested. You do not want to be operated on by a surgeon who has not been tested. The testing you face has the potential to make you stronger and better and prepares you to face new adventures and challenges in your future. And so, consider a revision of the verse by substituting the word *test* instead of *tempt*: *No one, when tested, should say, "I am being tested by God"; for God cannot be tested by evil and he himself tests no one.* God does not test you to teach you a lesson.

After Jesus emerged out of his thirty silent years, he was cast into the wilderness to be tempted by the evil one: *Again, the devil took him to a very high mountain and showed him all the kingdoms of the world and their splendor; and he said to him, "All these I will give you, if you will fall down and worship me." Jesus said to him, "Away with you, Satan! For it is written, 'Worship the Lord your God, and serve only him.'"* (Matthew 4:8-10). Jesus was tempted to choose the wrong path. He was tested by tempting ideas that could have led to an alternative lifestyle than to the cross. He knew what testing feels like.

The Apostle Paul also wrote about testing, using the same Greek word which James used – it was translated as *tempt* in James but *test* from Paul: *"No testing has overtaken you that is not common to everyone. God is faithful, and he will not let you be tested beyond your strength, but with the testing he will also provide the way out so that you may be able to endure it"* (1 Corinthians 10:13).

Perhaps you have known people who don't buy this because they feel like they have been tested beyond their strength. A widow who lost her beloved husband after decades of happy marriage said *"I am not able to endure it. Where is the way out?"* In Paul's verse, it does not say that God caused the testing but that God will provide the way out so that you may be able to endure it.

Many have faced loss, illness or tragedy that seems beyond anyone's endurance. We cannot blame them for having a hard time with this verse.

A somewhat confusing verse in the Lord 's Prayer causes us to wonder about God's role in the testing of our souls: *"And lead us not into temptation, but deliver us from evil"* (Matthew 6:13, KJV). These may be the most droned words in the English language. The verse makes little sense to us. What kind of Heavenly Father, like a loving parent, would lead his beloved children into temptation? What sort of God have we if worshipers have to beg not to be led astray? That does not make sense. Would God lead you into temptation? No wonder some hold the view that God causes everything and therefore God might cause bad things to happen to me. On the other hand, if God does not lead people into temptation, then why would Jesus teach a prayer that asks God not to do what God does not do anyway?

The word *lead* can also mean *"let us not be led into."* It can mean to be carried into. That has a different flavor. Let us not be led into temptation rather than lead us not into temptation takes God out of the leading. There is a Jewish prayer that goes *"Allow me not to go into the hands of temptation."* You can be tempted to do dumb things. You may choose to do things which you know are not good for you, which is known as self-defeating behavior. And yet you do them anyway. This interpretation makes a little more sense, to pray: *"Allow us not to be led into doing bad things or making bad choices."*

Notice something important in the Lord's Prayer: the pronoun. It is not the first-person singular, as you might expect. Who prays in the plural? Do not most of us pray using *"I"*, *"me,"* or *"mine"*? My Father, who art in heaven… Give me this day my daily bread… forgive me my debts… lead me not into temptation but deliver me from evil. But that is not how Jesus taught his followers to pray. He used *"us"* rather than *"me."* Who does the *"us"* in the prayer refer to? It does not refer to the general public. It does not refer to humankind, mankind or womankind.

The "*us*" stands specifically for Christ's followers. "Us" stands for the person who has chosen to pray, a few verses earlier *"Thy kingdom come, thy will be done."* Only someone who believes in God would pray for God's will to be done. A non-believer would not care to pray this prayer. This is a prayer prayed by someone who cares that they are in the right relationship to God. It is the person who loves God who prays not to be led into temptation.

We have already seen that the New Testament word for *tempt* is more like our word for *to test.* God does not test you but is with you in your time of testing. So *"lead us not into temptation"* does not mean *"God, please do not seduce me into sin."* God would not lead you into temptation. So, then, what could the verse from the prayer mean?

To get a clue, look at the other part of the verse, its parallel partner: *"but deliver us from evil."* This is a common Middle Eastern literary technique known as parallelism. Parallelism means that there is a nearby verse, before or after, which amplifies, clarifies, explains, builds up or defines the other verse. Jesus employed parallelism frequently in his teaching. It is like saying the same thing twice... *"in other words."* That is what happens in the Lord's Prayer. The second phase *"but deliver us from evil"* is the parallel partner to *"Lead us not into temptation."* They are conjoined. The second phrase helps to explain the first.

Deliver means to rescue from danger. More than 400 times from Genesis to Revelation, God is asked to deliver people or is thanked for delivering them. A hundred times, the Psalmist praises God for delivering him: *"For thou hast delivered me from every trouble..."* (Psalm 54:7). *Deliver us from evil* is the parallelism to *lead us not into temptation.* They have parallel meanings. It would be a contradiction for the God who delivers you from evil to lead you to be tempted. And so, we glean from the parallel partner an affirmation that God delivers you, rescues you and helps you in your times of testing. God rescues you from the testing you go through.

This meaning is consistent with the teachings about testing from James and from Paul:

"No one, when tempted, should say, 'I am being tempted by God'; for God cannot be tempted by evil and he himself tempts no one."

"No testing has overtaken you that is not common to everyone. God is faithful, and he will not let you be tested beyond your strength, but with the testing he will also provide the way out so that you may be able to endure it"

Return again to the pronoun in the Lord's Prayer, which is not in the first-person singular. It is not "Lead *me* not into temptation but deliver *me* from evil." It is plural: "*us*." There is a great message captured by the pronoun, because as "us" we help one another when he or she faces his or her time of testing. You might be a part of how God delivers. You are an instrument of God's deliverance! The "us" we speak in the Lord's Prayer recognizes that we help one another in times of testing. Look around to see who is currently walking through his or her own valley of dark shadows. Be helpful to them, a source of encouragement and support. You could become the long arm of God reaching out to deliver another when he or she faces a rough time.

And so, the treasure we mine from the New Testament verses is:
First, God does not cause bad things to happen to you.
Second, bad things that happen to you are not caused by God to test you or to teach you a lesson.
Third, God delivers you when you are tested.
Fourth, God may use you to help God deliver others in their time of testing.

What then shall we say about Psalm 66? *"For you, O God, have tested us; you have tried us as silver is tried."* It tells us that thoughts about God's nature and character were still evolving and continue to evolve today. God is still speaking. It tells us that the Psalmist believed his testing was caused by God. He was human. He hurt. He searched for some reason or explanation.

187

He needed to give meaning to his pain and in so doing attributed its cause to the Divine. Even when we hold the New Testament theology that God does not cause bad things or testing or tempting to happen, we are still human. We, like the Psalmist, when we face pain, need to give meaning to our pain. And so, perhaps, we attribute it to God, even blaming God for causing the event that pains us. We, like the Psalmist, may be mistaken in what causes the pain or the testing. But also like the Psalmist, and James, Paul and Jesus, we have no doubt that God is with us in our times of testing. God delivers us. The Bible never said there would not be valleys of dark shadows, but in one of the most important messages of the Bible it affirms "For Thou art with me."

PRAYER: O Lord, when I hurt because of something that happened to me, I look for reasons and sometimes blame you or think you are using this to teach me a lesson. Remind me that even in my darkest valleys, you are with me. Indeed, sometimes I feel closer to you in times like that than at any other time. In times of testing, may I be aware of your presence, guidance, and strength. Deliver me from trouble. Amen.

SIXTY-SEVEN

The earth has yielded its increase; God, our God, has blessed us.
67:6

The Psalmist knows he is blessed by God. It was he who penned the incredibly brief and poetic phrase *"My cup runneth over"* in the 23rd Psalm. People of faith know they are blessed and they thank God frequently for their blessings.

The Psalmist frequently set his thanksgiving and praise to music. There is an old gospel song written by Johnson Oatman, Jr., a New Jersey musician, that also puts this attitude to music:

When upon life's billows you are tempest-tossed,
When you are discouraged, thinking all is lost,
Count your many blessings, name them one by one,
And it will surprise you what the Lord has done.

Refrain:
Count your blessings, name them one by one,
Count your blessings, see what God has done!
Count your blessings, name them one by one,
Count your many blessings, see what God has done.

Are you ever burdened with a load of care?
Does the cross seem heavy you are called to bear?
Count your many blessings, every doubt will fly,
And you will keep singing as the days go by.

When you look at others with their lands and gold,
Think that Christ has promised you His wealth untold;
Count your many blessings, wealth can never buy
Your reward in heaven, nor your home on high.

So, amid the conflict whether great or small,
Do not be discouraged, God is over all;
Count your many blessings, angels will attend,
Help and comfort give you to your journey's end.

Count your blessings, name them one by one,
Count your blessings, see what God has done!
Count your blessings, name them one by one,
Count your many blessings, see what God has done.

PRAYER: Generous God, you have blessed me abundantly. Let me focus my spirit upon what I do have rather than what I do not have. Lead me to see through lenses of abundance rather than through lenses of scarcity. And every day, may I count my blessings, see what you have done, and give you thanks. Amen.

SIXTY-EIGHT

Blessed be the Lord, who daily bears us up; God is our salvation.
68:19

Also, from the NIV: *Praise be to the Lord, to God our Savior, who daily bears our burdens.*

The Psalmist praises God for bearing our burdens. We are grateful to God for helping us carry a burden. Out of that gratitude we are inclined to choose a God-like outreach of lifting a burden for another. This idea is captured in Galatians (6:2): *"Bear one another's burdens, and in this way you will fulfill the law of Christ."*

A story is told about Sadhu Sundar Singh, a Hindu convert to Christianity, who became a missionary in India. One late-afternoon Sadhu was traveling on foot through the Himalayas with a Buddhist monk. It was bitter cold and with night coming on, the monk warned Sadhu that they were in danger of freezing to death if they did not reach the monastery before darkness fell. As they were crossing a narrow path above a steep cliff, they heard a cry of help. Down the cliff lay a man, fallen and hurt. The monk looked at Sadhu and said *"Do not stop. God has brought this man to his fate. He must work it out for himself. Let us hurry on before we, too, perish."*

But Sadhu, the Christian, replied, *"God has sent me here to help my brother. I cannot abandon him."* The monk made off through the whirling snow while the missionary climbed down the cliff. The man's leg was broken and he could not walk. So Sadhu took his blanket, made a sling of it and tied the man on his back. Then, bending under his burden, he began a body-torturing climb. By the time he reached the narrow path again he was drenched with perspiration. Doggedly he made his way on through the deepening snow. It was dark now and it was all he could do to follow the path.

But he persevered and though faint with fatigue and overheated from exertion, he finally saw ahead the lights of the monastery.

Then, for the first time, Sadhu stumbled and nearly fell. But not from weakness. He had stumbled over some object lying in the road. Slowly he bent down on one knee and brushed the snow off the object. It was the body of the monk, frozen to death.

Years later a disciple of Sadhu's asked him: *"What is life's most difficult task?"* Without hesitation Sadhu replied, *"To have no burden to carry."*

Bear one another's burdens, and in this way you will fulfill the law of Christ, Paul wrote to the Galatians. That is what Jesus himself offered to do: *"Come to me, all you that are weary and are carrying heavy burdens, and I will give you rest"* (Matthew 11:28). This is shirtsleeves Christianity where we roll up our sleeves and help to carry a burden for another. A burden shared is a burden halved. A person who has faith in Jesus will want to do the work of bearing another's burden.

A seminary student admired so the life of Albert Schweitzer that he went to visit the great man at his jungle hospital at Lambarene on the banks of the Ogowe River. Schweitzer was eighty-five years old. Listen to this entry in the student's diary:
You can imagine the deep and profound effect of that visit, which included opportunity for some leisurely conversation with that great humanitarian, theologian, musician, and physician. But one event stands out in a special way. It was about eleven in the morning. The equatorial sun was beating down mercilessly and we were walking up a hill with Dr. Schweitzer. Suddenly he left us and strode across the slope of the hill to a place where an African woman was struggling upward with a huge armload of wood for the cook fires. I watched with both admiration and concern as the eighty-five year-old man took on the entire load of wood and carried it on up the hill for the relieved woman. When we all reached the top of the hill, one of the members of our group asked Dr. Schweitzer why he did things like that, implying that in that heat and at his age he should not.

Albert Schweitzer, looking right at all of us and pointing to the woman, said simply, "No one should ever have to carry a burden like that alone."

Perhaps when another person lifts you up by helping you, offering you a good word, a hug, a positive note of encouragement or aid in carrying your burden that is God working through another to bear you up. *Blessed be the Lord,* wrote the Psalmist, *who daily bears us up.*

PRAYER: Thank you, God, for helping me with my burdens. I would ask one thing more, and that is for you to use me to lift a burden for another. Guide me to opportunities to serve you in this way and grant me wisdom to know how to help. Amen.

SIXTY-NINE

They gave me poison for food, and for my thirst they gave me vinegar to drink.
69:21

There are two candles on the altar. One signifies the humanity of Jesus and the other signifies his Divinity. One man with two natures, human and divine. The human side of Jesus suffered pain, rejection and hurting on the cross when he was executed.

This was the Psalm Jesus quoted as he was dying and drew his final breath, as described by John: *After this, when Jesus knew that all was now finished, he said (in order to fulfill the scripture), "I am thirsty." A jar full of sour wine was standing there. So they put a sponge full of the wine on a branch of hyssop and held it to his mouth. When Jesus had received the wine, he said, "It is finished." Then he bowed his head and gave up his spirit.* (John 19:28-30). For his thirst, they gave him vinegar to drink.

There are times after a high salt meal that I am especially thirsty and will drink glass after glass of water. It tastes good, feels good going down, and refreshes my thirst. Can you imagine the cruelty in their hearts when instead of providing a last little bit of tender compassion by giving a sip of water they instead gave him vinegar? That must have been the final straw of unkindness, for as soon as he tasted it, he pronounced *"It is finished,"* bowed his head and died.

When John adds the editorial comment *"to fulfill the scripture"* he is referring to the Psalm 69: *"They gave me poison for food, and for my thirst they gave me vinegar to drink."* There is a deeper meaning as there often is with John. After Jesus said *"I am thirsty"* the next verse says *"A jar full of sour wine was standing there. So they put a sponge full of the wine on a branch of hyssop and held it to his mouth."* Only John tells that it was on a hyssop reed that they put the sponge containing the vinegar.

A hyssop reed was a stalk like a strong grass which was no longer than two feet. Why use a hyssop reed to affix a sponge? John is referring to Exodus 12:22: *"Take a bunch of hyssop, dip it in the blood that is in the basin, and touch the lintel and the two doorposts with the blood in the basin."* That was the instruction to the captive Israelites in Egypt for the first Passover when the angel of death was to pass by and slay every first-born son of the Egyptians. The Israelites were to slay the Passover lamb and smear the doorposts of their homes with its blood so that the angel of death would pass over their houses. It was the blood of the Passover lamb which saved the people of God. John is making a link: It was the blood of Jesus which was to save the world. When Christians celebrate the sacrament of Holy Communion, the words spoken also link to this verse: *"For this cup is my blood of the covenant, which is poured out... for the forgiveness of sins."* (Matthew 26:28)

The hyssop reed also provides an unexpected clue to an amazing fact. A soldier holding a two-foot stalk could reach Jesus' mouth. That means that Jesus on the cross was only a couple feet off the ground. At crucifixions, the beam with the body was lifted and tied to the already affixed upright pole which typically was eight or nine feet high. That is not so high. Imagine a six-foot-tall man on a crossbeam attached to an eight-foot pole. Jesus would have been only a couple feet off the ground so that a two-foot stalk of grass could touch his lips. He was in your face. Depictions of the Crucifixion by artists sometimes portray the cross way up high as if in the clouds and far removed from people. Not so. For Jesus' painful and cruel death, he was only a couple feet off the ground, close to people.

Like any people who hurt, Jesus too could cry *"I thirst."* He felt pain. Rejection and abandonment pierced his soul. When we feel pain, rejection or abandonment, we have a God who has been there, done that and knows how we feel. God is with us when we hurt, understands, and soothes our thirst with living water as only God can give.

195

We are deeply grateful for God who is with us in our hurting. But for a brief moment, turn your attention to the callousness of those who gave a suffering Jesus vinegar instead of water for his thirst. Human meanness is not restricted to a couple centuries ago at Golgotha. It is reenacted every time a human thirst is met with a wrong response. It can be individual, as when we encounter another in need and give them something or nothing instead of the cup of water they crave. It can by corporate, as when our nation or our culture does not provide care for those in need. Mahatma Gandhi said *"A nation's greatness is measured by how it treats its weakest members."* This message is badly needed at a time when some incumbents in the highest offices here and around the world have lost this vision. We might paraphrase Gandhi, to make it personal, to say that a person's greatness is measured by how he or she treats "the least of these." Whether individual or corporate, our response to the weakest among us can either be a cup of water or a hyssop of vinegar. Kindness or meanness. When we quench the thirst of a thirsty person, or provide food, shelter, health care, education, and safety nets, what we do for them we do for Him.

PRAYER: Loving God, when I think of how Jesus hurt and thirsted for a cup of water, I wonder what I would have done had I been there. Open my eyes to the needs of others and help me to respond with kindness, care and help to meet their need. When I see my own government responding to those in need with vinegar instead of water, may I do whatever I can as a citizen to encourage my nation to become great by how it treats its weakest members. Amen.

SEVENTY

Let all who seek you rejoice and be glad in you. Let those who love your salvation say evermore, "God is great!"
70:4

You have met or known of people who lost their joy. Perhaps it happened because of the loss of a loved one, a conflict with someone they cared about, a wrong turn in a decision or a job, or being a victim of an unfortunate circumstance. Bad things that happen can cause us to lose our joy. They rob us of something we value. We may be able to move on and learn to manage with increased effectiveness, but the ghost of the incident never fades. How blessed are we when we can see live with a new perspective and regain the joy we once had. Deep joy comes as a gift from God. Sometimes we simply open our eyes and our arms to receive it and then, a have joy again. We re-joice. Rejoice. Our lost joy is re-found and renewed.

When we recognize the renewal of our joy, all we can do is to proclaim "God is great!" and sing to God a hymn of praise:

To God be the glory, great things He hath done,
So loved He the world that He gave us His Son,
Who yielded His life our redemption to win,
And opened the life-gate that all may go in.

Praise the Lord, praise the Lord,
Let the earth hear His voice;
Praise the Lord, praise the Lord,
Let the people rejoice;
Oh, come to the Father, through Jesus the Son,
And give Him the glory; great things He hath done.

Great things He hath taught us, great things He hath done,
And great our rejoicing through Jesus the Son;
But purer, and higher, and greater will be
Our wonder, our transport when Jesus we see.

197

Praise the Lord, praise the Lord,
Let the earth hear His voice;
Praise the Lord, praise the Lord,
Let the people rejoice;
Oh, come to the Father, through Jesus the Son,
And give Him the glory; great things He hath done.

PRAYER: Giving God, thank you for restoring joy in my life. I thank you, praise you and give you glory for great things you have done in my life. And on those days when, try as hard as I can, I am unable to feel the joy, renew in me the resolve to find something that I am glad about and rejoice with whatever it is I can find to be grateful for. Amen.

SEVENTY-ONE

I will also praise you with the harp for your faithfulness, O my God. I will sing praises to you with the lyre, O Holy One of Israel.
71:22

Nine times in the Psalms, the Psalmist tells about the lyre, a stringed instrument of the harp class having a U-shaped frame and used as one of the most ancient of instruments. Indeed, many images of the Psalms focus upon the Psalmist playing the lyre in praise of God. God is praised with music. There are so many ways we use to praise God –music, prayer, service, giving, liturgy, poetry, art, wandering about nature, reading, writing, pottery and every sort of creative endeavor. But, as Jonathan Edwards noted, *"The best, most beautiful, and most perfect way that we have of expressing a sweet concord of mind to each other is by music."* The Psalmist praised God with music and so do we. One of the most moving expressions of praise to God is found in the hymn <u>How Great Thou Art:</u>

O Lord my God, when I in awesome wonder
Consider all the worlds Thy hands have made
I see the stars, I hear the rolling thunder
Thy power throughout the universe displayed

Then sings my soul, my Savior God, to Thee
How great Thou art, how great Thou art
Then sings my soul, my Savior God, to Thee
How great Thou art, how great Thou art!

When through the woods, and forest glades I wander
And hear the birds sing sweetly in the trees
When I look down, from lofty mountain grandeur
And see the brook, and feel the gentle breeze

Then sings my soul, my Savior God, to Thee
How great Thou art, how great Thou art
Then sings my soul, my Savior God, to Thee
How great Thou art, how great Thou art!

And when I think, that God, His Son not sparing
Sent Him to die, I scarce can take it in
That on the Cross, my burden gladly bearing
He bled and died to take away my sin

Then sings my soul, my Savior God, to Thee
How great Thou art, how great Thou art
Then sings my soul, my Savior God, to Thee
How great Thou art, how great Thou art!

When Christ shall come, with shout of acclamation
And take me home, what joy shall fill my heart
Then I shall bow, in humble adoration
And then proclaim: "My God, how great Thou art!"

Then sings my soul, my Savior God, to Thee
How great Thou art, how great Thou art
Then sings my soul, my Savior God, to Thee
How great Thou art, how great Thou art!

PRAYER: O Lord my God. My soul sings and my spirit proclaims with every musical fiber within my that you are my Savior God. How Great Thou Art! You are great, O God. I behold in awesome wonder your creation and praise you with everything cell in my body, with music, praise, art, wonder and thanksgiving. Amen.

SEVENTY-TWO

Give the king your justice, O God.
72:1a

O Lord my God, I pray for you to give our leader your justice. Indeed, may every person on the planet pray the same. May all of our leaders be infused with your justice. It does not seem to be happening. Just when one country seems to get it right, another goes astray of your way of love, mercy, compassion and justice. Job (34:17a) asked the question *"Shall one who hates justice govern?"* Sadly, it happens. The neglect of justice was one of the sins that Jesus of Nazareth hated most. He called them hypocrites and proclaimed *"But woe to you Pharisees! For you tithe mint and rue and herbs of all kinds, and neglect justice and the love of God. It is these you ought to have practiced, without neglecting the others."* (Luke 11:42)

In an earlier Psalm (33), the Psalmist wrote about God: *"He loves righteousness and justice."* God loves justice. In the best case, justice is used in the Old Testament for how people are treated, especially those on the margins of society. Justice involves meeting their needs.

Give the king your justice, O God. In the United States, we have witnessed the best and the worst of justice advocated by our heads of government. The one who needs this prayer the most is the one who fails to seek the betterment of each individual or who undermines systems of safety nets to care for those with the least.

At times, citizens feel helpless to do anything to counter the one who ignores God's love of justice. Elie Wiesel, Nobel Laureate and Holocaust survivor, said *"There may be times when we are powerless to prevent injustice, but there must never be a time when we fail to protest."* And even when the king or head of government practices or advocates for injustice, people of faith are called to stand with and speak for the oppressed and for those on the margins of society.

Let rulers of nations and states hear and heed the wisdom of the ages about justice:

Justice will not be served until those who are unaffected are as outraged as those who are.
Benjamin Franklin

"The arc of the moral universe is long, but it bends towards justice."
Theodore Parker

Where justice is denied, where poverty is enforced, where ignorance prevails, and where any one class is made to feel that society is an organized conspiracy to oppress, rob and degrade them, neither persons nor property will be safe.
Frederick Douglass

In matters of truth and justice, there is no difference between large and small problems, for issues concerning the treatment of people are all the same.
Albert Einstein

We are not to simply bandage the wounds of victims beneath the wheels of injustice, we are to drive a spoke into the wheel itself.
Dietrich Bonhoeffer

Justice is the constant and perpetual will to allot to every man his due.
Domitius Ulpian

Justice is a contract of expediency, entered upon to prevent men harming or being harmed.
Epicurus

Injustice anywhere is a threat to justice everywhere.
Martin Luther King, Jr.

Justice consists not in being neutral between right and wrong, but in finding out the right and upholding it, wherever found, against the wrong.
Theodore Roosevelt

Justice is conscience, not a personal conscience but the conscience of the whole of humanity.
Alexander Solzhenitsyn

Throughout history, it has been the inaction of those who could have acted, the indifference of those who should have known better, the silence of the voice of justice when it mattered most, that has made it possible for evil to triumph.
Haile Selassie

Let the first act of every morning be to make the following resolve for the day: I shall not fear anyone on Earth. I shall fear only God. I shall not bear ill will toward anyone. I shall not submit to injustice from anyone. I shall conquer untruth by truth. And in resisting untruth, I shall put up with all suffering.
Mahatma Gandhi

Do not mistreat or abuse foreigners who live among you. Remember, you were foreigners in Egypt.
Exodus 22:21

Learn to do good; seek justice, rescue the oppressed, defend the orphan, plead for the widow.
Isaiah 1:17

He has told you, O mortal, what is good; and what does the Lord require of you but to do justice, and to love kindness, and to walk humbly with your God?
Micah 6:8

PRAYER: O God, give kings, presidents and rulers everywhere your justice. And when they lack a decent sense of justice, use me as your instrument and voice to speak for and stand with those who are victims of their injustice. Amen.

SEVENTY-THREE

Truly God is good to the upright, to those who are pure in heart.
73:1

We have seen how Jesus quoted some Psalms on the cross as his last words. The Psalms influenced his theology, teaching and preaching. He would have known this Psalm and used it as the basis for one of his beatitudes in his Sermon on the Mount: *"Blessed are the pure in heart, for they will see God."* (Matthew 5:8)

The Sermon on the Mount (in Matthew 5, 6, and 7) occurs shortly after Jesus recruited his twelve disciples. Up to this point, they knew little about what he stood for, who he was or what he believed. Something magical must have happened when he looked into each one's eyes and invited them to "Follow me." Now, on the Mount, he provides them with his basic orientation to discipleship. This is where they first learn about the core of his teachings. He begins with a series of teachings that begin with "Blessed are..." These are known as beatitudes. Can you imagine the newly minted disciples reacting when Jesus came to "Blessed are the pure in heart..."? Perhaps Peter quizzically looked as his brother Andrew and whispered "What have you gotten us into?" Pure in heart? Not us. If you were asked the question *"Are you pure in heart?"* would you raise your hand? My first inclination is to think that this is not me. Pure in heart? How many of us ever feel we are pure in heart?

The word for *pure* here was what was said about wine which was pure wine, unmixed with water. In Palestine, they did not drink the water and neither would you if you went there today. At meals, they drank wine. But you cannot drink too much wine or you know what happens. So they watered it down. The basic meaning of the word *pure* used in this beatitude is *unmixed* or *unadulterated*. Scottish New Testament professor Dr. William Barclay explained in his <u>Daily Bible Study</u> commentary that *pure in heart* refers to those whose motives are unmixed or to those who do things for the right reasons. That is integrity.

Sometimes no one else sees or knows that you are doing things for the right reasons but God.

Blessed are you when you do things from the right motives, because when people do things from the right reasons, they see God in a way that others cannot. Have you ever found yourself saying *"People see what they want to see?"* People see things different ways: A biologist and an artist look at a plant in different ways. A poet and an astronomer do not look at the stars in the same way. When you choose the course of doing things from the right reasons, you climb a little higher and see a little more of God's face. As the Psalmist wrote, *Truly God is good to the upright, to those who are pure in heart.*

PRAYER: Dear God, I have never felt myself to be pure in heart. You know my thoughts and how some are not so good. Lead me, guide me, push me and help me to choose to do things from the right motives and for the right reasons. Amen.

SEVENTY-FOUR

How long, O God, is the foe to scoff? Is the enemy to revile your name forever? Why do you hold back your hand; why do you keep your hand in your bosom?
74:10, 11

How long, O God. Why do you hold back you hand? Our country is divided, polarized, building up the rich, tearing down the poor, wrecking its environment, decreasing availability of health care, undermining and underfunding education, declining in its fight against racism, and replacing hospitality and a God-like welcome with "Keep Out" signs. This is not your way, O God. Why don't you do something? Is not that what the Psalmist seems to be asking? Why, O God, does it seem like evil is winning?

As I was leaving my visit with a parishioner, Muriel, and standing in the doorway, she said to me "When I watch TV news, it feels like evil is winning." That caught me off guard. How do you discuss hours' worth of systematic theology while you are buttoning up your coat? But I had to answer with something. So, I responded with Jesus' I AM statement from the Gospel of John (8:12): *"I am the light of the world. Whoever follows me will never walk in darkness but will have the light of life."* I tried to reassure Muriel that no matter how bleak things appear, the darkness will not overcome the light. Now, years later, I think my best intentions were misguided. I think I was wrong. What are we to say when leaders of a nation, society or culture seem to promote darkness rather than light?

Perhaps Muriel was correct: it feels like evil is winning. Like John, the prophet Isaiah proclaimed *"Then your light shall break forth like the dawn, and your healing shall spring up quickly."* (Isaiah 58:8). Light may have eventually dawned years after the Holocaust or South Africa's apartheid, but that gave small comfort to those who suffered tragic loss, pain or death. For a long time, darkness prevailed and there are signs today of a pervasive evil in our land.

The hundreds and maybe thousands of children dragged away by the US government from their migrating parents seeking to fall into the arms of the Statue of Liberty may find little relief from words about darkness not overcoming the light. The millions cascading down out of the middle class while the upper one percent increases their wealth geometrically may rightly wonder just when is the light supposed to break forth? Perhaps not in time to do them any good.

Consider when Jesus spoke these words about being the light of the world and how *"Whoever follows me will never walk in darkness but will have the light of life."* Jesus entered the world when an evil-minded Herod ordered all young children to be killed in order to hopefully eliminate Jesus. *"When Herod saw that he had been tricked by the wise men, he was infuriated, and he sent and killed all the children in and around Bethlehem who were two years old or under, according to the time that he had learned from the wise men."* (Matthew 2:16). This is the dark side to Christmas which rarely if ever makes it into the annual Christmas pageant. Thirty-three years later, leaders of darkness sought and obtained Jesus' death. How would you explain to someone that the Light of the World was sent by God to our planet, and we killed him? You couldn't blame the earliest followers of Jesus to question just when the light is supposed to break forth like the dawn.

When Jesus refers to being the light, perhaps he is not applying this to political, social or cultural experience but to something else. But what? He speaks in metaphor, uses figures of speech and frequently employs Middle Eastern teaching techniques like hyperbole, parallelism, patterns and parable. How are we to understand? Perhaps when Jesus spoke about the darkness not overcoming the light, he was not speaking about a nation's politics or governance.

Jesus came into the world to bring us the good news and to teach us the truth about God. That is the light. When John began his gospel, he talked about the mind of God becoming flesh and dwelling among us to enlighten us. *"The true light, which enlightens everyone, was coming into the world."*

When Jesus said *"Whoever follows me will never walk in darkness but will have the light of life,"* notice the pronoun: *whoever*. This is personal. This applies to you, me and anyone who follows him. Our following him, which is good news, is not likely to be shown on TV news. It is the nature of TV news for viewers to witness more darkness than light. It is also the nature of TV news to focus disproportionately on politics and politicians. Jesus was speaking personally... *whoever follows me*. He was not speaking politically or culturally. He did not say that when the light of the world arrives, our politics and society will change dramatically for the better. In many cases it did not. However, when the light of the world arrives, the light has the potential to change people, and people have the potential to change society and culture for good. The goal for people of faith is not to make our nation great again, but to make our nation good again. Therefore, how fantastically critical it is for followers of Jesus to let their lights shine, especially in the darkest of places and at the darkest of times. A critical mass of followers who reflect God's radiated light become a model and a warm glow when it is needed most. They serve as an example of the best of people aspiring to the goals of love, joy, peace, patience, kindness, goodness, faithfulness, gentleness and self-control – the fruit of the spirit.

We understand the Psalmist's lament... *How long, O God... Why do you hold back you hand?* There are times we feel that way too. We wonder why God does not intercede. Do not let the TV news or even national leadership going in the wrong direction draw you into darkness. Welcome into your soul the light of The Great I AM and trust that *"Whoever follows me will never walk in darkness but will have the light of life."*

PRAYER: O Lord, fill me with the light of your spirit. Infuse in me a desire to be a good person. Then, help me to do whatever I can to help make my country good again. When it feels like evil is winning, grant me trust that this is your world, which you so love. Use me in your service to shine my light whenever there is opportunity. Amen.

SEVENTY-FIVE

We give thanks to you, O God; we give thanks; your name is near. People tell of your wondrous deeds.
75:1

The Psalmist never fails to say thank you to God. His inspiration encourages us to remember to say thank you.

Do you ever think about if your house or office were on fire, what would you save, once the people were out? Usually it is the personal things, like pictures, mementoes, or art.

If it were my home, one thing I would save would be my file of thank-you notes which people have sent to me: cards, letters, emails, scribbles. Just seeing this collection fills me with a warm glow and makes me grateful to have been a part of their life. I keep this file close by my side and if my home was on fire that is one of the things I would rescue. It is one of my treasures. You see, nobody is required to thank you. But when they do, how cherished it is. Proverbs 15 says *A word in season, how good it is!*

Sometimes they do not thank you, and you notice that too. When they do not thank you, it can cause funny feelings, confusing feelings. You cannot help but notice what appears to be their ingratitude. It is not that you do things for the thanks. It is not that you feel you deserved to be thanked. It is just that sometimes the silence of ingratitude thunders with discordant noise.

I had that happen to me when I conducted at a funeral. The woman and her husband were members of the church. I visited in their home numerous times. When the husband had a heart attack, I rushed to the critical care unit. I visited him steadily. When he came home, I sat on his porch and drank ice tea with them. When he died, I conducted his funeral. Then, when his widow was lonely, I visited her. When she became sick, the church took her meals. Our prayer chain prayed for her daily. Our deacons delivered communion to her once a month. I telephoned her every week and visited every few weeks.

This church was there for her at every high point and low point of her life. It comforted her, strengthened her, and lifted her spirit. People cared and showed it. This was her "other family."

It cost. It cost us time, especially. It cost us money, even for the meals. But we sent her money too. She did not have much, so when she had big medical bills, we helped and sent her money. She was very grateful and said so.

When she was dying in a distant hospital, I called her daily. I spoke to her an hour before she died. Then, I conducted her funeral.

That is when I came in contact with her three daughters. They were good children. They were close to their mother and they loved her. I suppose here is where human vanity gets mixed up in the picture… my vanity.

I wanted this woman's three children to know how much we had all done for their mother. I wanted to tell them, in a sense, about her "other" family – her church – and about all the caring, sharing, and loving their mother received. This was a textbook case for how well a church could care for its people in their time of greatest need.

It did not feel like the daughters were hearing me. They did not nod. They did not say *Gee, that is great.* They did not say *thank you.*

In fact, they raved about a Nun who stopped by the woman's hospital room for ten minutes, how a neighbor had brought her a meal once, and how wonderful another church was. When her obituary was printed, in lieu of flowers, contributions were encouraged to another church, the church where she went for a few weeks on vacation.

All I could do was shake my head. After the service, I spoke once more to the daughters. Nothing. Not a *nice service* or *glad the church was here for mom.* Later, weeks later, there was no thank you card.

These three adult daughters seemed to be walking models of ingratitude: The three ungrateful children.

You've had that happen to you, haven't you? When ingratitude comes from a family member, a neighbor, from your church or your employer, it leaves you feeling unthanked. It affects your feelings. Do you ever wonder, *Does GOD have feelings?* I think so! Remember the Ten Commandments (in Exodus 20:5): *For I the LORD your God am a jealous God...* God has feelings.

My reaction to these three daughters troubled me. Then it troubled me that I was troubled. What's the big deal? But I couldn't let go of it. It was not so much like a slap on the face, but it stung. It was not so much that they did not thank me, but they did not appear to have any gratitude for all the church had done.

I tried to re-direct my energy from the sting of ingratitude to lessons I could learn from this experience. There were two lessons which shook me by the shoulders and made me pay attention.

LESSON #1: I did not do it for their gratitude. I did it for God. Lesson: *Do not expect to be thanked.* Do not do good things for the thanks. Colossians 3:23 says *Whatever you do, work at it with all your heart, as working for the Lord, not for people.* Do things for the Lord, not for the thanks.

LESSON #2: This was the big lesson that struck me: Could I be like them TO GOD... not saying thank you... being so obviously and obliviously ungrateful? Oh, yes! Oh, no! I have been just like them!

There is a powerful story in Luke 17 where Jesus healed ten lepers and only one returned to thank him. Jesus was on the border between Galilee and Samaria and was met by a band of ten lepers. Since we do not have much first-hand experience with lepers, we might substitute something else, like AIDS.

The tension on the border then was like the tension between Jews and Palestinians today. Their mutual dislike went back a thousand years. The Bible points out in another story that Jews had no dealings with the Samaritans. They considered them foreigners... unclean. Not one of us.

As he entered a village, ten lepers approached him. Keeping their distance... (Luke 17:12). The lepers stood far off. It was required that, when a leper was to windward of a healthy person, the leper must stand at least fifty yards away: half a football field. That is why this little band of ten lepers approached him but still kept their distance. That shows the lonely isolation in which lepers lived. The lepers themselves would have seen themselves as people, not as Jews or Samaritans. They were just people in need and their being victims of this awful disease created in them something of a bond. The lepers congregated at a distance. They could not work to earn a living, of course. They could not go home. Never again would they have a home, a room of their own or privacy. They would have no friends, no spouse, and no children. All they could do is hang around together and beg, hoping for the mercy of a few who would toss them a shekel or two.

Into their world walks Jesus. Keeping their distance, they called out, saying, *Jesus, Master, have mercy on us!*

When he saw them, he said to them, *Go and show yourselves to the priests.* And as they went, they were made clean.

No fireworks there! No magic wand. Go show yourselves to the priests and as they went, they were made clean. Healed. They could work again. They could go home. They would have family. Instead of outcasts, they were now people. That changes everything.

Nine out of ten never came back to say thank you. Only one Samaritan returned to express his gratitude. Even Jesus felt the ingratitude of the other nine. It was not so much that it hurt him personally, but like the three daughters who never said thank you, it stunned him: *Then Jesus asked, Were not ten made clean? But the other nine, where are they? Was none of them found to return and give praise to God except this foreigner?* (Luke 17:17). The only one who bothered to say thank you was the Samaritan.

Often, we are ungrateful to other people. Somebody helps us. We believe we would never forget, but we do, sometimes without a word of thanks. It would have meant so much to them for us to send a card or note, to make a call, or even just to say those two words *Thank you.*
Blow, blow, thou winter wind,
Thou art not so unkind
As man's ingratitude. (W. Shakespeare, *As You Like It*)

And, of course, we forget to say thank you to God. In a time of need, we pray for what we want, with the utmost of intensity. Time passes and we forget God. We forget to say thank you. Psalm 103 (2) reminds us to *Bless the LORD, O my soul, and do not forget all his benefits*. Do not forget all God's benefits: God's gifts, what God has done for you and how God has helped you.

Of this error, I am guilty and perhaps you are too. I forget to say thank you. I am like the three ungrateful daughters. I am like the nine healed lepers. I have been ungrateful and I cannot imagine that God does not have some of those funny feelings I experienced when the three daughters appeared ungrateful for the care their mother received. Perhaps my ingratitude, or yours, stuns God.

The hope we have comes from a verse in Luke 6 (35), which says about God: *"...for he is kind to the ungrateful and the selfish."* May you and I try to be like that too, like God: kind to others who are ungrateful or selfish.

The ingratitude of the nine lepers may have stunned Jesus, but it did not change his nature. And so, may you and I never give up our own nature to do good and to be kind to others, even if they are ungrateful or selfish.

Whenever we experience the ingratitude of another, may it remind us that like the nine lepers, perhaps we too have forgotten to say thank you to God.

So... thank you to God for all God's blessings to us. And thank you to the Psalmist for being a model of one who gives thanks to God: *We give thanks to you, O God; we give thanks; your name is near. People tell of your wondrous deeds.*

PRAYER: I give you thanks, O God, for your love, your blessings and your grace. Thank you too for loving me anyway even when I am an ungrateful person. Amen.

SEVENTY-SIX

Make vows to the Lord your God, and perform them; let all who are around him bring gifts to the one who is awesome,
76:11

Let all who are around him bring gifts to the one who is awesome.
If this Psalm was authored by David, his beautiful attitude about giving has a fascinating connection to a story about King David in 2 Samuel, chapter 24. In the story, King David believed he was instructed to build an altar to the Lord on the threshing floor of Araunah the Jebusite. We do not know anything about Araunah except he owned the threshing floor that David wanted to buy.

One day Araunah looked up to see the King and his entourage approaching. Can you imagine the feeling you would have if you looked up to see the ruler of your nation approaching in order to visit you? As they drew near, he laid prostrate with his face on the ground to show respect for his King. Araunah asked the obvious question: *"Why has my lord the king come to his servant?"*

David said, *"To buy the threshing floor from you in order to build an altar to the LORD, so that the plague may be averted from the people."*

Overwhelmed that his King wanted something he owned, Araunah essentially said: *"Take it. It's yours. I give it to you."* If David accepted it as a gift from Araunah, it would be Araunah's gift to the Lord, not David's. So, the King said to Araunah, *"No, but I will buy it from you for a price. I will not offer burnt offerings to the LORD my God that cost me nothing."*

In *The Message*, it is told this way: *"I'm not going to offer God, my God, sacrifices that are no sacrifice..."*

The point: our giving to God costs. What good is an offering that cost me nothing? That is no sacrifice. That is not a gift. When you love someone, you want to give to them. You want your gift to be a significant gift, a special sacrifice made out of love.

People of faith desire to give God a sacrifice that is a sacrifice. Our giving is faith-based. We give, not to meet a budget or pay an institution's bills, but to give to God. When we give, we consecrate our giving, which means, we make our act of giving holy. David not only demonstrated the sincerity of his giving but encouraged others to do the same when he wrote in this Psalm *Let all who are around him bring gifts to the one who is awesome.*

PRAYER: Awesome God, build up in me a spirit of generosity. May I make gifts to others and to you out of my love. Help me to think of ways, Dear God, that I can make gifts to you which cost me something... gifts of financial resources, time, talent, sharing and caring. Amen.

SEVENTY-SEVEN

Your way was through the sea, your path, through the mighty waters; yet your footprints were unseen.
77:19

One of our favorite summer vacations was when my wife and I went fossil hunting in Nova Scotia. We got tourist information which talked about how some of the earliest fossils known to humans have been found at Joggins, Nova Scotia, so we set out to explore. Within the past few decades, fossilized dinosaur footprints have been discovered at Joggins.

On the way, driving up Route 1 along the Maine coast, we listened to National Public Radio. There was an interview on with Neil Armstrong, reflecting on the first moon landing. If you were alive in 1969, do you remember where you were when the "Eagle" landed on the moon? That was one of the most significant happenings of the last millennium: It was the first time two people ever landed on another world. About seven hours later, I was hundreds of millions of years away, from Tranquility Bay on the moon to the Minas Basin in Canada – a journey back in time.

The Minas Basin is at the head of the Bay of Fundy, which has the highest recorded tides in the world. It has 50' tides. These record tides wash up to the sandstone cliffs and erode away the sand, leaving precious heirlooms in stone – fossils – scattered on the beach... only to be washed away to the sea in a few hours.

That evening by dusk, we walked the beach of one of the richest fossil sites in the Western Hemisphere. Just about every stone on the beach was a 200-million-year-old fossil. We'd pick one up, stuff it in our pockets, then find a better one, and then an even better one, one fossil after another. You're not allowed to do that anymore, but we could on our first visit. The fossils cracked under our feet when we walked on them... which was a sound of horror – to think of a paleontological record lost forever, although it would be gone anyway at the next tide, only to be ground into sand.

It felt like a sacred site, and it struck me that I was walking into a fascinating study of Genesis 1:1: *"In the beginning God created the heavens and the earth."* For weeks, my thoughts centered upon that verse and the fossils at Joggins, for they are among the earliest record of God's creation. If you believe Genesis 1:1, then every fossil you hold in your hand contains God's thumbprint in stone. It may look like a stem from the earliest sea plant life, the trail of a crab, a small dinosaur's footprint, or – would you believe this: fossilized raindrops – but God's fingerprints are all over God's creation.

In Psalm 77 the Psalmist tells how *"Thy way was through the sea, thy path through the great waters; yet thy footprints were unseen."* God was there. The Creator's footprints, though unseen, are present all over the earth and all throughout time.

Geologist J. William Dawson said: *"It has often happened to geologists, as to other explorers of new regions, that footprints in the sand have guided them to the inhabitants of unknown lands."* Dawson said that in 1863, but it wasn't until 1986 that dinosaur footprints from the Triassic-Jurassic boundary were discovered in the red sandstone cliffs of the Minas Basin in Nova Scotia.

Let me back up a couple hundred million years here and tell you why the Minas Basin is so significant. In the beginning, there was only one big land mass with a body of water in the center. Scientists call this super-continent *"Pangea."* "Pangea" means, simply, "all the earth." Pan = all. Gea, as in geology = earth. All the earth.

Over time, the Atlantic rifts gradually pushed the land masses away from each other. At that time, Nova Scotia was then wedged near the equator between South America and Africa. Nova Scotia was smack dab in the middle of Pangea.

The Fundy Geological Museum says: *"The land masses were like huge rafts of land on molten magma."* What was once the shores of this big pond pushed away, twisted around, and became Africa, Brazil, Europe, and North America as the rafts of land floated away from each other.

As the continental plates began to pull apart, great rift valleys formed. These valleys gradually filled with sediments that today make up the Newark Supergroup, which extends from Nova Scotia to South Carolina. The tides have eroded through the Triassic-Jurassic sediments, opening a window for geologists into the world of 240 to 175 million years ago.

The dinosaurs which roamed around Pangea's big pond left their footprints in the stones, which are now found in the sandstone cliffs of... Africa, Brazil, Europe, and Joggins, Nova Scotia... once the center of this Ancient Rift Valley.

The Apostle Paul wrote in Romans (8:22) how *"the whole creation has been groaning in labor pains until now."* When you hear about continental plates pulling apart, great rift valleys forming, and huge rafts of land mass floating on molten magma, Paul's language seems fitting, doesn't it: *"the whole creation... GROANING in travail together..."* (KJV).

The continents are still moving. The rifting continues to spread the floor of the Atlantic Ocean, pushing Europe and North America apart at a rate of 2 centimeters a year. In your lifetime, the continents will push apart about the height of a basketball player, about 6 ½ feet. The rift still spreads. The rafts still float... at the same speed as when Pangea broke apart 350 million years ago. Then, God was there. God's creation continues into the present. Future citizens of planet earth will look back on the beginning and on today's times as well and affirm that God's fingerprints are all over God's creation: *Your way was through the sea, your path, through the mighty waters; yet your footprints were unseen.*

PRAYER: Grant me eyes to see, Creator God, that your fingerprints and footprints are all over your creation, from the tiniest plant to the most distant star. Help me too to recognize your footprints and to know that you have been with me in every chapter of my life. Amen.

SEVENTY-EIGHT

He established a decree in Jacob, and appointed a law in Israel,
which he commanded our ancestors to teach to their children;
that the next generation might know them, the children yet
unborn, and rise up and tell them to their children, so that they
should set their hope in God, and not forget the works of God,
but keep his commandments;
78:5-7

There is a song with words and music by Steve Romanoff, a Maine singer-songwriter, that reminds of this Psalm about teaching your children and encouraging them to teach their children. Its title is *Teach Your Children to Sing*.

Somewhere between your noon hour and alarm clock setting day,
If you are lucky, must be lucky, but we're all lucky anyway,
Set aside your routine pleasures for this most important thing,
And take the time to teach your children to sing.

Oh, you know it's not like working and the kids will call it play,
And as you teach them, they will teach you, we're all teachers
*   in a way.*
Set aside your routine pleasures sit together in a ring,
And take the time to teach your children to sing.

Now I know what you are thinking, he's a dreamer, he's a fool,
I can't even sing myself, they used to keep me after school;
But if the parent is the playmate and the playground is your mind,
Take a lesson from the piper, kids choose music every time.

Before the fighting, or the silence that they find
*   when they're at home,*
And when they grow they turn to battle, or find some way
*   to be alone;*
Away from life, away from loving, away from nearly everything
That gives us all our own good reason to sing.

222

No, it won't take away your sorrows or be a cure-all for your pain,
It won't end all wars tomorrow, or bring all the deserts rain,
But if we start now with our children,
*   while we still have got the time,*
They'll be much less apt to quarrel when a song is on their minds.

Somewhere, somewhere, between your noon hour and
*   alarm clock setting day,*
If you are lucky, must be lucky, but we're all lucky every day,
Set aside your routine pleasures for this most important thing,
And take the time to teach your children,
Take the time to teach your children,
Take the time to teach our children to sing.

The Psalm encourages people of faith to teach their children to set their hope in God. Parents teach their children with words and also by example. If children see their own parents setting their hope in God, they will know it is an important family value. They, when they become parents, are encouraged to do the same... to keep the song and the psalm echoing throughout their family's spiritual history so that it is never lost.

There are so many values parents desire to instill in their children. This one may be the most important, for when they set their hope in God, they can not only survive but can thrive no matter what their future brings.

PRAYER: Eternal God, how easily I can forget your great works and to set my hope in you. Guide me back to the path which is rooted in hope and faith in you. Let the candle of hope in my life radiate out to bring a glow, a warmth and an example to others. Amen.

SEVENTY-NINE

Then we your people, the flock of your pasture, will give thanks to you forever; from generation to generation we will recount your praise.
79:13

There may be an unintended warning of danger which is signaled by the first word in this verse: *then*. The word often follows the word *if* and becomes a part of a conditional phrase: IF this, THEN that. A conditional phrase means there are conditions. Imagine someone saying "I will love you if..." Uh oh. That means they have conditions to loving you. You must do something to satisfy their conditions in order to be loved. Or, the phrase if-then becomes part of a deal: I will agree to the deal IF... The settlement and closure need to be negotiated.

In the Gospel of John (14:15) Jesus told his disciples *"If you love me, you will keep my commandments." If you love me...* The word *if* presumes a condition. The *if* is not a requirement. It is a choice. Jesus does not require anyone to love him. No person can require another to love him or her. But IF you do, THEN certain behavior or action will follow. IF you love another person THEN you will want to give them the bigger piece of the cookie when you break it to share. IF you love your child or grandchild THEN you will sacrifice for them. So Jesus starts by saying *"IF you love me..."* If you do THEN you will keep my commandments. People do things for love that they would never do if it was simply required.

The Psalm beginning with the word *then* could sound like the Psalmist is imposing conditions upon God. If... THEN we will give thanks to you. THEN we will praise you. While he probably did not intend it to mean this, it has a familiar ring to it because we sometimes do just that. We bargain with God. We make a half-hearted promise that IF we get what we want, THEN we will praise God. Our thanks and praise become conditional.

224

It can feel like we are trying to make a deal with God in order to get something we want. Otherwise, we withhold our part of the deal, our thanksgiving to God and our praise.

Thinking about placing conditions upon our thanks to God can also remind us of something wonderful, and that is that God possesses unconditional love for you. In the Parable of the Prodigal Son – which might be better titled the Parable of the Loving Parent – the parent demonstrates unconditional love for the prodigal child. When the child returns home, the father runs out to greet him, throws his arms around him, hugs and kisses him. This unconditional love is demonstrated, not with a word but with a hug. That is how God loves you, unconditionally.

While the word *then* was likely not intended by the Psalmist to place conditions on thanking God, it serves as a reminder for us to watch our language, for we would never want to bargain with God to get what we want. That is not the way of loving and faithful children. Ask for what you want, but do not place conditions on it.

PRAYER: Gracious God, do I do that? Do I sound like I place conditions on thanking or praising you? If I do, please forgive me. Give to me a simple and child-like faith that loves, trusts, and obeys you. And thank you, God, for your unconditional love for me. Amen.

EIGHTY

Restore us, O God; let your face shine, that we may be saved.
80:3

I once asked the governing board and also the deacons of the church I was serving "Who is praying for our church?" They did not have an answer, not even a guess. I continued "If you are not praying for our church, who is?" This time a discussion evolved with some suggesting that perhaps when the governing board or the deacons meet, they might make a time to pray for our church.

The Psalmist, in Psalm 80, prays for Israel to be restored. Three times in this brief Psalm the verse is repeated: *Restore us, O God; let your face shine, that we may be saved.* He is praying for a nation and a people. In so doing, he causes us to think about our prayers. We pray for people, especially those whom we care about. Usually we pray for individuals rather than groups or classes of people. We pray for ourselves. Again, we are praying for an individual. But what if we also prayed for groups: our church, our community, our state, our nation, or our planet? It feels less personal. Perhaps we wonder if our prayers make any difference. And yet, why would we believe that our prayers make a difference for someone we care about but not so for an institution, like our church? Besides, don't we already have so many things to pray for that this seems to add more to our prayer time?

If you were praying for your church, for what would you pray? Using the Psalmists prayer, we might pray for our church to be restored. Restored to what? As churches tend to be in decline in attendance and membership, we tend to think that filling the pews may symbolize restoration. On the one hand, church membership is linked more to a congregation's zip code and cultural shifts. Congregations in growing communities are more likely to be growing, and congregations in declining populations are likely to be declining. Also, culturally, participation in membership-based organizations is in decline in this phase of the 21st Century.

226

People on the whole are opting not to go to church, so obviously congregations are in decline. On the other hand, this may be a sign that churches are not meeting needs. When visitors attend a church, too often they hear about decline in members, in choir participants, and in church school. There are many empty seats. Worshippers get bombarded with how the church needs more money. It feels needy and if there is any reality, it is that people do not want to belong to a needy organization. Rather, people want to belong to an organization that meets needs. And so, our prayer could be for God to restore our churches to meeting the spiritual needs of people and to guide congregations to know how to meet needs. Think of the important role you play when you pray for your church to meet the spiritual needs of people.

You might also pray for your church to grow in faithfulness. A judicatory leader of a church denomination went out visiting churches in her area. She returned to tell her supervisor, "It feels like the Holy Spirit has departed from our churches." What if people turned to churches to guide them into an encounter with the Divine, but what they find instead are congregations centered upon chili cookoffs, bean suppers, rummage sales, musical or theatrical productions, the preservation of infrastructure and tradition, worship services which begin with ten minutes of announcements and skits, and the deification of the word "community" as they crave a place to meet their belongingness needs. In some places, the worship of God and the teaching and learning about faith has slipped silently into second place. And yet, national polls show a very high percent of Americans believe in God. Nine-in-ten Americans believe in a higher power, according to a Pew Research Center poll. The Gallup Poll results show that 89% of Americans believe in God, although people's concept of God can vary dramatically. Whatever the percent, there is a large section of our population who say they believe in God, but only a sliver attends a community of worship. And so, our prayer may be for God to restore our churches to faithfulness and meeting the spiritual needs of those seeking to know God better and love God more.

If you were praying for your nation, for what would you pray? There is an illustration which is sometimes attributed to French writer Alexis de Tocqueville. It is said that he was curious about what made America tick. What made it a great nation? Legend has it that he considered America's harbors and fields, its vast world commerce, public school system, institutions of higher education and even its democratic Congress. His conclusion which has been oft credited to him: *"Not until I went into the churches of America and heard her pulpits flame with righteousness did I understand the secret of her genius and power. America is great because America is good, and if America ever ceases to be good, America will cease to be great."* The prayer for people of faith is not to make America great again but to make American good again. May God grant that we desire to be good people and a good nation. In the words of the Psalmist, Restore us, O God.

PRAYER: Restore us, O God. I pray for my church and for it to be led by your spirit into faithfulness. May it be a healthy and vital congregation. Lead my church to be faithful in meeting the spiritual needs of people. I pray for my nation and its leaders. May their highest priority be to make our nation good and to seek the best interests of its citizens. Help me to strive to be a good person, a faithful member of my community of faith, and a good citizen. Amen.

EIGHTY-ONE

*"But my people did not listen to my voice; Israel would not
submit to me."*
81:11

This verse is Psalmist's understanding of God speaking. It has the
tone of a parent saying "You are not listening to me." That can be
taken figuratively, as the parent explains that "I told you the right
way to live and you didn't listen. You didn't obey." It can also be
taken literally, almost as though the Divine Parent says "Just stop
talking so much and listen. Listen to me. You will not be able to
hear me if you are doing all the talking." In that, we are reminded
that in our prayers to God, communication is a two-way street. We
talk. But how well do we listen? Perhaps silence makes us
uncomfortable. Perhaps we want to hurry on and get it done, but
miss the presence of God which is found in silence.

Mother Teresa wrote that God is the friend of silence:
*If we really want to pray we must first learn to listen, for in the
silence of the heart God speaks. And to be able to see that silence,
to be able to hear God we need a clean heart; for a clean heart
can see God, can hear God, can listen to God; and then only from
the fullness of our heart can we speak to God. But we cannot
speak unless we have listened, unless we have made that
connection with God in the silence of our heart.*

*We need to find God and God cannot be found in noise and
restlessness. See how nature, the trees, the flowers, the grass grow
in perfect silence. See the stars, the moon and the sun, how they
move in silence. The more we receive in silent prayer, the more we
can give in our active life. Silence gives us a new outlook on
everything.* [from *Seeking the Heart of God: Reflections on
Prayer* by Mother Teresa and Brother Roger].

In the Psalm, God says *Israel would not submit to me.* Submitting
to God is an engaging idea. When you study world religions and
come to the Muslim faith, you discover that the word *Islam* means
submission. Islam requires a complete submission to Allah.

When you examine the teachings of Jesus, the same could be said of Christianity: Jesus expects submission to the God's will: *"Thy will be done."* If we drone those words when saying the Lord's Prayer, we miss the understanding that we are asking God to have God's way with us. In this prayer we pray to submit ourselves to God and to God's will. In the Sermon on the Mount, Jesus used the word *"first"* only three times to emphasize what he prioritized for followers. The first and most important *first* comes in Matthew 6:33 (KJV): *"Seek ye first the kingdom of God, and his righteousness."* Some Christians have considered this the most important verse in the Bible. This is what followers of Jesus should put first in our lives. Is this not the same as choosing to submit ourselves to God?

And so, from this Psalm, we get two important messages. One is the encouragement to listen to God... to actively listen and to embrace silence as a pathway into the presence of the Divine. Listen more, talk less. The second is the radical call to submit ourselves to God, to mean it when we pray "Thy will be done."

PRAYER: Awesome God, I guess I don't do a lot of listening. I am more inclined to do the talking, to tell you what I want or hope for. I don't give you a chance to get a word in edgewise. There is so much to prayer and I understand so little about it. Give me patience and peace to be able to sit with you, to be with you in silence, and to listen to your still small voice speaking to me. May each day be a recommitment for me to submit myself to you and to pray with sincerity "Thy will be done." Amen.

EIGHTY-TWO

Give justice to the weak and the orphan; maintain the right of the lowly and the destitute. Rescue the weak and the needy; deliver them from the hand of the wicked."
82:3, 4

John Bradford, a 16th Century English Reformer, watched as a group of prisoners were led to the gallows. As he looked at their faces, he exclaimed *"There but for the grace of God goes John Bradford."* We too might look upon those who are troubled and exclaim "There but for the grace of God go I." Whenever we witness another who is hungry, a stranger, a person escaping danger and seeking a hospitable welcome, one who is sick, needy or hurting, this is a worthy saying upon which to center our spirituality: *There but for the grace of God go I.* And that is a great motivation to give justice to anyone in need, for it could have been us. If we were the one in need, we would hope for people of faith to give justice and compassion to us. Justice in the Old Testament is thought of as how you treat another.

People of faith are called to care for others. Justice is the care and advocacy of those on the margins, those least able to advocate for themselves, those with the least power, least voice, least security, least safety, least access to safety nets, and the least wealth.

The prophet Amos wrote *"Let justice roll down like waters, and righteousness like an ever-flowing stream."* (Amos 5:24). These prophetic words from Amos were a favorite text of Martin Luther King, Jr. When King accepted the Nobel Prize for Peace on December 10, 1964, he questioned why they were giving the prize to a work which was unfinished. King said: *I must ask why this prize is awarded to a movement which is beleaguered and committed to unrelenting struggle; to a movement which has not won the very peace and brotherhood which is the essence of the Nobel Prize.* He was essentially asking... why are you giving this prize to a movement which has not won? The job is not done, although, he said in the speech: *I still believe that we shall overcome.*

231

Four years after the Nobel Prize, the work remained unfinished and the struggle felt like pushing a bolder uphill. *"We've got some difficult days ahead,* he said in Memphis to sanitation workers on strike in April 3 1968. *But it doesn't matter with me now. Because I have been to the mountaintop. And I don't mind. Like anybody, I would like to live a long life. Longevity has its place. But I'm not concerned about that now. I just want to do God's will. And He's allowed me to go up to the mountain. And I've looked over. And I've seen the promised land. I may not get there with you. But I want you to know tonight, that we, as a people will get to the promised land. And I'm not fearing any man. Mine eyes have seen the glory of the coming of the Lord"*

The following day, April 4, 1968, King walked out the door of the Lorraine Motel and
drew his last breath. He did not get to the promised land and the work is still unfinished, but what a powerful foresight... that we shall overcome... someday. Someday... *Justice will roll down like waters, and righteousness like an ever-flowing stream.*

Puccini, the Italian composer, wrote a number of famous operas, including La Boheme, Madame Butterfly, and La Tosca. In 1922 he was stricken by cancer while working on his last opera, Turandot – which many now consider his best. Puccini told his students, *"If I don't finish Turandot, I want you to finish it for me."* Shortly afterward he died. Puccini's students studied the opera carefully and after considerable work, completed it. In 1926 the world premiere of Turandot was performed in Milan with Puccini's student, Arturo Toscanini, directing. Legend tells how everything went beautifully until the opera reached the point where Puccini had been forced to put down his pen. Tears ran down Toscanini's face. He stopped the music, put down his baton, turned to the audience, and announced, *"Thus far the Master wrote, and then he died."* Silence filled the opera house. It was an unusual, uncomfortable interruption. Then Toscanini picked up the baton again, smiled through his tears, and exclaimed, *"But the disciples finished his work."*

When Turandot ended, the audience burst into thunderous applause and that performance became one of the most memorable in the distinguished history of opera.

Such is the nature of our calling, as people of God: We are called to finish the work so that someday *"justice may roll down like waters, and righteousness like an ever-flowing stream."* We, people of faith, commit ourselves to be advocates for those on the margins of society and to help finish the Master's work, especially to those he named "the least of these… my children."

PRAYER: God of justice and mercy, use me in your service to carry on your work in giving justice to those who are most in need. When I am not sure how to do this, show me the way and lead me. Amen.

EIGHTY-THREE

Let them know that you alone, whose name is the Lord, are the Most High over all the earth.
83:18

Psalm 83 does not seem very God-like. He is praying for God to make bad things happen to his foes and to teach them a lesson. That is not the right prayer. Jesus taught his followers to love their enemies and to pray for those who persecute them. That is the right prayer, although it is one of the hardest things asked of people who follow the way of Jesus.

So, the Psalmist is human. His foes seem to be causing him great pain. It feels like he is losing and they are winning. If you have ever had a foe who sought to undermine you, spread poison about you, betray you or do you harm, perhaps you have felt the same way. You and the Psalmist wish for bad to happen to them for what they've done to you. But of course, that is not the right way to prayer. We wonder what God would think of us if we were to pray for evil to befall another. It is the lowest of prayer rather than the highest.

The Psalmist, however, concludes his prayer on a high note, praying for his foes to know that God alone is the Most High over all the earth. Think about what that means. If God causes your foes to know the goodness and truth about God, and if that leads them to want to love and obey God, then they cease to be foes because their values are now centered upon love and forgiveness. Love, *agape* in Greek, is the desire for the highest and best interests of the other. If your foes become children of God, they are compelled to desire for you that which is your highest and best interest. That is a 180 degree turn from them wishing you harm. And so, perhaps, this is the highest prayer one can pray for his or her foes, that the foe comes to know that God alone is the Most High over all the earth. And so, think about anyone who might wish you unwell and pray for them to turn around and become practitioners of the love and forgiveness of God.

PRAYER: Loving God, I pray for someone I'm thinking about whom I might consider a foe and I pray that they may know that you are God and the Most High over all the earth. Teach me to forgive as you forgive, and to love as you love. Help my open wounds caused by another to heal, help me to forgive them and pray for them, and to pray that they might come to know you and wish to practice your ways. Amen.

EIGHTY-FOUR

How lovely is your dwelling place, O Lord of hosts! My soul longs, indeed it faints for the courts of the Lord; my heart and my flesh sing for joy to the living God. Even the sparrow finds a home, and the swallow a nest for herself, where she may lay her young, at your altars, O Lord of hosts, my King and my God. Happy are those who live in your house, ever singing your praise.
84:1-4

Your dwelling place... the courts of the Lord... a nest... your altars... your house – these are all metaphors for the place where God is. God's presence. In the most poetic of language, the Psalmist rejoices and celebrates being in the presence of the Divine. This is the same meaning of his 23rd Psalm (KJV)... *"and I shall dwell in the house of the Lord forever."* The Psalm recognizes that the person who recognizes himself or herself in God's presence is not only happy, but wants to sing God's praises.

How do you know if you are in God's presence? What does it feel like? Is it a mystical or magical experience? Now, of course, God is omnipresent which means that God is everywhere. So, in the Psalm we witness a heightened sensitivity to being in God's presence or to feeling that God is by our side. Perhaps we anticipate too much, wondering if there will be some kind of spiritual fireworks, a bright white light or trumpets and clashing cymbals. More likely, it is an inner confidence and a knowing that God is near. A hymn by Cleland B. McAffee goes...
There is a place of quiet rest,
Near to the heart of God;
A place where sin cannot molest,
Near to the heart of God.

Refrain:
O Jesus, blest Redeemer,
Sent from the heart of God;
Hold us, who wait before Thee,
Near to the heart of God.

There is a place of comfort sweet,
Near to the heart of God;
A place where we our Savior meet,
Near to the heart of God.

There is a place of full release,
Near to the heart of God;
A place where all is joy and peace,
Near to the heart of God.

O Jesus, blest Redeemer,
Sent from the heart of God;
Hold us, who wait before Thee,
Near to the heart of God.

Where do people feel nearest to the presence of the Divine? A fly fisherman told about the river and said "That is my sanctuary, where I feel closest to God." Others have felt that way in nature, through music or poetry, in meditation or quiet reflection, in prayer or in worship services, or through devotional reading or contemplative thought. When we have that sense that we are near to the heart of God, we are likely to break out in poetic celebration, like the Psalmist saying *How lovely is your dwelling place, O Lord of hosts! My soul longs, indeed it faints for the courts of the Lord; my heart and my flesh sing for joy to the living God.*

PRAYER: O Lord, I long to be in your presence. Let me be still and know that you are God. Allow me to drink of your living water and to sense your spirit within me. Grant that I may be happy to be in your house and sense you by my side. Amen.

EIGHTY-FIVE

Steadfast love and faithfulness will meet; righteousness and peace will kiss each other.
85:10

Consider two important words in this Psalm: *righteousness* and *peace*. They kiss each other.

RIGHTEOUSNESS: We have seen from previous Psalms that the word *righteousness* is one of the most-used and least-understood words in the Bible. *Righteousness* is well-translated as *right relationships*. The theme of the entire New Testament is right relationships. Seek first to be in the right relationship with God, as a child who desires to love, trust and obey. Seek also to see every woman and man, every girl and boy as a unique wonder, never to be repeated in all of human history, and to treat each one as God's most sacred creation. As people of faith desiring to be righteous, we seek first of all to be in the right relationship with God and secondly to be in the right relationship with others, all of God's children.

PEACE: If you study the places in the gospels where Jesus used the word *peace*, you will discover there are twenty-six times in twenty-two verses. Each time, underneath the English word, is the Greek word *eirene*. The word does not mean world peace or peace-making activities. There are other Bible words for that. Jesus' teachings encourage non-violent resolution to conflict. This word for *peace* essentially refers to inner peace. It is translated *"to set at one again,"* as when everything is whole, good and reset to start anew. It feels like the confidence that everything is going to be okay. Synonyms include: harmony, tranquility, quietness, rest or to be set at one again. To feel peace is to sense that everything is okay. Is that not the medicine we crave when feeling anxious... to possess a sense of peace within?
It is like the hymn that reminds *"It is well, it is well, with my soul."* There are no self-help books or courses that lead to that kind of peace. It comes to you by gift.

Jesus said *Peace I leave with you; my peace I give to you. I do not give to you as the world gives. Do not let your hearts be troubled, and do not let them be afraid.* (John 14:27). Consider his use of the word *give* three times on one sentence. His peace within you comes by gift. That is the kind of peace where your heart is not troubled nor afraid.

Now, consider the stunningly creative poetry of this Psalm: *"Righteousness and peace will kiss each other."* Who kisses? Those who love. Righteousness and peace love each other. Look then at the verse in terms of its deeper meaning: Right relationships and a sense of inner peace in your soul are inner connected. They kiss each other. When you set as your goal to be in the right relationship with the Divine and to make your relationships right with others, you have an inner feeling of "it is well, it is well, with my soul." Conversely, when relationships are not right, you are not at peace. The message: place highest your pursuit of right relationships. A sign on an Amish barn in the Pennsylvania Dutch countryside said *"Get right with God."* It could hardly be said better. And, even though it may be hard, get right with others. Then, your efforts to make relationships right and your resulting sense of inner peace will kiss each other.

PRAYER: O God, let me get right with you. May I truly pray for your will to be done in my life. May I commit, like a child, to love, trust and obey you. Then, guide me to get right with others, to make even difficult relationships healed and healthy. Then I shall know peace. Thank you, O God. Amen.

EIGHTY-SIX

Give ear, O Lord, to my prayer; listen to my cry of supplication.
In the day of my trouble I call on you, for you will answer me.
86:6, 7

I saw a refrigerator magnet with this Psalm printed on it. It served
as a daily reminder that *In the day of my trouble I call on you, for
you will answer me.* Not every day is a day of trouble. Most are
not. But when we face a day of trouble, how energizing to know
that when you call on God, God will answer you.

Sometimes God's answer is yes. Sometimes no. Sometimes wait.
And sometimes God's answer is that God has something better in
store for you. Whichever the answer, God always has your best
interest at heart and desires nothing but the best for you.

Like any art or skill, we improve our praying with practice and
experience. And yet, there is always more to learn about prayer.
In the Sermon on the Mount from Matthew 6, Jesus taught his new
disciples how NOT to pray before giving them a model prayer for
how TO pray. He explained: *"And whenever you pray, do not be
like the hypocrites; for they love to stand and pray in the
synagogues and at the street corners, so that they may be seen by
others. Truly I tell you, they have received their reward. But
whenever you pray, go into your room and shut the door and pray
to your Father who is in secret; and your Father who sees in secret
will reward you. "When you are praying, do not heap up empty
phrases as the Gentiles do; for they think that they will be heard
because of their many words."* (Matthew 6:5-7)

In Jesus' Sermon on the Mount, he was speaking to people who
pray, not to people who do not. His audience consisted of people
already intent on wanting to talk with God and believing that God
hears our prayers. Perhaps his tone was that of a kindly teacher
who gently guided them in the right direction and reminded them
of a few things to avoid when praying.

FIRST, there could be a tendency to try to flatter God. One famous prayer began: "Blessed, praised, and glorified, exalted, extolled and honored, magnified and lauded be the name of the Holy One." It is right to begin every prayer with praise... Hallowed be thy name. The praise should be sincere and not hurried, as though wanting to get through the necessary preliminaries before getting to the good stuff. Many teachers put their instruction in the positive. When Jesus put it in the negative (how not to give, not to pray, not to fast), he must have wanted to call heightened attention to the dangers of approaching these spiritual disciplines the wrong way.

SECOND, there could be a tendency to use long prayers. Have you ever noticed from conversation that when a person is not quite sure what to say, he or she may talk at great length? Perhaps that is why we think it necessary to use long prayers. But many of the Bible's greatest prayers are brief. Consider the beautiful prayer of placing all into God's hands, which we saw in Psalm 31: "*My times are in thy hand.*" The best prayer can be brief and comes from the heart.

A pastor was called to the bedside of a man who was quite ill. As he entered the sickroom and sat down, he noticed another chair on the opposite side of the bed, a chair which had been drawn close. The pastor said, "Well, Donald, I see I'm not your first visitor for the day." The old man was puzzled for a moment and then recognized from the nod of the head that the pastor had noticed the empty chair. "Well, Pastor, I'll tell you about that chair. Years ago I found it difficult to pray, so one day I shared this problem with my minister. He told me not to worry about kneeling or finding the right words. Instead, he said 'Just sit down, put a chair opposite you, and imagine Jesus sitting in it, then talk with Him as you would a friend.'" The old man added, "I've been doing that ever since." A while later the daughter of the man called to inform the pastor that her father had died. She said that she had gone to take a short nap and when she woke up and checked her father, he was dead. "He died peacefully in his sleep," she said, "and he looked so comfortable... except for one thing: his hand was on the empty chair by the side of his bed."

THIRD, there could be a tendency to struggle to find the exact right words. Relax, advised the Apostle Paul in Romans 8:26: *"...the Spirit helps us in our weakness; for we do not know how to pray as we ought, but that very Spirit intercedes with sighs too deep for words."* You do not have to know the right words to say in prayer because God can hear your heart. The Spirit carries your feelings, yearnings and thoughts to the ears of God. When you pray, try times of silence where you take a break from struggling to find the right words and allow the Spirit to reach deep within and pull out your prayers to God. When praying for another person and you are unsure of what to say, it can be enough to say *"I pray for the best possible outcome..."* or *"I lift up in prayer..."* That prayer is just as powerful and received by God as one where words may be more precise or technical.

Jesus gave an example of hypocrites who were putting on an act more than they were praying. He said don't pray like that. Don't show off. Don't use flattery. Long prayers are no better than short prayers. God is not impressed by your vocabulary or by the length of your prayer. Don't be formal in your praying. Just talk to God as you would to a friend. Don't restrict where you pray. You can pray in a worship space, but can also go into your room, shut the door, and be alone with God. When you pray, make it private, personal, and to God.

Then he gave them an example which has become a beloved and perhaps the most prayed prayer of all time. We call it *The Lord's Prayer*. It might be better named *"The Believer's Prayer"* because this prayer can only be prayed by someone who believes in God. Why would a person who did not believe care to hallow God's name? Why would a person who did not care about God dare to pray for God's will to be done?

Our Father which art in heaven, Hallowed be thy name. Thy kingdom come, Thy will be done in earth, as it is in heaven. Give us this day our daily bread. And forgive us our debts, as we forgive our debtors. And lead us not into temptation, but deliver us from evil: For thine is the kingdom, and the power, and the glory, forever. Amen. (from the King James Version).

In a group of clergy, I once asked each to go around in turn to address the question: *"How do you center yourself spiritually?"* I was genuinely curious. Here were woman and men called by God to be spiritual leaders. They were well-educated, highly experienced, and knew the Bible as experts. They had read dozens or hundreds of devotional readings. So how did they center themselves spiritually? I was surprised to find that almost all centered themselves by using the Lord's Prayer, sometimes many times a day. It was neither rote nor routine but the simple beauty of the prayer served to lift these women and men of God into an encounter with the Divine.

The model prayer is in counter-point to Jesus' teaching about how not to pray. He could have provided them with tips, pointers or guidelines. Instead he gave them an example. The flow of the prayer can be used as a jumping off point for adding your own thoughts and words, or it can stand alone as a powerful mantra to lead into God's presence.

A story is told of how when Robert Louis Stevenson lived in the South Sea Islands, he would conduct family worship in the mornings for his household. It always concluded with the Lord's Prayer. One morning in the middle of the Lord's Prayer he rose from his knees and left the room. His health was precarious, so his wife followed him thinking that he was ill. *"Is there anything wrong?"* she said. *"Only this,"* said Stevenson, *"I am not fit to pray the Lord's Prayer today."*

Such is the response of a person of faith who conscientiously thinks about the meaning of each part of Jesus' model prayer for believers. Stevenson's answer also serves to remind with humility how we sometimes feel too unworthy even to pray the prayer.

And yet, by the grace of God, we are forgiven, renewed and restored so that we can approach God, hallow God's name, and offer ourselves to yield to God's will.

Perhaps it is on our roughest days that we want to pray with the Psalmist *Give ear, O Lord, to my prayer; listen to my cry of supplication. In the day of my trouble I call on you, for you will answer me.* Trust that God will hear you, for you are God's beloved child.

PRAYER: Dear God. Hallowed be your name. I worship you, I love you, and I desire to try my best to yield to your will. God, there are some things I cannot speak to any other person, but I bring them to you and place them into your hand. Hear my prayer, O God. Listen who what I want to say from the depths of my soul... Amen.

EIGHTY-SEVEN

Singers and dancers alike say, "All my springs are in you."
87:7

As a counterpoint to psalms about foes and days of trouble, this psalm arises like a fresh spring breeze. To the Psalmist, God's springs of living water inspire singing and dancing. His view of a relationship with God evokes a sense of joy.

The Psalm reminds of the classic Shaker tune written by Elder Joseph Brackett in 1848. Brackett was a lifelong resident of Maine. It was his father's farm that helped to form the nucleus of the Shaker settlement. The tune, to which Shakers danced with joy, is known as *Simple Gifts*:

'Tis the gift to be simple, 'tis the gift to be free
'Tis the gift to come down where we ought to be,
And when we find ourselves in the place just right,
'Twill be in the valley of love and delight.

When true simplicity is gained,
To bow and to bend we shan't be ashamed,
To turn, turn will be our delight,
Till by turning, turning we come 'round right.

A more recent tune, written by English songwriter Sydney Carter in 1963, is *Lord of the Dance* which tells the gospel story in the first person voice of Jesus of Nazareth, portraying his life and mission as a dance:

I danced in the morning when the world was begun,
And I danced in the moon and the stars and the sun,
And I came down from heaven and I danced on the earth:
At Bethlehem I had my birth.

Dance, then, wherever you may be,
I am the Lord of the dance, said he,
And I'll lead you all, wherever you may be,
And I'll lead you all in the dance, said he.

It is music that reminds us to sing, dance, and to celebrate our faith with joyful celebration. One of the great hymns of joy, by Henry J. van Dyke and set to Beethoven's Ode to Joy, is *Joyful, Joyful, We Adore Thee*:

Joyful, joyful, we adore Thee,
God of glory, Lord of love;
Hearts unfold like flow'rs before Thee,
Op'ning to the sun above.
Melt the clouds of sin and sadness;
Drive the dark of doubt away;
Giver of immortal gladness,
Fill us with the light of day!

PRAYER: God of glory and God of love, may my faith inspire me to sing and dance and celebrate with joy the life with which you have blessed me. It is so easy for religion to degenerate into stern seriousness. Remind me every day to enjoy the gift to be simple and the gift to be free as I sing praises to you. With joy I adore you. Amen.

EIGHTY-EIGHT

But I, O Lord, cry out to you; in the morning my prayer comes before you.
88:13

In the morning my prayer comes before you. There is a message for us in this Psalm, for what we do first in the morning has the potential to shape our day. The Psalmist started his day with prayer. Other than biological needs, how do you start your day? Do you rush to the internet to check Facebook, news, sports, weather, and emails? That is not a great way to start your day. That is just busy stuff. That is a common beginning, but not very enlightening. Why not begin instead by practicing a few, very brief mantras to shape how you will see things in your new day?

The word *mantra* is a sound, syllable, word or group of words that is considered capable of creating transformation. In the case of people of faith, the goal would be a spiritual transformation. You could just as easily call them spiritual practices, disciplines or even reminders. They are Bible verses that remind us of something, especially when uttered at the right time or spoken repeatedly until they sink in and become a part of our spirit.

Transformation… to transform… means to change. What changes? Well, repeating these mantras daily changes how you see things. That makes all the difference in the world. How you see things affects your attitude, your mood, your spirit, your inner nature, your perspective on life, and your devotion to God. It is truly amazing that changes of this magnitude can result simply from repeating some of these verses every day. Use these mantras to shape your day. Indeed, as you come to own them, they begin to shape your whole life.

Why bother? Who wants to change? Answer: The person of faith who desires to know God better and to love God more. Out of your devotion, you are motivated to want to please God, to communicate with God, and to glorify God.

These mantras have the potential to lift you out of a daily routine or even a rut into a higher spiritual plain that reframes how you see things... including how you see yourself and your purpose.

A woman told how every morning when her toes touch the floor, she repeats a couple of these mantras as her morning prayer. Use that for your inspiration: Toes touching the floor. Train yourself to associate toes touching the floor with reciting a couple of these suggested mantras. Toes, floor. Toes, mantra. Let it sink in as a routine. It becomes your prayer, your pledge, and your goal for the day. You can use any favorite verse, but following are a few suggestions to memorize and repeat when your toes touch the floor. Do not try to say them all. Just pick one or two.

This is the day that the Lord has made. Let us rejoice and be glad in it.
Psalm 118:
It might be helpful to change the pronoun, which makes it your will or your determination to do this in the current day: "I will rejoice and be glad in it."

My cup runneth over.
Psalm 23:5, King James Version
Begin your day by focusing on your gratitude to God for all that you have. When you are longing to want just a little bit more, remind yourself that your cup already overflows.

But the fruit of the Spirit is love, joy, peace, patience, kindness, generosity, faithfulness, gentleness, self-control...
Galatians 5:22, 23
An important list of nine qualities that radiate in a person when God's spirit dwells within. Worth memorizing and setting them as your goals and as a reminder to invite God's spirit into your soul and to treat it as an honored guest.

And the king will answer them, 'Truly I tell you, just as you did it to one of the least of these who are members of my family, you did it to me.'
Matthew 25:40

This is what counts in God's book – how you treat another, especially those most in need. When you do something good for another, you do it for God. What you do for the child, you do for the Parent.

I lift up my eyes to the hills – from where will my help come? My help comes from the Lord, who made heaven and earth.
Psalm 121:1,2,

A beautiful psalm to remind you to look up, look at nature, stop to appreciate beauty and to know that your help comes from God.

My soul is bereft of peace, I have forgotten what happiness is... but this I call to mind, and therefore I have hope: The steadfast love of the Lord never ceases, his mercies never come to an end; they are new every morning; great is thy faithfulness.
Lamentations 3:17, 22, 23

What would it be like to awaken every morning and think *I wonder what new mercies God is going to give me today?* People are always asking *What's new?* Here's what's new: God's mercies to you. God's blessings, gifts, and surprises are new every morning and encourage you to see that, for you, the best is yet to come.

Strive first for the kingdom of God and his righteousness...
(Matthew 6:33a, NRSV)

This, from the Sermon on the Mount, is what Jesus placed first. He even used the word *first*. In the Lord's Prayer, he taught *"Thy kingdom come, thy will be done."* This is a parallelism. Both phrases mean approximately the same thing. To be in God's kingdom is to seek to do God's will. And so, strive first to do God's will and to be in the right relationship with God.

PRAYER: Dear God, *in the morning my prayer comes before you.* Help me to begin each day with a prayer or a verse that transforms how I see things and shapes my day, to launch into the day as your faithful child. Amen.

EIGHTY-NINE

You rule the raging of the sea; when its waves rise, you still them.
89:9

David was an ancestor of Jesus of Nazareth, which is why Joseph and Mary returned to Bethlehem, the City of David, for the census. That, of course, is where Jesus was born. In the Psalm, David praises God's power and might, even over nature: *You rule the raging of the sea; when its waves rise, you still them.* Centuries later, Jesus stilled the waves and the storm:

One day he got into a boat with his disciples, and he said to them, "Let us go across to the other side of the lake." So they put out, and while they were sailing he fell asleep. A windstorm swept down on the lake, and the boat was filling with water, and they were in danger. They went to him and woke him up, shouting, "Master, Master, we are perishing!" And he woke up and rebuked the wind and the raging waves; they ceased, and there was a calm. He said to them, "Where is your faith?" They were afraid and amazed, and said to one another, "Who then is this, that he commands even the winds and the water, and they obey him?"
Luke 8:22-25

The story of Jesus calming the waters reminds of a gospel pop song by Gene MacLellan (February 2, 1938 – January 19, 1995), a Canadian singer-songwriter from Prince Edward Island:

Put your hand in the hand of the man
Who stilled the water
Put your hand in the hand of the man
Who calmed the sea
Take a look at yourself
And you can look at others differently
Put your hand in the hand of the man
From Galilee

In the gospels, Jesus stilled the water. In the Psalms, it is God: *You rule the raging of the sea; when its waves rise, you still them.* Now, that may be true in a literal sense, but there is also a message to us as we consider the deeper meaning of these texts and that is, when you face the storms of life, it is God who stills the waves coming at you and it is God who is in charge of all in your life.

Sometimes God calms the storm. Other times God lets the storm rage and calms you, but in your storms, he reaches out his hand and encourages you to trust and to put your hand in the hand of the One who stills the water.

PRAYER: Almighty God, you are the ruler of the raging seas and you are the ruler of my life. When I face storms, let me trust you to either calm the storm or to calm me so that I can face the waves knowing that you are with me and on my side. Amen.

NINETY

So teach us to count our days that we may gain a wise heart.
90:12

Companion verse: *Satisfy us in the morning with your steadfast love, so that we may rejoice and be glad all our days.* (90:14)

Make every day count. Live, not in the past nor in the future, but in the present. The Psalmist, perhaps better than any other biblical writer, encourages you to live in the moment. That does not preclude thinking about the past or planning for the future, but as he said he Psalm 118 (24) *"This is the day that the Lord has made; let us rejoice and be glad in it."* This day. Now, in Psalm 90, he again speaks of rejoicing and being glad all of our days. Live that way and you will gain a wise heart.

Sometimes our rejoicing and being glad is tempered by regrets we have over something in the past. A palliative nurse in Australia named Bronnie Ware recorded the top five regrets of the dying. Her job was to care for patients in the last twelve weeks of their lives. That led her to observe the phenomenal clarity of vision that people gain at the end of their lives, and how we might learn from their wisdom. "When questioned about any regrets they had or anything they would do differently," she says, "common themes surfaced again and again."

This led Ware to record their dying epiphanies in a blog. That blog caused such a stir of attention that she put her observations into a book called *The Top Five Regrets of the Dying*. Here are the top five:

FIRST: "I wish I'd had the courage to live a life true to myself, not the life others expected of me."
This was the most common regret of all. Ware wrote "When people realize that their life is almost over and look back clearly on it, it is easy to see how many dreams went unfulfilled. Most people had not honored even a half of their dreams and had to die knowing that it was due to choices they had made, or not made.

It is very important to try to honor at least some of your dreams along the way. From the moment that you lose your health, it is too late. Health brings a freedom very few realize, until they no longer have it."

SECOND: "I wish I had not worked so hard."
"This came from every male patient that I nursed," wrote Bronnie Ware. "They missed their children's youth and their partner's companionship. Women also spoke of this regret, but as most were from an older generation, many of the female patients had not been breadwinners. All of the men I nursed deeply regretted spending so much of their lives on the treadmill of a work existence." Isn't that true today for men and for woman? Nobody wants written on their tombstone the words "I should have spent more time at the office." Ware commented: "By simplifying your lifestyle and making conscious choices along the way, it is possible to not need the income that you think you do. By creating more space in your life, you become happier and more open to new opportunities, ones more suited to your new lifestyle."

THIRD: "I wish I'd had the courage to express my feelings."
The nurse observed: "Many people suppressed their feelings in order to keep peace with others. As a result, they settled for a mediocre existence and never became who they were truly capable of becoming. Many developed illnesses relating to the bitterness and resentment they carried as a result. We cannot control the reactions of others, she says. However, although people may initially react when you change the way you are by speaking honestly, in the end it raises the relationship to a whole new and healthier level. Either that or it releases the unhealthy relationship from your life. Either way, you win."

FOURTH: "I wish I had stayed in touch with my friends."
"Often they would not truly realize the full benefits of old friends until their dying weeks and it was not always possible to track them down. Many had become so caught up in their own lives that they had let golden friendships slip by over the years. There were deep regrets about not giving friendships the time and effort that they deserved.

Everyone misses their friends when they are dying. It is all comes down to love and relationships in the end. That is all that remains in the final weeks, love and relationships."

FIFTH: "I wish that I had let myself be happier."
"This is a surprisingly common one. Many did not realize until the end that happiness is a choice. They had stayed stuck in old patterns and habits. The so-called 'comfort' of familiarity overflowed into their emotions, as well as their physical lives. Fear of change had them pretending to others, and to their selves, that they were content. When deep within, they longed to laugh properly and have silliness in their life again."

We all hold regrets that haunt us. There is nothing you can do about the past. You cannot change decisions you made, actions you took or words you said in the past. All you can do is to give yourself grace, forgive yourself and, as the Psalmist advised, count your days that you may gain a wise heart.

PRAYER: Giving God, whom I praise and adore, guide me to live in the present, to determine that I will rejoice and be glad in this day which you made for me, and to make my day count. Cleanse me of regrets from my past, heal me and lead me to gain a wise heart so that I may live fully into the abundant life that you desire for me. Amen.

NINETY-ONE

For he will command his angels concerning you to guard you in all your ways. On their hands they will bear you up, so that you will not dash your foot against a stone.
91:11, 12

The Psalmist frequently employs metaphor and symbolic language, so the interesting question here is whether his talk of angels is literal or metaphorical. In other words, do angels really exist?

Every time the word *"angel"* appears in the New Testament, the word written in Greek is *"aggelos."* The translation of *aggelos* is *messenger.* It does not say it is a supernatural messenger. Any messenger is an aggelos. The guy next door brining you some news is an aggelos. A messenger from God is an aggelos. In verb form, the word means to announce, to report, to bear a message, to bring tidings or news, to proclaim. In the New Testament, the word *"angel"* means, simply, *"messenger."* Angels deliver a message.

Where in the Bible should you turn to find out about angels and what they do? Answer: nowhere. There is no single place. It is all disconnected. The word appears about 300 times in the Bible. Biblical scholars will tell you that there is no clearly defined *angelology* anywhere in the Bible.

Let us consider two sides to the questions "Do angels really exist?" The PRO and the CON. Note carefully that there is no value judgement to either argument. Both are held by faithful Christians. One is not better, more faithful or more biblical than the other.

The CON view is not questioning about God, Jesus Christ, or the Holy Spirit – just about angels. Think of this view as a faithful, thinking, devoted Christian who has trouble with the idea of angels... especially the kind hovering around up there in white robes, sparkle, and wings who light up when they start to get emotional. The PRO view accepts the existence of angels.

This does not imply that people who hold the PRO view are better than those who do not. Let us give both positions a fair hearing, because both views are held by intelligent, faithful followers of Jesus the Christ.

THE CON POINT OF VIEW: You don't have a guardian angel. You have a guardian God.

Angels, says this view, are a figment of the imagination. Wishful thinking. They are in the same category as UFO's, ghosts, headless horsemen, and the Loch Ness monster. They represent a fantasy... a good fantasy, but a flight of the imagination. When good luck happens or if there is some coincidence, people attribute that to angels. When random chance occurs, they think an angel did it. Wishful thinking. People wish they had some guardian angel up there to look after them, but that's a fanciful longing.

The Holman Bible Dictionary says *"Some passages imply that a heavenly counterpart represents each person in heaven. This evidence is commonly used to assert that each individual has a 'guardian' angel assigned to him or her by God. The term 'guardian angel', however, is not biblical, and the idea is at best only implied."*

You do not have a guardian angel, says this view. Rather, you have a guardian God. It is God who guards and protects, not angels. That is what the Bible says. I Peter (2:25) says *"For you were straying like sheep, but have now returned to the Shepherd and Guardian of your souls."* The Lord your Shepherd is your guardian. If God knows your name, considers you precious, loves you and cares about you... why would God need angels? Do people who believe in guardian angels believe that God is too busy to tend to you, so has angels do the day-to-day interpersonal work?

This view holds that people who believe in angels are getting their theology confused with popular culture. It is like the classic love song "*True Love*" that goes... "*for you and I have a guardian angel on high with nothing to do, but to give to you and to give to me, love forever true.*" That is a song, not the Bible. The notion of a guardian angel is not biblical and not necessary.

The CON view asks "Have you ever seen one?" Do you know anyone who has ever seen an angel? What do they look like? Do they have wings stapled to their backs? Are their wings made of feathers, like a bird? Or fabric? Cotton or polyester?

Billy Graham wrote a book titled <u>*Angels*</u>. Billy Graham said he never saw an angel, but he wrote a book about them anyway. He begins the book with some far-fetched illustrations of people who thought they saw angels. The CON view believes in God, but just cannot swallow those stories. It is not that this view places sophistication over faith, or science above belief. It is just too remote from reality for a thinking person to accept.

There are no angels captured on video tape, none measured by any technological devices, none photographed. When people in hospitals undergo tests – and that's when you would think angels are needed most – the angels do not show up on X-ray, sonar, or any kind of magnetic imaging. You never saw one, I never saw one, and Billy Graham never saw one. The world possesses no empirical evidence of the existence of angels.

It is quite possible to believe in the power of God, the divinity of Jesus Christ and the mysterious work of the Holy Spirit without needing to attribute God's work and care to angels.

THE PRO POINT OF VIEW: The entire Bible acknowledges the existence of angels.

The PRO view holds that the soul of the people – which is represented in their art, literature, music, stained glass windows, greeting cards, home decorations – the soul of the people appears to believe in angels. We are not talking here about just a small handful of people. Belief in angels cuts across cultures, races, continents, generations, and miles. There is a great weight of testimony that there is something there... something which it recognizes as angels.

Our hymns are filled with references to angels:
Angels, from the realms of glory
Angels we have heard on high
Hark! The Herald Angels Sing
The First Nowell, the angel did say
It came upon the midnight clear... The world in solemn stillness lay
to hear the angels sing.

Look at the overwhelming references to angels in the Bible – almost 300 verses about angels, from Genesis to Revelation. In the Old Testament, angels appeared to Hagar, to Abraham, and to Moses at the burning bush. Job wrote about how angels witnessed creation. The New Testament never questions the existence of angels, but simply states the fact. Angels exist. Jesus often spoke of them. He told us that: They rejoice over the penitent, they bear up souls to paradise, angels announced the birth of Jesus and angels rolled away the stone from the tomb and announced his resurrection.

If the Bible were one single book written by one person in a short span of time, you might be able to write-off angels as that author's imagination. But the Bible is a library of sixty-six books, written over a span of centuries. The whole collection records the activity of angels.

The PRO view begins with the weight of an overwhelming number of references to angels in the Bible, in hymns and music, in literature, and in art. You cannot fool that many people, nor could you dismiss so many people in so many lands as simply engaged in wishful thinking or religious hallucinations.

The PRO view acknowledges that it has never seen an angel, at least as they are depicted by classical art. But there are a lot of things never seen that cannot be explained. The PRO view might say: I've never seen electricity, but my lights go on when I turn the switch. I've never seen air waves, but I hear voices and see pictures from halfway around the world on my radio and TV. I cannot see or explain microwaves, but that box cooks my dinner in just seconds. I've never seen the face of God, but I believe in God. One of the main reasons for that belief is because I believe in Jesus Christ and in how Jesus described God.

Much of science, technology, and mathematics is based upon accepting theories, assumptions, hypotheses, postulates, axioms, principles, precepts and premises that cannot be proved. They must be taken on faith. A considerable amount of the physical world is based upon faith in what we think we know.

Beyond the physical world is the realm of the spirit. In the spiritual world, it is not a matter of proof. The PRO view chooses to have faith in Jesus Christ. It trusts his words, and his words indicate that he accepted the presence of angels. Jesus had plenty of opportunity to deny their reality if he wanted to, but nowhere did he say to his twelve disciples, *"Men, get real. Angels do not really exist."*

The PRO view considers: Have I ever seen an angel? I believe that at times in my life, people... *messengers*... have been sent to *"look after me,"* to guide me, to help direct my steps, and – as they keep me from going the wrong way – to protect me. I have experienced how, sometimes, people appear to be *"sent"* to speak to me a good word. If they are "sent" by God, then they are, by definition, *"messengers,"* so I believe in angels. Did they have wings? No, I didn't see any. Did they have halos?

Well, when they came to me by surprise, when they lifted me up, carried me when I was weak, and helped me when I was in trouble... yes... maybe they did have halos. And after they came to me, I feel like I could say with Psalm 91: *"For he will give his angels charge of you to guard you in all your ways."*

Vermont writer Frederick Buechner (in his book <u>Wishful Thinking</u>) says: *Sleight-of-hand magic is based on the demonstrable fact that as a rule people see only what they expect to see. Angels are powerful spirits whom God sends into the world to wish us well. Since we do not expect to see them, we do not. An angel spreads his glittering wings over us, and we say things like "It was one of those days that made you feel good just to be alive" or "I had a hunch everything was going to turn out all right" or "I do not know where I ever found the courage."*

WHICH VIEW IS CORRECT?

Belief in angels is not critical to your faith. Angels are not mentioned in Statements of Faith nor in any of the church's historic creeds like the Apostles' Creed or the Nicene Creed. Believing in angels is not a litmus test of whether or not you are a good Christian.

There are good arguments for both points of view. Perhaps the question is more about whether the Psalmist and the Bible spoke of angels as metaphor or as literal beings. Either way, be careful because you could miss the whole point. The whole point is not the MESSENGER, but the MESSAGE. That is what we should be paying attention to: The message. The message and the messengers point to God. Instead of focusing too much on the messenger, listen instead for the message. It is about God... and you It has to do with what is best for you, what guides you, and what protects you. Most frequently, the message of the angels in the Bible is *"Do not be afraid."* *Do not be afraid* is the most common message of angels in the Bible.

The Psalmist wrote: *For he will command his angels concerning you to guard you in all your ways. On their hands they will bear you up, so that you will not dash your foot against a stone.* Whichever way God does it, it is God and the beings God uses – angelic or human – which guide you, guard you and bear you up.

PRAYER: Creator of the Universe, thank you for watching over me, guarding me and bearing me up. May I be ever alert to the messages you give me, through divine or human messengers. Tune my ears to hear their message not to be afraid, and to trust you. Amen.

NINETY-TWO

It is good to give thanks to the Lord, to sing praises to your name,
O Most High; to declare your steadfast love in the morning, and
your faithfulness by night, to the music of the lute and the harp,
to the melody of the lyre.
92:1-3

The Psalmist never tired from praising God, which is a lesson for
us too. Let us never grow weary of praise or feel like we have
already done this enough. Psalm 92 mentions declaring God's
steadfast love to the music of the lute, the harp and the lyre. It is
often music that guides our praise and adoration best of all, as does
the hymn *Holy, Holy, Holy!* by Reginald Heber and tune by John
B. Dykes:

Holy, holy, holy! Lord God Almighty!
Early in the morning our song shall rise to Thee;
Holy, holy, holy, merciful and mighty!
God in three Persons, blessed Trinity!

Holy, holy, holy! All the saints adore Thee,
Casting down their golden crowns around the glassy sea;
Cherubim and seraphim falling down before Thee,
Who was, and is, and evermore shall be.

Holy, holy, holy! Though the darkness hide Thee,
Though the eye of sinful man Thy glory may not see;
Only Thou art holy; there is none beside Thee,
Perfect in pow'r, in love, and purity.

Holy, holy, holy! Lord God Almighty!
All Thy works shall praise Thy Name, in earth, and sky, and sea;
Holy, holy, holy; merciful and mighty!
God in three Persons, blessed Trinity!

PRAYER: Holy God, like the Psalmist, I can never praise you too
much. May my song rise to you early in the morning, affirming
my desire to know you better and love you more. Amen.

NINETY-THREE

The Lord is king, he is robed in majesty; the Lord is robed, he is girded with strength. He has established the world; it shall never be moved; your throne is established from of old; you are from everlasting.
93:1, 2

David finds the highest analogy he can think of – king – to attribute as a description of God. The Lord is king. He is robed in majesty. *Majestic is his name,* he wrote in Psalm 8, which is chosen as the title of this book. Then he tells of God's work: He established the world. God is the Creator of the heavens and the earth. The first verse of the Bible tells how it was God who called the worlds into being: *"In the beginning God created the heaven and the earth."* (KJV). Each time God created a part of the heavens and the earth, he pronounced it good. Everything God created, God created good. *"God saw everything that he had made, and indeed, it was very good."* (Genesis 1:31). All men and woman are created good. No one is created evil, although some might come to do evil deeds. We all fall short.

This is God's world. God created it, God sustains it, and God loves it. Everything God created, God created good. Note that Hebrew verbs have no tense: you have to tell from the context what the tense is, so it is appropriate to say that God created, God IS creating, and God WILL continue to create. God's creation is a continual work in progress.

The Psalmist's phrase "He has established the world" reminds of the hymn *This is My Father's World:*
This is my Father's world,
And to my list'ning ears
All nature sings, and round me rings
The music of the spheres.
This is my Father's world:
I rest me in the thought
Of rocks and trees, of skies and seas—
His hand the wonders wrought.

263

This is my Father's world:
The birds their carols raise,
The morning light, the lily white,
Declare their Maker's praise.
This is my Father's world:
He shines in all that's fair;
In the rustling grass I hear Him pass,
He speaks to me everywhere.

This is my Father's world:
Oh, let me ne'er forget
That though the wrong seems oft so strong,
God is the ruler yet.
This is my Father's world,
The battle is not done:
Jesus who died shall be satisfied,
And earth and Heav'n be one.

The hymn affirms that God is like a loving parent. Jesus referred to God as "*Abba*." There are other words for the formal word "*father*." *Abba* is much more personal and affectionate – more like the word *dad* than father. In the carpenter shop, Jesus would have called Joseph *Abba*. All Jewish girls and boys would have called their dad by that title. The night before his crucifixion, Jesus went to the garden to pray, calling God *Abba*. The next day on the cross, Jesus cried out *Abba*! Other religions did not call God *Abba* or see God as a loving parent. In one of his greatest teachings about the nature and character of God – the Parable of the Prodigal Son – it is the parent who represents God. Abba knows, cares for, and loves unconditionally each of God's children. When they fall short, the Loving Parent welcomes them home with a hug.

The hymn affirms that everything that God created is connected – all nature and all humans. *All nature sings and round me rings the music of the spheres*. This is God's world and everything is connected.

Native American Chief Seattle said...
This we know.
All things are connected
like the blood which unites one family.
All things are connected.
Whatever befalls the earth
befalls the sons and daughters of the earth.
We did not weave the web of life;
We are merely a strand in it.
Whatever we do to the web,
we do to ourselves.

Everything is connected and all nature points to God. He has established the world, wrote the Psalmist. *"In the rustling grass I hear him pass, He speaks to me everywhere."*

The hymn, like Psalm 93, affirms that God is in charge. "God is the ruler yet." He is robed in majesty, wrote the Psalmist. God is in charge. This is God's world and God continues to be in control. Those who desire to walk faithfully as God's children not only grasp that God is in control, but personalize it as to say "God is in control of me too."

PRAYER: Creator God, you are the ruler of the universe. This is your world. I want to yield to you and allow you to be in control of me too. Help me to practice good stewardship of this world which you have created, for all things are connected and what we do to the web, we do to ourselves and to those who follow us. Amen.

NINETY-FOUR

When the cares of my heart are many, your consolations cheer my soul.
94:19

We worry. A behavioral scientist studied what people worried about and found that 40% of what an average person worries about will never happen. 30% of what they worry about concerns things in the past that cannot be changed. 12% of the worry was about criticism by others, mostly untrue, and 10% was about health, which gets worse with worry. Only 8% of the worries were about real problems that need to be faced. Do the math: 92% of worry is wasted.

Mark Twain wrote *I am an old man and have known a great many troubles, but most of them never happened.* Most troubles never happen and most worry is wasted. Worry dissipates energy, muddies focus and zaps vitality.

There are times when we face troubles, a failure, or a conflict with another and that is when we most need consolation which comes only from God's touch. Consider these words about the consolation which cheers the soul:

My child, I am the Lord Who gives strength in the day of trouble. Come to Me when all is not well with you. Your tardiness in turning to prayer is the greatest obstacle to heavenly consolation, for before you pray earnestly to Me you first seek many comforts and take pleasure in outward things. Thus, all things are of little profit to you until you realize that I am the one Who saves those who trust in Me, and that outside of Me there is no worth-while help, or any useful counsel or lasting remedy.
Thomas à Kempis, The Imitation of Christ

Cast all your anxiety on him because he cares for you.
1 Peter 5:7

In the midst of the awesomeness, a touch comes, and you know it is the right hand of Jesus Christ. You know it is not the hand of restraint, correction, nor chastisement, but the right hand of the Everlasting Father. Whenever His hand is laid upon you, it gives inexpressible peace and comfort, and the sense that "underneath are the everlasting arms," (Deuteronomy 33:27) full of support, provision, comfort and strength.
Oswald Chambers

When the cares of your heart are many, sing to God to seek God's consolation:

Precious Lord, take my hand
Lead me on, let me stand
I am tired, I am weak, I am worn
Through the storm, through the night
Lead me on to the light
Take my hand, precious Lord
Lead me home

When my way grows drear
Precious Lord, linger near
When my life is almost gone
Hear me cry, hear my call
Hold my hand lest I fall
Take my hand, precious Lord,
Lead me home.

When the shadows appear
And the night draws near
And the day is past and gone
At the river I stand
Guide my feet, hold my hand
Take my hand, precious Lord,
Lead me home.

Precious Lord, by Thomas A. Dorsey

PRAYER: Precious Lord, when the cares of my heart are many or when I cannot stop worrying, take my hand. Lead me on and give me strength to stand. May I find consolation in you which I can find nowhere else. Not only does your touch comfort me, but your consolations cheer my soul. Thank you, Dear God. Amen.

NINETY-FIVE

O come, let us worship and bow down, let us kneel before the Lord, our Maker! For he is our God, and we are the people of his pasture, and the sheep of his hand.
95:6, 7

This Psalm is a common Call to Worship, gathering God's people of faith to prepare themselves to bow down and kneel before the Lord.

If you changed the pronoun to the first-person-singular, you could adapt this as a great opening to your prayer: *O God, let me worship and bow down. Let me kneel before You, my Maker! For You are my God, and I am a person of Your pasture, and a sheep of Your hand.*

As noted in Psalm 64, Napoleon Bonaparte said *If Socrates would enter the room, we should rise and do him honor. But if Jesus Christ came into the room, we should fall down on our knees and worship Him.* Standing ovations are given to fine theatrical or musical performers, all rise when the President enters the room or a judge enters the courtroom, and we stand up for those whom we respect or honor. But for whom would we bow down? Who is worthy of our worship? The Psalmist answers the question. Only for the Lord our Maker do we bow.

Then he proclaims his credo, declaring *"For he is our God."* This is similar to his 23rd Psalm – *"The Lord is my shepherd."* There is a world of difference between saying the Lord is <u>A</u> shepherd and the Lord is <u>MY</u> shepherd. Anyone can acknowledge that the Lord is A shepherd, but to say that *he is our God, and we are the people of his pasture,* that statement declares that he is the one I follow and to whom I bow down.

We are… the sheep of his hand. A worship service begins with a Call to Worship and concludes with a Benediction. Psalm 95 does both in this gem, starting with a call to *Let us worship and bow down*. It then ends with a benediction about being *the sheep of his hand*, almost like the beautiful Irish benediction which blesses:
May the road rise up to meet you.
May the wind always be at your back.
May the sun shine warm upon your face,
and rains fall soft upon your fields.
And until we meet again,
May God hold you in the palm of His hand
May God hold you in the palm of His hand

PRAYER: You are my God, O Lord. You I worship and for you I bow down in humility. Be Thou my Shepherd, lead me, guide me, care for me and own me. Amen.

NINETY-SIX

***O sing to the Lord a new song; sing to the Lord, all the earth.
Sing to the Lord, bless his name; tell of his salvation from day to
day. Declare his glory among the nations, his marvelous works
among all the peoples.***
96:1-3

Sing to the Lord, the Psalmist repeats lyrically in Psalm 96. His
inspiration reminds us that our praise to the Lord does not need to
be spoken words. Sometimes our prayer is better as a hymn. Sing
or hum your praise to God, which is much like praying a psalm. A
nice example is <u>*For the Beauty of the Earth*</u> by Folliott S. Pierpoint
which declares God's glory and blesses God's name in song...
Lord of all, to thee we raise, this our hymn of grateful praise.

*For the beauty of the earth,
for the beauty of the skies,
for the love which from our birth
over and around us lies,
Lord of all, to thee we raise
this our hymn of grateful praise.*

*For the beauty of each hour
of the day and of the night,
hill and vale, and tree and flower,
sun and moon and stars of light,
Lord of all, to thee we raise
this our hymn of grateful praise.*

*For the joy of ear and eye,
for the heart and mind's delight,
for the mystic harmony
linking sense to sound and sight,
Lord of all, to thee we raise
this our hymn of grateful praise.*

For the joy of human love,
brother, sister, parent, child,
friends on earth and friends above,
for all gentle thoughts and mild,
Lord of all, to thee we raise
this our hymn of grateful praise.

For each perfect gift of thine,
Unto us so freely given,
graces human and divine,
flowers of earth and buds of heaven,
Lord of all, to thee we raise
this our hymn of grateful praise.

PRAYER: Dear God, may I sing songs of praise to you. Whether I say the lyrics or hum the tune, hear the depths of my soul blessing your name and singing of my adoration. Instill in me a desire to want to do all to your glory. Amen.

NINETY-SEVEN

The Lord loves those who hate evil.
97:10a

In childrearing, there is the school of thought which encourages parents to love the child but to dislike the behavior. This position holds that a parent should never tell a child that she or he is bad. Rather, the child is told that she or he has done a bad thing. The child is then guided to learn what is the right behavior. The child should never be told by the parent "I don't like you." Rather, the child should be told "I don't like what you did." See the child as good, the behavior as not good. The Divine Parent – God – does this. God sees the child as good and loves the child, but hates the evil done by the child. To be God-like is to love the person, hate the behavior.

The Greek word for *love* in the New Testament is *agape*. One of the best meanings of *agape* means to desire that which is truly in the other's highest and best interests. Agape is not necessarily feelings of affection or attraction, but rather, seeing the other person's best interest. As Paul wrote in 1 Corinthians 13, love does not rejoice at wrong, but rejoices in the right. Agape rejoices in the right. There are people we do not like, especially people who consistently do evil behavior, but we can still tower above our dislike to love them in the sense of desiring their highest and best interest. Love the person, hate the behavior.

This seems to be the sense of Psalm 97: *The Lord loves those who hate evil.*

Who is being written about here? Perhaps we take it to mean that we are on the same bandwagon with God. We too, of course, hate evil and evil behavior. But what if we are on the receiving end of this psalm? What if we are the ones who have committed evil behavior? We are certainly not evil people, we believe, but we have to confess to having done some evil things. Does the Psalm mean that God loves those who hate us or what we have done? "All cruelty springs from weakness," wrote Seneca.

We have experienced some weak moments in our life. "All human beings are commingled out of good and evil," wrote Robert Louis Stevenson. We are hardly all pure and good. Thank God for God's grace and forgiveness, for God still loves us anyway and forgives evil we have done. God loves us, but hates our evil behavior.

Let us join with God in hating evil behavior. Let us also join with God in loving the person and forgiving their deeds, for that is exactly how we would wish God to love and forgive us. That is the first thing Jesus said after he taught the Lord's Prayer: *"For if you forgive others their trespasses, your heavenly Father will also forgive you; but if you do not forgive others, neither will your Father forgive your trespasses."* (Matthew 6:14, 15).

This kind of forgiveness is not easy or cheap. It can come with pain or a high price. Martin Luther King, Jr. knew that. He and many of those who fought for civil rights with him had to endure beatings, nastiness, church burnings, hangings, bigotry and hatred. And yet he could tower above human nature's desire for retaliation to proclaim: *"We must develop and maintain the capacity to forgive. He who is devoid of the power to forgive is devoid of the power to love. There is some good in the worst of us and some evil in the best of us. When we discover this, we are less prone to hate our enemies."* Martin Luther King, Jr.

The Lord loves those who hate evil. Let us too strive to be God-like in hating evil deeds and behavior. Let us too practice love, grace and forgiveness as we discover that there is some good in the worst of us and some evil in the best of us.

PRAYER: Dear Lord, I hate the evil I see in persons, in institutions, in corporations and in national leaders who promulgate evil ways. Help me to not hate them as individuals, but to hate their behavior and work for helping them to become good. Help me to remove the log from my own eye, so I may be aware of my own choices or acts which are evil. I ask for your forgiveness, Dear God, and ask that you would lead me to become a person who forgives others as I would wish to be forgiven. Thank you. Amen.

NINETY-EIGHT

With trumpets and the sound of the horn make a joyful noise
before the King, the Lord. Let the sea roar, and all that fills it;
the world and those who live in it. Let the floods clap their
hands; let the hills sing together for joy
98:6-8

With trumpets and the sound of the horn make a joyful noise before
the King, the Lord. There is a hymn that begins with a fanfare of
trumpets before each stanza which makes a joyful noise before the
Lord. It is <u>God of Our Fathers, Whose Almighty Hand</u> by Daniel
C. Roberts:

God of the ages, whose almighty hand
leads forth in beauty all the starry band
of shining worlds in splendor through the skies,
our grateful songs before thy throne arise.

Thy love divine hath led us in the past;
in this free land with thee our lot is cast;
be thou our ruler, guardian, guide, and stay,
thy Word our law, thy paths our chosen way.

From war's alarms, from deadly pestilence,
be thy strong arm our ever-sure defense;
thy true religion in our hearts increase;
thy bounteous goodness nourish us in peace.

Refresh thy people on their toilsome way;
lead us from night to never-ending day;
fill all our lives with love and grace divine,
and glory, laud, and praise be ever thine.

There is so much inspiration, energy, and theology which arises from this hymn:

.. our grateful songs before thy throne arise. Sing this tune with gratitude for God's leading. We are prone to ask God to lead us. How many times have we paused to thank God for answering us and leading us in the past?

.. be thou our ruler, guardian, guide, and stay. This stanza can only be sung by the one who invites God to be my ruler, guardian, guide and stay. You rule me, sings the verse.

.. thy true religion in our hearts increase. What is God's true religion? Is it not, from both Testaments of the Bible, to love the Lord your God and to love your neighbor as yourself? That is what God wants most from us. That is what Jesus named the Great Commandments. The verse asks that our hearts increase with love for God and for God's children.

.. Refresh thy people on their toilsome way. God refreshes you for the journey. Your faith in God renews and restores.

.. fill all our lives with love and grace divine. If you were asked to describe your religion in two words, you would not miss with the words *love* and *grace*. Even people who do not believe in God can look at Christians to see love and grace radiating outward. Love and grace are two of the most God-like characteristics to which we aspire to imitate.

.. and glory, laud, and praise be ever thine. The Psalmist never tires of heaping praise, glory and laud upon the Lord and neither should we. May our prayers begin and end with praise for God.

PRAYER: Lord, I praise you this day and pray that I may bring glory to your name. Thank you, God, for all the times you have led me, guided me, and helped me. I am truly grateful. Refresh me for the day ahead and lead me into opportunities to show love or grace to another. Amen.

277

NINETY-NINE

Let them praise your great and awesome name. Holy is he!
99:3

Holy is God. Let us consider the nature of holy.

Moses stood before the burning bush. God spoke to him and said: *"Come no closer! Remove the sandals from your feet, for the place on which you are standing is holy ground."* (Exodus 3:5). This verse inspired the hymn *On Holy Ground* by Geron Davis:

When I walk through the doors I sensed God's presence
When I knew this was a place where love abounds
For this is a temple Jehovah God abides here
and we are standing in His presence on holy ground.

We are standing on holy ground
For I know that there are angels all around
Let us praise Jesus now
For we are standing in His presence on holy ground.

In His presence I know there is joy beyond all measure
And at His feet sweet peace of mind can still be found
For when we have a need He is still the answer
Reach out and claim it for we are standing on holy ground.

We are standing on holy ground
For I know that there are angels all around
Let us praise Jesus now
For we are standing in His presence on holy ground.

To stand on Holy Ground is to encounter God. Worship can be defined that way: to encounter God in some spiritual way.

Native Americans tell about Indian dances, how each step of each foot means something. The Indian first touches the earth very gently – just taps it – to signify a recognition that the earth is sacred. Then he puts his whole foot down. Each step begins with a touch. Touch. Step. Touch. Step. Touch the earth twice.

That is a beautiful recognition that the earth is sacred because all things are connected and created by the Divine Creator. Each step of the dance is a celebration that *The Earth Is the Lord's* and therefore it is holy. Touch. Step. Touch. Step. Every step is preceded by a ceremonial touch of the holy ground.

What makes something holy? For Native Americans, the most sacred of places are where Indians believe they were created or where they received a special message or insight. The greatest joy for the Indian is to dance at a sacred place. The drums throb with the steady beating, the Indians chant or sing, and dancers in ceremonial costume touch the earth twice to recognize that they are on holy ground.

What makes a place sacred? If one place is sacred, are others not? Isn't it all sacred?

A place becomes sacred because someone has made it so. A ground becomes holy because it was treated as holy by another or a group of others, or by God.

Where are your holy places? Where are places that you treat as sacred? Perhaps it is in nature, in the sanctuary, or in the still small silences of your day that you encounter the Sacred. A place or object becomes holy because you treat it as holy. When that place is experienced, it makes it so holy that you just about want to take off your shoes and touch the floor twice.

A poem by Kenneth Caraway goes: *"There is no box made by God nor us but that the sides can be flattened out and the top blown off to make a dance floor on which to celebrate life."* Perhaps you cherish some sacred dance floors in your life where you celebrate life and touch the earth twice.

Wherever you encounter the Divine, that becomes a holy place for you. When you experience that, you can say with the Psalmist *"Holy is he."*

PRAYER: Holy God, lead me into your presence where I may experience The Holy. Let me think about places in my life where I feel close to you. Guide me to invest less time staring into an electronic screen and to spend more of my precious moments looking outward, upward, and into the eyes of others. Holy are you, O God. Amen.

ONE HUNDRED

Make a joyful noise to the Lord, all the earth.
100:1

This may be the greatest Psalm of praise in all the Bible. It is an all-time favorite for many people of faith and really cannot be limited to one verse – the whole Psalm is as one living and breathing song:

Make a joyful noise to the Lord, all the earth. Worship the Lord with gladness; come into his presence with singing. Know that the Lord is God. It is he that made us, and we are his; we are his people, and the sheep of his pasture. Enter his gates with thanksgiving, and his courts with praise. Give thanks to him, bless his name. For the Lord is good; his steadfast love endures forever, and his faithfulness to all generations. (100:1-5)

Do you ever find it difficult to find the right words for your prayers? Or, do you find your prayers are all about yourself? For a change of pace, pray the Psalms. Make Psalm 100 your prayer and simply recite it as your prayer, perhaps adding onto it with other things or people for whom you wish to lift up in prayer. Beginning your prayer with the 100th Psalm elevates the beauty and thoughtfulness of your praise for God.

It is a worthy prayer of thanksgiving and stimulates us to consider the question – for what do I give thanks this day?

Make a joyful noise. Rejoice and be glad. Find something today to be joyful about. Joy is best found in relationships, and that is the kind of joy the Psalmist describes – an intimate relationship with God.

Worship the Lord with gladness. On your best days as well as your worst, ask yourself – for what am I truly glad about today? When your mind dwells on problems, regrets or worries, change your polarity by entering his gates with thanksgiving. Tally a mental list of the positive things for which you are grateful.

Can you list ten things that make you glad? Give thanks to him. Never forget to say "Thank you."

Come into his presence with singing. Music lifts up our spirits into God's presence. Store up in your mind some tunes which you can sing or hum which draw you closer to the Divine. This is one of the great benefits of belonging to a community of faith, for week after week you are exposed to hymns which you store in the recesses of your mind and can call upon them when they can be used to seek God's presence.

We are his. When he was chaplain of the United States Senate, Dr. Richard C. Halverson spoke at Princeton Theological Seminary about what it means to belong to the Kingdom of God. He said: *I have recaptured something that came to me early in my Christian experience: that Jesus Christ owns me because he created me, owns me because he purchased me with his sacrifice on the cross and has a right to possess me totally.* This is the kind of thinking that led the Apostle Paul to develop his personal credo: "*...I have been crucified with Christ, and it is no longer I who live, but it is Christ who lives in me..."* (Galatians 2:19, 20).

We are his people, and the sheep of his pasture. In the 23rd Psalm, the Psalmist describes four things the Shepard does for those who follow:
He maketh me to lie down in green pastures.
He leadeth me beside the still waters.
He restoreth my soul.
He leadeth me in the paths of righteousness for his name's sake.

Phillip Keller, who spent years in agricultural research, land management and ranch development in Canada, wrote in *A Shepherd Looks at Psalm 23* how there are four retirements for sheep to lie down. They must be:
Free from fear.
Free from friction with others of their kind,
Free from pests, and
Free from hunger.

That sounds like us! Fears keep us from settling down. Friction with others causes us to lose sleep. Pests are like the little things that cause us to worry, even when we know that most of what we worry about will never happen or will not be helped by our anxiety. Hunger, for food or for fulfillment, keeps us craving for new ways to pursue our appetites.

How then can you become free enough from those ever-present needs to go to a green place, to lie down and to get some refreshment for your body, mind or soul? Phillip Keller explained the answer: when the sheep become aware of the shepherd's presence, they feel safe enough to lie down in green pastures. He wrote *"When my eyes are on the Master they are not on those around me. This is the place of peace."*

Invite Psalm 100 to guide you into that place of peace, where you gain a sense of joy in being the Shepherd's. You are included as a cherished and loved part of his flock. You belong.

For the Lord is good. Visit a museum of archeology or anthropology to witness how cultures throughout the eons have conceived of God. For some, their view of God was a demanding god, even demanding human sacrifices. For some, their view of God was a critical judge, watching your every word, thought and deed to judge you and to determine your eternal future. Our God, the Shepherd, is good. A good God wants nothing but the best for each member of his flock. This is a God of love, grace, and forgiveness.

PRAYER: Dear God, my Shepherd. May I enter your presence everyday with thanksgiving and a joyful noise to worship you, praise you and love you. Guide me to grow in joy because of our relationship. As a sheep in your flock, let my eyes be upon you rather than upon all the little things that bug me. Lead me to lie down in green pastures and discover the place of peace. Amen.

I will sing of loyalty and of justice; to you, O Lord, I will sing.
101:1

This is an interesting song to sing unto the Lord. It might cause us to wonder: "Am I loyal to God?"

Loyalty, like love or respect, is something that is given. It cannot be required or demanded. The one who requires loyalty will find only a superficial appearance of loyalty on the surface. While people may think they can require loyalty, God knows better.

Loyalty to God, like our love for God, is a choice. Mark (8:34) wrote how Jesus *"called the crowd with his disciples, and said to them, 'If any want to become my followers, let them deny themselves and take up their cross and follow me'."* Notice Jesus' use of the conditional word *"if."* A conditional word means that a choice is involved. A conditional phrase often has an *if* and a *then*: IF this, THEN that. IF you want to become his follower, THEN you will deny yourself, take up your cross, and follow him. You cannot be required to follow him but if you want to, you will choose to sacrifice your self and voluntarily give your love and loyalty.

Notice how Jesus never made following him sound like an easy choice. Just the opposite: *let them deny themselves and take up their cross.* There will be sacrifices involved. Former U.S. president Woodrow T. Wilson said *"Loyalty means nothing unless it has at its heart the absolute principle of self-sacrifice."* That is true for loyalty to God. Morihei Ueshiba, Japanese martial artist, taught *"Loyalty and devotion lead to bravery. Bravery leads to the spirit of self-sacrifice. The spirit of self-sacrifice creates trust in the power of love."* That too is true for those who desire to sing a song of loyalty unto the Lord. There will be the spirit of self-sacrifice and trust in the power of love.

Loyalty to God is a sentiment captured well by Earl Marlatt's hymn *Are Ye Able*:

"Are ye able," said the Master,
"to be crucified with me?"
"Yea," the sturdy dreamers answered,
"to the death we follow thee."

Refrain:
Lord, we are able. Our spirits are thine.
Remold them, make us, like thee, divine.
Thy guiding radiance above us shall be
a beacon to God, to love, and loyalty.

Why would anyone offer to follow the Master even unto death – an ultimate self-sacrifice – except for the reason of love? We pledge our loyalty to God because of our love for God.

Former columnist Ann Landers equates love with loyalty: *"Love is friendship that has caught fire. It is quiet understanding, mutual confidence, sharing and forgiving. It is loyalty through good and bad times. It settles for less than perfection and makes allowances for human weaknesses."*

For many of us, our loyalty to God is rarely put to the test. When bad times come, we hope and pray that our song of loyalty unto the Lord continues.

PRAYER: Dear God, I love you and sing to you of my loyalty. Remold my spirit to be strong and brave, so when it called upon it is willing to deny itself, to sacrifice, and to bear a burden as a beacon to you, to love and loyalty. Amen.

Hear my prayer, O Lord. Let my cry come to you. Do not hide your face from me in the day of my distress. Incline your ear to me. Answer me speedily in the day when I call.
102:1, 2

The Psalmist is hurting and feels in distress. He calls upon God and begs God to hear and to answer his prayer, calling for help. This is similar to other Psalms but is also a counter-balance to the many Psalms that begin with praise, adoration and thanksgiving. In the previous Psalm he sang to the Lord of his loyalty. In the one before that he wrote of making a joyful noise to the Lord, worshipping God with gladness, and entering his gates with thanksgiving. In a way, this counter-balance captures the essence of the Psalms and perhaps of our lives too – a see-saw of love, praise and gratitude on one end and a cry for help in times of trouble on the other. Faith is a living, breathing inhale and exhale, an ebb and flow of praise and thanksgiving with difficulties and needs.

This might describe the life and faith of Henry F. Lyte, who was born in Scotland in 1793. Lyte was educated at Trinity College in Dublin, Ireland and was a member of the Church of England. Throughout his lifetime, Lyte was known to be frail in body but strong in faith and spirit. His health was continually threatened by asthma and tuberculosis. Despite his physical frailties he was a tireless worker with an established reputation as a poet, musician, and minister. It was Lyte who coined the phrase, "It is better to wear out than to rust out."

Lyte pastored a poor parish church among fishing people in Devonshire, England, where his health continued to grow worse. Near the end of his life, Lyte wrote a hymn which reflects the counter-balance of his distress and his faith in God. It first appeared in America when it was included in Henry Ward Beecher's hymnal titled "Plymouth Collection," in 1855, with the notation that *"this hymn was meant to be read and not sung."*

He titled his hymn *Abide with Me*. Hum it quietly in your mind, but read the words to make them your prayer:

Abide with me; fast falls the eventide;
The darkness deepens; Lord, with me abide;
When other helpers fail and comforts flee,
Help of the helpless, oh, abide with me.

Swift to its close ebbs out life's little day;
Earth's joys grow dim, its glories pass away;
Change and decay in all around I see—
O Thou who changest not, abide with me.

I need Thy presence every passing hour;
What but Thy grace can foil the tempter's pow'r?
Who, like Thyself, my guide and stay can be?
Through cloud and sunshine, Lord, abide with me.

I fear no foe, with Thee at hand to bless;
Ills have no weight, and tears no bitterness;
Where is death's sting? Where, grave, thy victory?
I triumph still, if Thou abide with me.

Hold Thou Thy cross before my closing eyes;
Shine through the gloom and point me to the skies;
Heav'n's morning breaks, and earth's vain shadows flee;
In life, in death, O Lord, abide with me.

PRAYER: Hear my prayer, O Lord. When I am in distress, incline your ear to me. Abide with me. I need your presence. Shine through the gloom and point me to the skies. Amen.

ONE-HUNDRED-AND-THREE

Bless the Lord, O my soul, and all that is within me, bless his holy name.
103:1

Bless the Lord? Isn't that backwards? Usually we ask God's blessing on us, our family, our friends or on anything that moves. But here is the Psalmist, not asking for God's blessing, but he is blessing God.

There is a traditional Jewish prayer goes *"Blessed art Thou, Jehovah, King of the Universe, who bringest forth bread from the earth."* It is likely that Jesus used this prayer when he blessed the food at a meal. When we say grace over a meal, we tend to ask God to bless the food, the guests, and anything else we can think of to bless. In this traditional blessing of the bread, it is God who is blessed. The prayer also acknowledges that God is King of the Universe. This is a personal faith statement, for the one who prays this prayer professes that God is his or her ruler. This short traditional prayer also acknowledges God is the Creator, who bringest forth bread from the earth. Even if we are the ones who planted the seeds, harvested the crop and baked the bread, it is the Creator who is responsible for everything needed to create the bread and therefore, it is Jehovah who is to be blessed. How beautiful it was and is to use a simple, common liturgy for blessing God, acknowledging God as the King of the universe and the one who brings forth bread from the earth. This is not a bad model for us, for sometimes we feel we must create a prayer and we are not always sure what to say next. There is nothing wrong with finding a grace like this and repeating it at every meal.

It is God who gives us our daily bread – Praise God from whom all blessings flow. This verse also illustrates that God cares about the little things in your life, even on a daily basis. Sparrows are a dime a dozen, Jesus taught, yet not even a sparrow falls without God's knowledge and care. Sometimes we have a tendency to not want to bother God about little things in our lives.

288

When we consider all the big problems of the world, our small daily concerns seem too trivial to bring to God. Perhaps we feel that God is like an overworked customer service representative who cannot possibly handle or deal with all of the calls. That conception of God is too small. Your God is big enough to care about both the major problems of the world as well as your daily needs and your daily bread.

Bless the Lord, wrote the Psalmist. Bless God. When God blesses people, they are helped, strengthened, or made better off than they were before. But when people bless God, God is not helped, strengthened, or made better off. God is not changed. So why bless God? In the scriptures, when God is blessed, it is another way of offering God praise or thanksgiving. Perhaps the one who blesses God desires to express overflowing gratitude for all the blessings he or she has received and so uses the same word to thank God. She or he exalts God's holy name and pays tribute to God for God's blessedness.

When we bless God, we do something unusual: we draw attention away from ourselves and our needs or wants. Do not our thoughts and prayers often begin with ourselves? Learning to Bless God shifts the focus and priority to God first, ourselves second. *Hallowed be Thy name* starts with God and later gets to our needs.

This gem from Psalm 103 inspires us to lift our sights high and bless God… Blessed art Thou, Jehovah, King of the Universe!

PRAYER: My soul magnifies you, O Lord. Blessed art Thou! Please give me the attitude to put you first in my prayers and in my life and help me to find language worthy of using to bless you and hallow your holy name. Amen.

ONE-HUNDRED-AND-FOUR

You set the earth on its foundations, so that it shall never be shaken. You cover it with the deep as with a garment; the waters stood above the mountains.
104:5, 6

The Psalmist is an environmentalist! He sees in nature God's creation. He does not worship nature, but worships the one who created nature… and continues to create nature. God set the earth on its foundations. There is in Psalm 104 the recognition of God's power and magnificence.

This sentiment is captured by Isaac Watts in his classic hymn *I Sing the Mighty Power of God*:

I sing the mighty power of God,
That made the mountains rise,
That spread the flowing seas abroad,
And built the lofty skies.
I sing the wisdom that ordained
The sun to rule the day;
The moon shines full at His command,
And all the stars obey.

I sing the goodness of the Lord,
That filled the earth with food,
He formed the creatures with His word,
And then pronounced them good.
Lord, how Thy wonders are displayed,
Where'er I turn my eye,
If I survey the ground I tread,
Or gaze upon the sky!

There's not a plant or flower below,
But makes Thy glories known,
And clouds arise, and tempests blow,
By order from Thy throne;
Creatures that borrow life from Thee
Are subject to Thy care;
There's not a place where we can flee,
But God is present there.

PRAYER: O God, Creator of all that is awesome and beautiful. Every plant and flower, every mountain and sea, testifies to your goodness and care. Sharpen all of my senses to be more aware of your presence. Amen.

ONE-HUNDRED-AND-FIVE

Seek the Lord and his strength; seek his presence continually.
105:4

A common Hebrew word for *presence* is translated as *face*. To be before God's face is to be in God's presence. God is always present, which is the meaning of omnipresent. We may not be tuned in to God's presence, but God is still there. To seek God's presence is often described in the Bible as setting the mind and heart on God... a conscious focusing of our mind's attention and our heart's affection on God. The Psalmist earlier wrote *"My soul thirsts for God, for the living God. When shall I come and behold the face of God?"* (42:2). To behold the face of God is to recognize being in the presence of the Almighty.

1 Chronicles 22:19 says *"Set your mind and heart to seek the Lord our God."*

Colossians 3:1-2 encourages believers to *"Seek the things that are above, where Christ is, seated at the right hand of God. Set your minds on things that are above..."*

The desire is to know God better and to love God more. As we *seek God's presence continually*, we endeavor to do no less than to seek an encounter with the Divine. That activity sounds incredible, like Moses standing before the burning bush when God said to him *"Come no closer! Remove the sandals from your feet, for the place on which you are standing is holy ground."* (Exodus 3:5). Perhaps we think "Me? Beholding the face of God? Having an encounter with the Creator of the Universe?" Would it be too much for us? And yet, sometimes we have that inner sense where we are close to God. Perhaps it happens in the most special or beautiful places of our lives and we say "I felt close to God at that time."

In the meditation for Psalm 16, I noted a plaque that said *"That which you are seeking is causing you to seek."* The majestic and mysterious wonder of God may be reaching down to touch you and cause you to seek God's presence. Something may be beckoning you, as it did the Psalmist. It is not so much that we arrive in front of God's very presence, but we remain on the journey of the pursuit of that encounter... to *"seek his presence continually."* And by whatever methods we use to do that, our hope is to climb a little higher on the mountain and to see a little more of God's face. In your seeking, recognize that you are standing on holy ground.

PRAYER: O God, I want to seek your presence and to see a little more of you. Sometimes I struggle so hard to seek you and nothing seems to happen. Bless my seeking, draw me closer to you, and guide me even in silence to know that I am standing on holy ground. Amen.

Both we and our ancestors have sinned; we have committed iniquity, have done wickedly.
106:6

The Psalmist confesses that he has sinned. In so doing, he reminds that confession belongs in our prayers. A good prayer has four parts: praise, thanksgiving, confession and petition.

Praise. Jesus began his prayer with praise: *"Hallowed be thy name."* The Psalms are filled with praise. *"Let everything that breathes praise the Lord,"* wrote the Psalmist (150:6). Praise will feel most genuine if you do not hurry through it as though it were an obligation.

Thanksgiving. A good prayer thanks God, from whom all blessings flow. We need to say "thank you." Let your prayers lead you to an attitude that *"My cup runneth over."* Prayers of thanksgiving want to be authentic without expecting anything in return, but there is a fringe benefit to an attitude of gratitude: it leads to contentment. Is that not one of our highest desires, to be content?

Confession. The Psalmist in 106 reminds us to confess our sins. The Apostle Paul wrote to the Romans (3:23): *"All have sinned and fall short of the glory of God."* It is not that we like the word *sin* or being reminded that we have done it, but the stark reality affirms two things: we have all done it and we all fall short. For a person to think that he or she has not fallen short of God's glory is itself a falling short. God knows your secrets, yet loves you anyway. Confession precedes forgiveness. *"If we confess our sins,"* says the epistle 1 John, *"God is faithful and just and will forgive us our sins and cleanse us from all unrighteousness."* Just like there is the need to say "thank you," there is also the need to say "I'm sorry."

Petition. This is the asking part. Should you pray specifically for what you want or should you pray for God's will to be done? Jesus answered that question by his example. He did both. In his Garden Prayer following the night before the cross, he asked God... if it were possible... for him to not have to go through with the crucifixion. He prayed: *"O my Father, if it be possible, let this cup pass from me: nevertheless not as I will, but as thou wilt."* (Matthew 26:39, KJV). Pray for what you want, but let that "nevertheless" be in every one of your prayers: "not what I want, but what you want."

The Psalmist has demonstrated abundantly the importance of our prayers and our lives being filled with praise and thanksgiving. He has also abundantly petitioned God for what he wants. Now, he adds for fourth part to a good prayer: confession. May we follow his lead to confess our sins too, to come clean before God and to be renewed by God's grace and forgiveness.

PRAYER: O Lord, my God. I have sinned. I confess to you now my sins and failures, asking for your forgiveness, cleansing of my soul, and renewal of my spirit. I am sorry for knowing the right and choosing the wrong, by my actions or inactions. Amen.

O give thanks to the Lord, for he is good; for his steadfast love
endures forever.
107:1

Psalm 107 inspired the hymn *Eternal Father, Strong to Save*,
which is also known as the Navy Hymn. At the funeral of that
Navy veteran, President John F. Kennedy, this was the hymn.

It was written by William Whiting, born in 1825 in London. He
was headmaster at the Winchester College Chorister's School for
thirty-five years, a member of the Anglican church, and author of a
book of poems titled *Rural Thoughts*.

The hymn's composer was John Bacchus Dykes, born about the
same time as Whiting, in Hull, England -- a graduate of Cambridge
and an honorary doctorate of music from Durham University.
Dykes also composed the well-known hymns
Holy, Holy, Holy
I heard the Voice of Jesus Say
Jesus, the Very Thought of Thee, and
Ride On! Ride On in Majesty!

Dykes titled the tune "Melita," after the island where the Apostle
Paul was shipwrecked (Acts 28:1). Today that island is named
"Malta."

One of the most interesting things about this hymn is its theology
of the Trinity. Each verse tells about a part of the Divine Trinity:
The Father, the Son, and the Holy Spirit.
Verse 1 begins "Eternal Father"
Verse 2 begins "O Savior"... the son
Verse 3 begins "O Holy Spirit"
Verse 4 begins "O Trinity of love and power."

The Father, Son, and Holy Spirit.

The inspiration for Whiting's hymn comes from Psalm 107 (23-28): *Some went down to the sea in ships, doing business on the mighty waters; they saw the deeds of the Lord, his wondrous works in the deep. For he commanded and raised the stormy wind, which lifted up the waves of the sea. They mounted up to heaven, they went down to the depths; their courage melted away in their calamity; they reeled and staggered like drunkards, and were at their wits' end. Then they cried to the Lord in their trouble, and he brought them out from their distress.*

That is the message of *Eternal Father, Strong to Save*: God hears you when you cry out of the depths, God brings you out of your distresses, God's power – *whose arm doth bind the restless wave* – gives you strength, and by faith there is joy, for even out of the depths you are able to raise to God *glad hymns of praise from land and sea.*

While not necessarily nautical, we too face distresses in our lives and are glad to know that God hears our cry, brings us out of our distress, and gives us strength. Look back at all the times that has happened in your life and sing to God glad hymns of praise.

Eternal Father, strong to save,
Whose arm does bind the restless wave,
Who bids the mighty ocean deep
Its own appointed limits keep;
O hear us when we cry to Thee
For those in peril on the sea.

O Savior, whose almighty word
The winds and waves submissive heard,
Who walked upon the foaming deep,
And calm amid the rage did sleep;
O hear us when we cry to Thee
For those in peril on the sea.

O Holy Spirit, who did brood
Upon the waters dark and rude,
And bid their angry tumult cease,
And give for wild confusion peace;
O hear us when we cry to Thee
For those in peril on the sea.

O Trinity of love and pow'r,
Your children shield in danger's hour;
From rock and tempest, fire, and foe,
Protect them where-so-e'er they go;
Thus, evermore shall rise to Thee
Glad hymns of praise from land and sea.

PRAYER: Eternal God, you have delivered me in times of distress more than I could ever remember. I prayed, you heard my cry and you gave me strength. Let me not forget to say thank you for all those times and to *give thanks to the Lord, for he is good; for his steadfast love endures forever.* Amen.

ONE-HUNDRED-AND-EIGHT

My heart is steadfast, O God, my heart is steadfast; I will sing and make melody. Awake, my soul! Awake, O harp and lyre! I will awake the dawn.
108:1, 2

Now there is an uplifting way to wake up in the morning: *Awake, my soul! Awake, O harp and lyre! I will awake the dawn.* Actually, how you wake up in the morning and the first things you do set the tone for the day and have the potential to shape it. Consider a dozen ideas for starting your day with a steadfast heart:

ONE. Begin your day by repeating a favorite Bible verse that draws you closer to God. A great beginning to any day is to start with a verse like Psalm 118:24: *"This is the day that the Lord has made; let us rejoice and be glad in it."* For a change of pace, switch the pronoun to the first-person singular: *This is the day that the Lord has made. I will rejoice and be glad in it.* When you first awaken, let your first thoughts be of your relationship with God.

TWO. Begin your day with a favorite tune. Think of a hymn and hum the tune, perhaps remembering some of the words. This is how the Psalmist awakens: *I will sing and make melody.* A woman asked her church administrator to order her a hymnal, which cost about the same as a lunch out. She kept the hymnal by her bedside, eventually marking pages of favorites. Each morning as she woke up, she read the verses to the hymn, planted the tune in her mind and hummed it throughout the day.

THREE. Read something uplifting or positive. Keep a good book or a devotional publication by your bed or desk. Instead of rushing to see the news, which is almost always negative, start with a good reading to center your spirit for the coming day.

FOUR. Take a fifteen-minute retreat from looking at a screen, be it a TV, computer or phone. Allow yourself a brief sabbatical to choose to start your day gentle and easy rather than checking emails, news, or messages.

That will all come flooding in soon enough and you will look at them all day long. Start your day in control of your time and your spirit. Rushing to the screen is reactive behavior. Choosing how you spend your awakening moments is proactive and puts the control into your hands.

FIVE. Get even ten minutes of exercise, stretching, yoga or meditation. You do not need to do all your exercise at one time, but at least get started on exercising your body and centering your mind. For some, exercise comes naturally. For others, even small accomplishments are a success to get the day moving. Getting exercise is counter-intuitive. When you feel too tired to exercise, that is when you need it most and when it will combat tiredness.

SIX. Eat a healthy breakfast. It is worth making sure you fuel yourself properly. Breakfast improves your metabolism, regulates weight better, improves your mood and fuels your ability to manage your life effectively. Manage your energy, not your time, and watch creativity flow more freely.

SEVEN. Set some goals. Allow time to look at the forest as well as the trees. What are important life goals that you might touch upon this day? When you review your day at its conclusion, what would you like to have accomplished? For example, today I would like to look people in the eye, linger for just a moment to engage with them, listen to them, and smile at them. Or, today I would like to lift a burden for another in some way.

EIGHT. Triage your TO DO list. Prioritize your TO DO list so that your day's list has only three to five items on it, ranked in order of priority to make sure you tackle the most pressing things first. Keep it simple and manageable. Better to categorize items under one heading than to be overwhelmed with a list too long to achieve in one day. One leader creates a long list of TO DO items on a 3 x 5 card but then adds a post-it note on top with never more than three items. After those three are completed, she repeats the process with the next three. That way, she is never overwhelmed by too much to consider at one time.

NINE. Hydrate. Drinking a glass of water in the morning after going hours without a sip is a good way to hydrate your body. If you could scan the entire body of medical advice for self-care, the top two items would be exercise and hydration. Start by hydrating after your toes touch the floor to begin a goal of six to eight glasses of water in the day.

TEN. Practice gratitude. Repeat the three-word mantra every morning: "*My cup overflows.*" Reflect upon who and for what you are grateful. Offer micro-brief prayers thanking God for a couple items for which you are especially thankful. Practicing gratitude reduces stress hormones, improves mood, and increases contentment.

ELEVEN. Smile and think something positive. When you smile, it signals your brain to release the feel-good neurotransmitters (dopamine, endorphins, and serotonin), which lift your mood, relax your body, and lower your heart rate. Smiling and thinking about something positive sets your spirit's polarity to begin in the right direction – the positive. For your first fifteen-minutes, tell yourself that you are banishing negative thoughts about weather, work, problems, or not feeling good. Start with a positive, smile, elevate your mood and control your polarity.

TWELVE. *Let the day's own trouble be sufficient for the day.* (Matthew 6:34, RSV). Do not start your day worrying about yesterday or being anxious about tomorrow. Learn from yesterday and plan for tomorrow, but set your energy on the present day before you. Consider not just how you hope to approach your tasks, but also how you intend to live as a person of faith, allowing your candle-power of one to radiate to those around you.

PRAYER: O God, my heart is steadfast. Guide me to sing and make melody. As I awake in the dawn, equip me to take control of the day's beginning by starting it with you and for you. Amen.

ONE-HUNDRED-AND-NINE

*But you, O Lord my Lord, act on my behalf for your name's
sake; because your steadfast love is good, deliver me.*
109:21

O Lord my Lord, act on my behalf. Does that actually happen?
Does God act or intercede for us? The Psalmist certainly hopes so,
for Psalm 109 details a long list of how people are against him. He
uses the plural pronoun, so he is thinking about more than one
person. After pleading with God to act on his behalf, his next
verse begins to tell God how bad it is: *For wicked and deceitful
mouths are opened against me, speaking against me with lying
tongues.* The nature of the Psalmist's problems is clear:
relationships. He has relationships which have gone bad and he
needs God to act on his behalf to help make them better.

God majored in relationships. That is what God does best and that
is what you do better when you invite God to act on your behalf.
The Bible is more about relationships than anything else – more
than laws, religious practices, commandments, history, stories,
rules or judgement. What God wants most from you and me is
right relationships, with God and with God's children.

It is likely that of all the challenges or problems you might
encounter, relationship problems sting the most. It is difficult to
resolve them, hard to forget them, and sometimes we are put to the
test by not being able to forgive them.

When you think about it, it might be much easier to try to obey
commandments than to maintain right relationships. It is hard to
keep relationships healthy. People, even those who love one
another most of all, experience times of conflict, disagreement or
hurt. There are some people with whom you could care less about
fostering a healthy relationship. Then there is the problem of
busyness. We get too busy to keep up with relationships. Good
relationships take work.

People in love can find that their relationship stretches to a breaking point and sometimes the relationship fails. It hurts the most when a relationship with someone you have loved goes bad. It is possible that the quality of your life depends more upon relationships than anything you might ever achieve, acquire or accomplish. At your funeral, they will speak only a sentence or two about what you did. Most of all, they will talk about what kind of a person you were and what you meant to them.

It is likely that the biggest relationship problems you encounter will be with a person whom you have know well, cared about greatly, or loved. Not every relationship will be healthy. Sadly, some may break. Great relationships can make your life great. Hurting relationships can overshadow your thoughts, and broken relationships can ache with inner pain.

Perhaps we have tried and failed to reconcile a troubled relationship. Maybe we do not know what to do next. It may feel like we have hit a dead end. The Psalmist felt that way. But then it occurred to him to ask God to do something… to *act on my behalf*. Sometimes when there is no way out, God makes a way out of no way. Never give up hope that God can change things. God may change you, even in ways you cannot change yourself, and that may lead to healing a relationship. God may change the other. Things may go bad and not resolve, but there can be those miraculous times in our relationships when it feels like the parting of the seas and a new path forward is illuminated for us to take. Reconciliation can be achieved, by God's hand. And so, think of a troubled relationship you might have and when there is nothing left to do, pray like the Psalmist *O Lord my Lord, act on my behalf for your name's sake.*

PRAYER: O Lord, my Lord, as I consider a broken or troubled relationship in my life, I pray that you would act on my behalf. If it is possible, restore the relationship to a healthy place. Guide me to do whatever I can do, even if it means coming more than half-way in order to repair things. And whatever happens, touch the wounds of mine and the other's that healing may occur. Amen.

The Lord says to my lord, "Sit at my right hand until I make your enemies your footstool."
110:1

If you open your Bible to Psalm 110 for inspiration, it is possible you would slam it shut before finishing, for it all seems to be about enemies and how God will shatter their heads. Hardly inspiring. It is all about enemies, a topic which pops up frequently in the Psalms. That may be hard for us to connect with, because if you really think about it, you might not be able to name three enemies. In fact, you might not even be able to name one person whom you consider to be an enemy. And so, here is where we have the potential to transform the Psalms into a heightened inspiration for us, if we take a bit of poetic license to reframe the word *"enemy"* or *"foe."*

Here is the idea. If you substitute the word *"problem"* or *"challenge"* for the word *"enemy,"* everything changes. Now you are not thinking of the Psalms applying to people out to get you or do you in, but rather, to everyday difficulties or worries that are constantly up on the rimrock waiting for a time when you are vulnerable. This substitution exercise causes the Psalms to jump off the page and into your daily experience, for we all encounter challenges, difficulties, obstacles, hurdles, adversity, burdens and problems. The message from Psalms is that God is with you, by your side, gives you strength beyond your own, advocates on your behalf, and helps you to conquer or at least to manage your problems. For those experiences, the Psalms are a soothing balm. Reread the Psalms making this substitution to see if this understanding does not help to deal with all the references to enemies or foes.

A story is told of a New York City minister who was stopped on the street by a man who said to him, "Reverend, I've got problems." The Pastor answered, "Well, I know a place near here that has a population of fifteen thousand people and not a person has a problem."

The troubled man said, "Where is that place? I'd like to live there." The minister answered, "It's Woodlawn Cemetery!" If you are alive, you face problems. Problems are our enemies. Sometimes they appear so large that we feel like a part of our life is ruined.

An artist went to visit a friend. When he arrived, he found her crying. He asked why? She showed him a handkerchief of exquisite beauty – a treasure that had been a gift from her father. The handkerchief had been ruined with a drop of indelible ink. The artist asked her to let him have the handkerchief. Several days later, he mailed it back to her. When she opened the package, she could not believe her eyes. The artist, using the inkblot as a base, had drawn on the handkerchief a design of great loveliness. Now it was more beautiful, more of a treasure, and more valuable than ever. With the handkerchief was a brief note, saying *I hope you will enjoy how I have restored the treasure from your father. Fondly, Oscar Claude Monet.*"

God can take our problems and refashion them. God can take a life with a blot on it and turn it into a work of art. And so, when we make the substitution from "enemies" to "problems," the Psalms come alive, speak to us anew, and we see that God can make your enemies your footstool.

PRAYER: Thank you, Loving God, for helping me to understand that when I face problems, you are with me, you give me strength, provide me wisdom, and help me to conquer these "enemies" that threaten the quality and balance of my life. May I place into your hand the worries and anxieties that upset me, and trust that you can take even the blots in my life and turn them into a work of beauty. Amen.

ONE-HUNDRED-AND-ELEVEN

The fear of the Lord is the beginning of wisdom; all those who practice it have a good understanding. His praise endures forever.
111:10

Just as the word "enemies" in the previous Psalm benefits from a substitution, so too does the phrase "fear of the Lord." As expressed in the meditation from Psalm 53, fear does not mean fear. The book of Proverbs (9:10a) notes that *"The fear of the LORD is the beginning of wisdom."* The word *fear* is an ancient word with a beautiful meaning. It does not mean being scared or afraid. A loving, compassionate God would not wish for believers to be afraid of God. The true meaning is "to revere." That makes sense. Revering God is the beginning of wisdom. In Proverbs, wisdom does not mean academic intelligence, content knowledge or the kind of wisdom that we associate with wise old sages. Rather, wisdom in the Bible is always intensely practical, not theoretical. Wisdom, in the Old Testament, is more like common sense or attitude. In many ways, the biblical meaning of wisdom is the art of being successful at life – understanding what about life is truly most important and worthwhile.

In Psalm 111, the writer tells how those who revere God have a good understanding. A good understanding of what? Well, presumably, those who revere God have a good understanding of what is most important. We may, for example, be so intensely focused upon what we are doing at the moment that we mistakenly think it is the most important thing in the world. When an interruption occurs, which may be of much greater importance in the long run, we can lack having a good understanding about which priority is greater. We become almost unable to put down the temporary item of importance for that which is truly more significant.

Those who revere God have a good understanding of which goals in life are most important. Achieve and acquire – those goals seem to be the way of the world.

The way for those who revere God does not discount those goals, but provides an enlightened understanding of what is most important: to love God and to love God's children, to practice kindness and forgiveness, and to treat others well – especially those in need. Those who revere God have a good understanding about what to think about and how to set their minds. Paul wrote to the Philippians (4:8) *"Finally, beloved, whatever is true, whatever is honorable, whatever is just, whatever is pure, whatever is pleasing, whatever is commendable, if there is any excellence and if there is anything worthy of praise, think about these things."*

That list of things to think about is the kind of understanding that results from revering the Lord.

PRAYER: Dear God, to you I bow down and it is you that I revere most of all. Plant within me a growing understanding of that which is good. Give me wisdom to discern what is really most important in life, so that I may think about and pursue that which is true, honorable, just, pure, pleasing, commendable and worthy of praise. Raise me up to hold excellence as my standard. Amen.

ONE-HUNDRED-AND-TWELVE

It is well with those who deal generously and lend, who conduct their affairs with justice.
112:5

The Psalmist lifts up those who are generous and conduct their affairs by treating others fairly and well. Generosity is one of the rich veins coursing throughout the Bible. People of faith are encouraged to have a generous spirit – to be givers of themselves, their resources, their energy and their time. Independent Sector's National Survey titled "Giving & Volunteering in the United States" documents that people of faith are much more likely to give financially and to volunteer their time than those who are not people of faith. If you are reading this book, it is highly likely that you are a giver and a volunteer. Our question now is: how can I grow my spirit of generosity?

Consider some of the Bible's encouragement for us to grow in our generosity:

For where your treasure is, there your heart will be also. (Luke 12:34)

Be generous. Give to the poor. Get yourselves a bank that can't go bankrupt, a bank in heaven far from bank robbers, safe from embezzlers, a bank you can bank on. It's obvious, isn't it? The place where your treasure is, is the place you will most want to be, and end up being. (Luke 12:33,34, The Message)

Give to... God the things that are God's. (Luke 20:25)

People who obey God are always generous. (Proverbs 21:326, Contemporary English Version)

Honor the LORD with your substance and with the first fruits of all your produce; then your barns will be filled with plenty, and your vats will be bursting with wine. (Proverbs 3:9, 10)

Each of you must make up your own mind about how much to give. But don't feel sorry that you must give and don't feel that you are forced to give. God loves people who love to give. God can bless you with everything you need, and you will always have more than enough to do all kinds of good things for others. (2 Corinthians 9:7, 8, Contemporary English Version)

Some give freely, yet grow all the richer; others withhold what is due, and only suffer want. (Proverbs 11:24)

The world of the generous gets larger and larger. (Proverbs 11:24a, The Message)

Sometimes you can become rich by being generous or poor by being greedy. (Proverbs 11:24, Contemporary English Version)

The one who blesses others is abundantly blessed; those who help others are helped. (Proverbs 11:25 (The Message)

In all this I have given you an example that by such work we must support the weak, remembering the words of the Lord Jesus, for he himself said, 'It is more blessed to give than to receive.' (Acts 20:35)

By everything I did, I showed how you should work to help everyone who is weak. Remember that our Lord Jesus said, "More blessings come from giving than from receiving." (Acts 20:35, Contemporary English Version)

"I'm not going to offer God, my God, sacrifices that are no sacrifice." (2 Samuel 24:24b, The Message)

Not only do we find encouragement from the Bible, but consider too the wisdom of the ages:

"We make a living by what we get. We make a life by what we give."
Winston Churchill

"To show great love for God and our neighbor we need not do great things. It is how much love we put in the doing that makes our offering something beautiful for God."
Mother Teresa

"The best use of life is to invest it in something which will outlast life."
William James

"You can give without loving, but you can never love without giving."
Robert Louis Stevenson

"Giving money is a very good criterion, in a way, of a person's mental health."
Karl Menninger

"Giving is true loving."
Charles H. Spurgeon

"Wealth unused might as well not exist."
Aesop

"In this world, it is not what we take up, but what we give up, that makes us rich."
Henry Ward Beecher

"The one who gives early gives twice."
Cervantes

"Give often, when you know your gifts are well placed."
Cato

"No one is useless in this world who lightens the burdens of another."
Charles Dickens

"You give but little when you give of your possessions. It is when you give of yourself that you truly give."
Kahlil Gibran

"The person who gives little with a smile gives more than the person who gives much with a frown."
Jewish Proverb

"The one who gives when asked has waited too long."
Seneca

"A bit of fragrance always clings to the hand that gives you roses."
Chinese Proverb

"What I gave, I have. What I spent, I had. What I kept, I lost."
Old Epitaph

"Give what you have. To someone, it may be better than you dare think."
Henry Wadsworth Longfellow

"God has given us two hands – one for receiving and the other for giving."
Billy Graham

"No person was ever honored for what s/he received. Honor has been the reward for what s/he gave."
Calvin Coolidge

"As the purse is emptied, the heart is filled."
Victor Hugo

"If you would like to take, you must first give."
Lao Tzu

"Thoughtful giving begins with thoughts on giving."
Arthur C. Frantzreb

"For it is in giving that we receive."
St. Francis of Assisi

PRAYER: Generous God, you have given me so much, for which I am truly grateful. Teach me how to be more generous. Grow my spirit of generosity so I am more incline to ask "What can I give" rather than "What can I get." Use me in your service, so that I may give back my church, community and the world. Inspire me to give of my resources freely and cheerfully, to support and help others as well as the institutions that make a great difference in our society. Instill your Spirit within me, so that I will want to be a good and generous person. Amen.

ONE-HUNDRED-AND-THIRTEEN

Blessed be the name of the Lord from this time on and
forevermore. From the rising of the sun to its setting the name
of the Lord is to be praised.
113:2, 3

This Psalm encourages us, from sunrise to sunset, to praise God.
We always benefit from this reminding to raise our sights from
dwelling upon our own needs to giving glory to God. Psalms and
hymns do this ever so well. A good example is one of Charles
Wesley's hymns: *O for a Thousand Tongues to Sing*.

Charles Wesley is considered one of the most influential writers of
English hymns. Hymns in the 18th century were dreary and
impersonal. Here is an example of a hymn in Wesley's time:
Ye monsters of the bubbling deep,
your Master's praises spout;
Up from the sands ye coddlings peep,
and wag your tails about.

To which Charles Wesley essentially replied "Yuk!" He started
writing hymns that were warm and personal. Wesley produced
what are called experiential hymns, because they described a
person's experience of living by faith. His hymns used the first-
person personal pronoun, which was a revolutionary shift in the
18th century.

Charles Wesley and his brother John, while students at Oxford
University, formed a religious "Holy Club" because of their
dissatisfaction with the spiritual apathy at the school. As a result
of their deliberate, systematic, and *methodical* habits of living and
studying, they were teased. Their friends gave them a derisive
nickname: they were called "METHOD-ists."

This is where the term "Methodist" came from. The Wesleys were
the founders of that denomination, but they never set out to start a
new denomination. They were Anglicans and they had no
intention of being anything but good Anglicans.

What they wanted to do was to breathe new life into what they felt had become a stodgy old shell of hollow form and practice.

After they graduated from Oxford, they were sent to America by the Anglican Church to help stabilize the religious climate of the Georgia Colonies and to evangelize the Indians. On the ship crossing the Atlantic, they came into contact with a group of German Moravians, a small evangelical group characterized by missionary concern and enthusiastic hymn singing. That started the Wesley's on a lifelong study of the theology and the hymns of the Moravians, which influenced their writings.

Charles and John Wesley hit the shores of America running, fell flat on their faces and they failed in their ministry. Disillusioned, the Wesley boys returned to England. There is a lesson here: those who accomplish great achievements get there over a road paved with failures, losses, and setbacks. Never give up!

The brothers traveled more than a quarter million miles in Great Britain – on horseback – to conduct 40,000 public services. Charles Wesley, the great Circuit Rider, traveled thousands of miles on horse and all the while writing hymns. Charles Wesley alone wrote 6,500 hymn texts... hymns such as *"Christ the Lord is Risen Today"* and *"Hark! The Herald Angels Sing."*

Wesley's hymn *"O for a Thousand Tongues"* was inspired by a chance remark by Peter Bohler, a Moravian leader, who exclaimed, *"Had I a thousand tongues, I would praise Christ Jesus with all of them."* The hymn originally had nineteen stanzas.

May God be praised in your prayers.
May God be praised in your thoughts.
May God be praised by how you live.
May God be praised in your songs.

Let the words of this hymn become your prayer and your praise:

PRAYER

O for a thousand tongues to sing
My great Redeemer's praise,
The glories of my God and King,
The triumphs of His grace.

My gracious Master and my God,
Assist me to proclaim,
To spread through all the earth abroad,
The honors of Thy name.

So now Thy blessed Name I love,
Thy will would e'er be mine.
Had I a thousand hearts to give,
My Lord, they all were Thine!

Tremble, O earth, at the presence of the Lord, at the presence of the God of Jacob, who turns the rock into a pool of water, the flint into a spring of water.
114:7, 8

Tremble at the presence of the Lord. The Psalmist talks about the earth trembling, a metaphor to indicate that God's presence is so awesome that even the planet shakes. It's a good thing it's a metaphor, because the earth physically trembling could have unfortunate consequences. That is the beauty of metaphors – they can express a dramatic hyperbole to make a point.

People tremble. Trembling is an involuntary response, brought on by fear, frailty, or anxiety. Trembling can also be brought on by excitement or being awe-struck. That is the sense of the haunting song *Were You There When They Crucified My Lord*:

Were you there when they crucified my Lord
Oh were you there when they crucified my Lord
Ooh sometimes it causes me to tremble, tremble, tremble, tremble, tremble
Were you there when they crucified my Lord

Were you there when they nailed him to the cross
Were you there when they nailed him to the cross
Ooh sometimes it causes me to tremble, tremble, tremble, tremble, tremble
Were you there when they nailed him to the cross

Were you there when they laid him in the tomb
Were you there when they laid him in the tomb
Ooh sometimes it causes me to tremble, tremble, tremble, tremble, tremble
Were you there when they laid him in the tomb

Well were you there when the stone was rolled away
Were you there when the stone was rolled away
Ooh sometimes it causes me to tremble, tremble, tremble, tremble,
tremble
Were you there when the stone was rolled away

As we consider being in the presence of The Almighty, we may or may not tremble, but we recognize that God's presence is so awesome that even the earth shakes. May that be the presence we seek.

PRAYER: O Lord, my God, lead me into your presence, so that I may experience more of that awe in being close to you, in knowing you better and in loving you more. Amen.

ONE-HUNDRED-AND-FIFTEEN

Not to us, O Lord, not to us, but to your name give glory, for the sake of your steadfast love and your faithfulness.
115:1

This gem captures the essence of faithful living with just a few words. Those who follow and love the Lord their Shepherd try their best to give glory to God rather than to themselves. The Psalmist begins the sentence with a negative to emphasize the behavior to avoid: promoting our own glory. That almost always backfires anyway. The person who attempts to bring glory to herself or himself rarely succeeds and people often think less of her or him rather than more.

Not that we wouldn't enjoy being appreciated, valued, cherished, praised, complimented, honored or glorified. At the least we would like to be noticed. And so, to call the faithful to deny themselves is a call to self-sacrifice. What could possibly motivate that kind of attitude that chooses to give glory to God above all? Love. It is our love for God that prompts us to seek first to glorify God.

In one of Paul's masterpieces, the Book of Romans, his concluding words are *"...to whom be the glory forever!"* What better conclusion could there be?

The word *"glory"* or *"glorified"* is one of Paul's favorite words, which he employs frequently in his epistles. Note that it is always God who is glorified. One of Paul's best verses about glory is *"So, whether you eat or drink, or whatever you do, do everything for the glory of God."* (1 Corinthians 10:31). Could there be a more fitting goal for the Christian than to do all to the glory of God?

As we seek to grow in faithfulness, consider questions we as people of faith might ask ourselves: Do my words glorify God? Do my choices glorify God? Do I intend each day to live my life to the glory of God? When problems or difficulties come my way, can I use them to the glory of God? How can I better adopt as my life goal to do all to the glory of God?

Doing all to the glory of God was Paul's and the Psalmist's life ambition. May their inspiration draw us into a heightened awareness of our intention to know God better, to love God more, to serve God and God's children, and to give God the glory.

PRAYER: O Lord, may I dedicate my life to giving you glory. I know that I will fail, but let me pick myself up again and continue to try as hard as I can to glorify you with my words, my attitudes, my values, my thoughts, my interactions with others, and my behavior. To you be the glory forever! Amen.

ONE-HUNDRED-AND-SIXTEEN

The Lord protects the simple. When I was brought low, he saved me.
116:6

When put together, these two phrases sound like the Psalmist, who was brought low, was protected and saved by God. But wait: is the Psalmist calling himself simple? Someone who crafted this exquisite literature, who devoted his life to praising, adoring, thanking and glorifying God does not sound simple to us. At least compared to us. If it was David, he was the heroic shepherd boy who slew Goliath and later became King. Simple? If that is simple, what are we?

No matter how the Psalmist perceived himself, his writing is right on target: God protects even the simplest of God's children and leads them into wholeness.

Sometimes religion is made more complicated than it needs to be. Jesus frequently chided the Scribes and the Pharisees for being on the wrong track when it came to faithfulness to God. And today, sometimes we can be our own worst enemies, thinking that faithfulness to God and seeking to be in the presence of God is too complicated for us. Maybe religious professionals and long-term people of faith get it better, but we see ourselves as, well, simple.

Jesus message was exactly that. Keep it as simple as a child-like faith. Faith is not obeying long lists of commandments, rules or practicing saintly behavior. It could not be simpler than this, as Jesus taught: *"Truly I tell you, unless you change and become like children, you will never enter the kingdom of heaven"* (Matthew 18:3). When Jesus took the children in his arms and blessed them, he uncomplicated the pathway to God for all time. Become like a child... in trust, love, faithfulness and obedience. That is what God wants most from you: your love and faithfulness. Like a child. When you embrace this idea, made simple by Jesus, you are on the pathway to a journey which will lead you into the presence of the Divine.

PRAYER: Forgive me, Dear God, for making my faith more complicated than it needs to be. I desire to follow you, to trust you, to love you, to obey you and to try as hard as I can to be faithful to you. And just as you love and care for the simple, may I too do whatever I can to be helpful to the simplest of your beloved children. Amen.

Praise the Lord, all you nations! Extol him, all you peoples! For great is his steadfast love toward us, and the faithfulness of the Lord endures forever. Praise the Lord!
117:1, 2

Psalm 117 has the distinction of being the shortest chapter in the Bible and also the exact middle of the Bible! Its theme is the praise of God. Of course! When you think of The Psalms, that is the first word that comes to mind. The chapter is so short that it could be memorized: *Praise the Lord, all you nations! Extol him, all you peoples! For great is his steadfast love toward us, and the faithfulness of the Lord endures forever. Praise the Lord!*

The Psalmist never tires of praising God and neither do we as his beloved children. There is an uplifting and upbeat traditional Caribbean praise hymn that beckons us to praise the Lord. There are many versions with different lyrics. One of the most popular is a tune composed by Hal H. Hopson

Halle, halle, halle-lujah.
Halle, halle, halle-lujah.
Halle, halle, halle-lujah.
Hallelujah, halle-lujah.

Praise God in this holy place,
every nation, every race.
Come, make joyful music to the Lord.
Sound the trumpet, sound it clear.
Sound it for the world to hear.
Come, make joyful music to the Lord.

Halle, halle, halle-lujah.
Halle, halle, halle-lujah.
Halle, halle, halle-lujah.
Hallelujah, halle-lujah.

Everything that breathes now praise;
sing your songs, let voices raise.
Come, make joyful music to the Lord.
Play the cymbals, play the lute;
play the timbrel, play the flute.
Come, make joyful music to the Lord.

Halle, halle, halle-lujah.
Halle, halle, halle-lujah.
Halle, halle, halle-lujah.
Hallelujah, halle-lujah.

PRAYER: Halle halle hallelujah, Dear Lord. Let my life make joyful music to you with an upbeat tempo and a positive spirit. I thank you for your steadfast love for me and your never-ending faithfulness. Amen.

ONE-HUNDRED-AND-EIGHTEEN

The stone that the builders rejected has become the chief cornerstone.
118:22

A verse that reoccurs through the bible is: *"The stone that the builders rejected has become the chief cornerstone."* In the New Testament, this refers to Jesus. He was rejected. He is the stone the builders rejected. Yet this rejected man has become the chief cornerstone: The head of the Church.

A keystone is the wedge-shaped piece at the crown of an arch that locks the other pieces in place. While it may not be the biggest stone, it is the most important. Can you imagine ancient builders of mighty arches sorting through their pile of cast-off rocks, searching for one of their rejects to use "up there" to hold it all together.

This passage from Psalm 118 fascinated the early Christian writers. It is quoted or referred to all over the New Testament: in Acts, I Peter, Romans, Ephesians, Matthew, Mark and Luke. Originally the Psalmist crafted this as a picture of the nation of Israel. Israel was the nation which was despised and rejected. The Jews were hated. They had been servants and slaves of many nations but the nation which was despised and rejected became the chosen people of God. The stone which the builders rejected, in the Old Testament, was the nation of Israel. Then, in the New Testament, the rejected stone came to refer to Jesus.

Jesus spoke about the rejected stone in Matthew, Mark and Luke which makes us wonder: did Jesus feel the rejection? Not appreciated? Not valued? Did Jesus have an ego? If the Word which became Flesh came to dwell among us and to feel what we feel and hurt like we hurt, would not he too have some bad days when it felt like he was not valued, not appreciated nor understood?

Matthew records that when Jesus taught in his hometown, listeners are astounded. They asked "Where did he get all this stuff? Is this not Joseph's and Mary's boy. We know his family. We know his brothers. Who does he think he is?" (Matthew 13:54-58, paraphrase). Matthew adds *And he did not do many deeds of power there, because of their unbelief."* There is a lesson for you there: you cannot do many great deeds when you do not feel valued.

We wonder how Jesus felt when the crowd cried for Pilate to release Barabbas rather than Jesus. That could not have made Jesus feel valued. And then, from the cross he spoke: *"My God, my God, why have you forsaken me?"* That sounds like a very human cry of rejection and if that is what it was, it assures that he can understand it when you and I do not feel valued, wanted, included, appreciated or needed.

The rejected stone first referred to Israel, then referred to Jesus and perhaps there are times when you feel like you are the stone which was rejected. When you have been rejected, perhaps it felt like a punch in the stomach. Rejection knocks the wind out of you and makes you dizzy and confused. Rejection feels like a slap in the face. It stings. It can make you angry. A natural reflex is to want to put up your fists and strike back. Look how we phrase it: *facing* rejection. It is in your face, open and exposed like a slap. Rejection can squash your self-esteem, rob you of control, strip away your power, whither your creativity and leave you feeling weak or vulnerable. Rejection has the potential to make you feel like you are not appreciated or valued. It can turn you into a door mat, allowing others to walk over you. It can de-inspire you to not care, to give up or to go cry.

Some have been rejected by a good friend and feel betrayed. Some carry the rejections of childhood: you were not the one they picked, you did not get in or you were not accepted. When the team was picking players, your name was not the one they called. Noel Paul Stookey – the Paul from legendary folk singers Peter, Paul, and Mary – sings a song about right fielders:

Saturday summers, when I was a kid,
we'd run to the schoolyard, and here's what we did,
we'd pick out the captains, we'd choose up the teams,
was always of a measure of my self-esteem,
cause the fastest, the strongest, played shortstop and first
the last ones they picked were the worst
I never needed to ask, it was sealed,
I just took up my place in right field.

... where he did not feel valued... out in right field.

Some face rejection by a spouse. It's been great in the past but something happened. Some feel rejected by one of their children: not consulted, not called or not cared for. You gave them so much of yourself and now it is like they do not care. Some feel rejected by their parents. They expect what you cannot deliver. All you want is a loving touch, an affirming hug or words that say "I accept you just as you are." But it feels like you cannot live up to what they want. Some were rejected by a mother or a father and that song plays in your head: *"Sometimes I feel like a motherless child."* Or, a fatherless child.

Some face rejection by your employer. You gave them everything. You were important. You modeled the organization's highest standards and values. You worked long and hard. Now you feel rejected. People are rejected by business partners, colleges they want to attend, jobs they hoped to get, committees on which they have served, colleagues with whom they work and some are rejected by none other than themselves. For some, it is hard to accept yourself. You know you should. You know God accepts you. But it is easier said than done.

When you experience rejection, trust God to use the rejected stone as a cornerstone for something else. Could it be that rejection is what shapes you, propels you, strengthens you, motivates you and even makes you great? Could it be that it is rejection that is the critical secret ingredient to your ultimate success?

Could God use the stones in your life which were rejected... to become the cornerstone for something else? The bible's message is *"The stone that the builders rejected has become the chief cornerstone."*

God did not cause the rejection. God does not cause bad things to happen to people. But could God use it? In Psalm 118 following the verse so often quoted about the rejected stone, look at the next verse: *"This is the Lord's doing; it is marvelous in our eyes."* Your rejection can be used by God. Later, as you look back upon it, you may see the rejection as a part of what recreated you into the fine person you have become.

PRAYER: Compassionate God, when I look back at rejections in my life, some of which still sting, help me to reframe them and see them as tough times which actually strengthened me. Guide me to trust that you can use all of my past, including rejection, to transform me into the cornerstone that you desire me to become. Let me commit my rejections into your hand and release the pain and heal the wounds. Amen.

ONE-HUNDRED-AND-NINETEEN

Hold me up, that I may be safe.
119:117a

If Psalm 117 is the shortest in the bible, Psalm 119 is the longest.
It has 176 verses. Ironically, the longest Psalm has the shortest and
one of the loveliest prayers: *Hold me up, that I may be safe.* This
brief prayer illustrates that the shortest and most simple prayers are
often the best. You can also pray this for one you love or care
about: *Hold them up and keep them safe.* When you pray this
prayer, you place your safety into God's hands. That prompts you
to trust God, to increase an inner sense of peace, and to know that
no matter what troubles may whirl around you, it is well with your
soul.

A man named Horatio Spafford discovered this power of trust and
its resulting gift of peace in his soul. Horatio Gates Spafford was
born in North Troy, New York and later moved to Chicago where
he became a successful attorney and business investor. He was
active in his Presbyterian church in Chicago, serving on boards and
in leadership roles. People who are attend a community of faith
get well-fed on God's word. They sing about and hear about
God's love and mercy and they develop resources for handling
whatever difficulties they might need to face. Horatio Spafford
grew in the spirit and would need all the resources he could
muster.

His young son died. There is nothing harder than losing a child.
His grief was deep. You never get over it. You wouldn't want to,
but life has to go on.

As senior partner in his law firm and an investor, Spafford invested
heavily in prime real estate on the shore of Lake Michigan. His
family's fortunes were tied up in Chicago real estate. And then...
*"One dark night, when people were in bed, Mrs. O' Leary lit a
lantern in her shed, the cow kicked it over, winked its eye, and
said, 'There'll be a hot time in the old town tonight'."*

The Chicago Fire did indeed start in the barn of Mr. and Mrs. Patrick and Catherine O'Leary, on Sunday evening, October 8, 1871. In two days, the fire had cut a path through Chicago three and one-third square miles in size. 100,000 people were left homeless, 300 people lost their lives, and Horatio Spafford's holdings were wiped out.

Spafford and his family needed a break from these troubled times in their lives, so he, his wife Anna, and their four daughters Maggie, Tanetta, Annie and Bessie planned a trip to Europe by luxury liner. The tickets were purchased, the bags packed, and they were ready to go, but at the last minute, Spafford had an unexpected business development which required him to stay in Chicago. The family decided that Anna and their four daughters would go on ahead as scheduled on the luxury ship, the S. S. Ville du Havre, and Horatio would catch up with them in a few days.

The S. S. Ville du Havre, at two in the morning on November 22, was struck by the English iron sailing vessel, the Loch Earn off the coast of Newfoundland. It sank in two hours with a loss of 226 lives, including the four Spafford daughters. When the survivors landed at Cardiff, Wales, Mrs. Spafford cabled her husband with two words, "Saved alone."

Spafford left to be with his bereaved wife. On the Atlantic crossing, the captain of his ship called Horatio to his cabin to tell him that they were passing over the spot where his four daughters had perished. Horatio walked out of the captain's cabin, stood at the rail as he passed over the watery grave of his beloved four daughters and on that spot, took out his pen and wrote the text for the hymn:
When peace, like a river,
upholds me each day,
When sorrows like sea billows roll,
Whatever my lot,
you have taught me to say,
"It is well, it is well with my soul."
It is well, with my soul,
it is well, it is well with my soul.

The name of the tune is named Ville Du Havre, the name of his daughters' ship.

A few years later, Anna and Horatio left their Chicago home to pursue a humanitarian mission in Jerusalem. They called themselves the American Colony and they set up medical clinics, orphanages, soup kitchens, schools and a pediatric hospital. They ultimately turned their villa into a hotel, which has been known since the 1960's as Jerusalem's American Colony Hotel. In 1992, in the hotel's garden courtyard, a meeting took place that led to the secret negotiations that culminated in the historic 1993 peace accord between Israel and the Palestine Liberation Organization. This story is told in Selma Lagerlöf Nobel-Prize winning novel _Jerusalem_, which lifts up the humanitarian work of Horatio and Anna Spafford and their American Colony.

Anna and Horatio did a lot of good despite all the troubles and loss they endured, and yet, it's Horatio's hymn which continues to carry the message of Christ's gift of peace: "_My peace I give to you. I do not give to you as the world gives. Do not let your hearts be troubled, and do not let them be afraid._" (John 14:27)

May His peace, like a river, uphold you each day.

PRAYER: Loving God, let your gift of peace flow like a river through me, to reassure me that no matter how rough are my seas, I can sing that it is well, it is well, with my soul. Amen.

Too long have I had my dwelling among those who hate peace.
120:6

You wonder, who could possibly hate peace? There are so many wonderful benefits to peace that it is hard to imagine anyone hating it. We do not know if the Psalmist was referring to individuals or to nations, for in the real world both can be found who seem to hate peace.

There are some people who are always lightning rods of trouble, conflict and divisiveness. Some are volatile. You must tiptoe around them carefully like walking on eggshells. You have to watch every word you speak to them so as not to set them off. Wherever they go they are either involved in tensions themselves or the cause of tensions between others. The person who divides people and tries to stir up division seems to be doing the devil's own work. Sad to say, they appear to hate peace.

Then there are nations who appear bent upon war. They do not have departments of peace, but rather, departments of war. They do not have peace academies, but war academies. War seems inconsistent with the Bible's teachings to overcome evil with good. The bible encourages us to live in harmony with one another... do not repay anyone evil for evil... live peaceably with all... if your enemies are hungry, feed them; if they are thirsty, give them something to drink; for by doing this you will heap burning coals on their heads. Do not be overcome by evil, but overcome evil with good. (Romans 12:16-21 selections). When Jesus said (Matthew 5:44) *"Love your enemies and pray for those who persecute you,"* it is hard to see that hating peace was what he had in mind.

Strategies for resolving conflicts are known, available, and effective. Look at what Senator George Mitchell did in Northern Ireland. Generations of warring conflict and both sides came to the table and talked. Mitchell later wrote a book titled *Making Peace* to teach how it can be done.

Communication is the basis of resolving conflict. Listening is the basis of resolving conflict. Probing to find what the other needs is the basis of resolving conflict. Searching to negotiate a win-win solution – a compromise where all sides benefit – is the basis for resolving conflict. Blessed are the peacemakers, taught Jesus.

We know how to make peace. We know strategies and techniques, and peace is far less expensive and costly in terms of lives than conflict. We know how to wage peace. What's missing seems to be the motivation. If trying to figure out what motivates a nation to prefer war, follow the money. Look at the lobbyists, political action committees, corporations, and their influence on lawmakers. Ask yourself who benefits financially from the war machine. A nation bent on war, or at least scaring people into believing we must always be prepared for war, is not necessarily the heart and soul of its people but rather the mind and pocketbook of those who would benefit financially.

The Psalmist laments having to dwell with those who hate peace. Then, in the next verse (7) he wrote: *"I am for peace."* So was Jesus. So was Paul. And so may we be. God grant that in our encounters with others and in our citizenship of a nation, may we endeavor to be peacemakers.

PRAYER: Loving and Compassionate God, who longs for all to live in a peaceable kingdom, teach me how to be your peacemaker. When there is conflict around me, use me as your ambassador to encourage reconciliation. In this world so full of conflict and saber rattling, I pray for peace. Instill in the hearts of leaders of nations a desire and a will to be for peace. Amen.

ONE-HUNDRED-AND-TWENTY-ONE

I lift up my eyes to the hills – from where will my help come? My help comes from the Lord, who made heaven and earth.
121:1, 2

This is one of the loveliest Psalms and a favorite for many people. Try this idea: when you see a hill or a mountain, or when you are in nature where you feel close to the Divine, say this verse to yourself: *"I lift up my eyes to the hills."* Repeat this verse to affirm that you know that your help comes from the Lord.

When the Psalmist wanted to feel close to God, he went outside. Perhaps as he gazed at the majestic hills, he reflected that they existed long before him and they would continue to look the same long after he was gone. Surrounded by a sense of permanence, perhaps he considered what a tiny speck he was in the universe of God's creation. And yet, the hills reminded him of the Creator's personal connection and help.

People have said that it is often when they are outdoors that they feel closest to God. For some it is the mountains, for others it is by the sea or in the forest. When our eyes behold the beauty of God's creation, our souls long to sing *"How Great Thou Art."*

Psalm 121 is an outdoors Psalm. Can you imagine the Shepherd tending his flock by day and by night, spending hours looking at the stars overhead... the purple mountain majesty in the distance... and feeling particularly close to God? When he felt troubled or anxious, he looked up to the hills. His religion came from the hills. That is where Moses went to meet God. Atop that mountain, God said... (Exodus 3:5) *"Remove the sandals from your feet, for the place on which you are standing is holy ground."* There is something holy about being in God's creation:

All nature sings, and round me rings, the music of the spheres
The morning light, the lily white, Declare their Maker's praise.
In the rustling grass I hear him pass, He speaks to me everywhere.

Jesus' life was surrounded by mountains. After his baptism, he
went to the mountain for forty days. That is where he was tempted
by the Evil One. When he chose his disciples, he took them apart
to teach them and they went up to the mountain. This collection of
his teachings is named The Sermon on the Mount. When he
wanted to be alone, the bible says, he *went up the mountain by
himself to pray.* When he was considering whether or not to go to
Jerusalem where he would be killed, he went to the mountain to
seek God's counsel. This mount is known as the Transfiguration.
Jesus lifted his eyes to the hills.

A caution: your help does not come from the hills. Your help
comes from God. This is not about nature worship. The hills are
not to be worshipped. The hills will not be your help and your
keeper, but the hills are reminders that *His hand the wonders
wrought.*

From where will my help come? The first verse raises the question
and the second verse answers it: *My help comes from the Lord,
who made heaven and earth.*

Consider what an amazing contrast these two phrases form: God is
as big as the universe and created the heavens and the earth and yet
God knows me and helps me. The juxtaposition of these two ideas
may make a person wonder if the Maker of the universe might be
too big or too busy to give you much help. Do you ever find
yourself pondering if God is too busy to handle all of the calls that
keep on coming? Or, have you ever thought that your needs or
worries were nothing compared to all the major tragedies, wars,
famines, and droughts that God has to tend to? So, you do not
want to bother God. This simple but profound Psalm tells us that
those ideas of God are too small. That is a small conception of the
greatness of the Divine. God is big enough to care about all of the
planet's big problems as well as the small things you are worried
about.

Allow this verse to expand your concept of God's greatness. God made the heaven and earth and yet, your help comes from the Lord.

God's help to you is a popular theme in the Psalms. Inhale and exhale a deep breath of comfort as you allow these affirmations of God's help to wash over your inner spirit:

"God is our refuge and strength, a very present help in trouble." (Psalm 46:1)

"Behold, God is my helper; the Lord is the upholder of my life." (Psalm 54:4)

"O LORD my God, I cried to thee for help, and thou hast healed me." (Psalm 30:2)

"The LORD is my strength and my shield; in him my heart trusts; so I am helped, and my heart exults, and with my song I give thanks to him." (Psalm 28:7)

"In my distress I called upon the LORD; to my God I cried for help... he heard my voice, and my cry to him reached his ears." (Psalm 18:6)

"I was pushed hard, so that I was falling, but the LORD helped me." (Psalm 118:13)

Could there be any clearer message from the bible that God helps you? This gem is an affirmation of faith by one who believes *The Lord is MY keeper*. And yet, we forget to ask.

A young girl was in her backyard trying to move a large rock while her mother sat nearby watching. The girl tried her hardest but she could not budge the rock. *"I can't do, mom. The rock won't move."* Her mother replied, *"Of course you can. You haven't asked me to help yet."* When you cannot move the big challenges in your life, do not make the same mistake. Ask for help.

335

I lift up my eyes to the hills is verse to reaffirm every time your eyes gaze to hills or mountains to remind you that your help comes from the Lord, who made heaven and earth.

PRAYER: Creator God, let me never forget that my help comes from you. I praise you for the beauty and majesty of your creation. When I next see a hill or a mountain, whisper to me the reminder that you are by my side and you are the source of my help. Thank you, Dear God. Amen.

ONE-HUNDRED-AND-TWENTY-TWO

For the sake of the house of the Lord our God, I will seek your good.
122:9

Psalm 122 is the writer's prayer for Jerusalem. It is Jerusalem he is thinking of when he writes *"I will seek your good."* However, this is a wonderful prayer to pray for others.

Imagine being on the receiving end of this seeking. Imagine others determined to seek your good. Imagine your boss set upon seeking your good. Imagine your teacher or your neighbor committed to seeking your good. Imagine the person on the phone helping you to fix your computer, the sales representative answering your questions, the doctor trying to diagnose your problem, or the government official in town hall having no mixed motives about seeking your good. How blessed we would be to be on the receiving end of others seeking our good.

In a world where it is almost a sport to try to out-do one another in using superlatives, the word *good* seems understated. It is almost as though good is not good enough. So, we pepper our sentences with words like *very, tremendous, fabulous, terrific, stunning, outstanding, superb, fantastic* – as though the word *good* cannot stand upon its own four letters. However, if we were to question another's motivation about helping us, we would be well-satisfied with *good* intentions. There are situations, like sales or politics, where the other's interest is usually placed before our best interests. They are, by trade, seeking to make the sale or get re-elected. Both parties understand that, which is the reason for the phrase *caveat emptor* – let the buyer beware. How wonderful it would be if we do not need to beware because we trust the other who truly seeks our good.

"I will seek your good," wrote the Psalmist. He said that about a nation, which prompts us to do the same about our nation and our planet, our church and organizations we care about, and our friends and neighbors. We will seek their good.

In place of self-serving motivations, we – who seek to be good people – will pursue their highest and best interests. That is one of the definitions of *agape*, the New Testament's word for *love*.

This phrase – *"I will seek your good"* – captures the nature and essence of God. It is a great summary of the Bible's teachings about what God is like. If we wonder if God is a judgmental God, a tempting God, or a God who causes bad things to happen to teach us a lesson, we can apply this simple phrase to find the answer is *no*. That is not the way of a God who seeks your good. While the Psalmist wrote the phrase, it could very well be the loving words to you coming out of God's mouth. God seeks your good.

PRAYER: Loving God, help me to be a good person. Let my love for you cause me to seek the good of others I encounter in my everyday life, especially those closest to me but also the stranger. Guide me to seek the good for my church, my community, my nation, and this beautiful world you have entrusted to us for our stewardship of the earth. Amen.

Have mercy upon us, O Lord, have mercy upon us.
123:3a

This verse is the basis of the liturgy known as the Kyrie Eleison, which is an invocation used in liturgical churches and often goes:
Lord, have mercy
Christ, have mercy,
Lord, have mercy upon us.

Father Richard Rohr, Founding Director of the Center for Action and Contemplation, wrote in Huffington Post (11/16/2013) *"Why We Need to Say 'Lord, Have Mercy!'"*

Is it any accident that the official liturgy begins with Kyrie, Eleison? It is the most common Christian short prayer, which is some form of "Have mercy on me!" This is not a self-demeaning prayer, nor a self-defeating prayer, nor is it a disempowering prayer. Relying upon mercy, in fact, protects you from the arrogance and pride that wants to judge others, even in your mind. It situates you in freedom from any sense of your own sufficiency or superiority, and affirms a non-need to justify yourself, and thus keeps your heart open for others and for God. It is basically a prayer for detachment from the self, both mind and heart, and its endless games of self-validation. "Lord, have mercy" seeks validation only from God and not from any inner or outer attempts to be worthy, independently "good," or not-in-need-of-mercy. Note that when you do not stand under the mercy, your mind almost certainly does one or all of three things: plays the victim, accuses others, or falsely exalts itself. When you honestly ask for mercy, you make all three of these responses unnecessary and, in a way, impossible.

The Psalmist inspires us by his example to include in our prayers "O Lord, have mercy upon us." One of Jesus' Parables, the Parable of the Pharisee and the Tax Collector (Luke 18:9-14), teaches us that a plea for mercy like this is what God values.

The one who prayers "God, be merciful to me, a sinner!" is the one who is justified and exalted:

He also told this parable to some who trusted in themselves that they were righteous and regarded others with contempt: "Two men went up to the temple to pray, one a Pharisee and the other a tax collector. The Pharisee, standing by himself, was praying thus, 'God, I thank you that I am not like other people: thieves, rogues, adulterers, or even like this tax collector. I fast twice a week; I give a tenth of all my income.' But the tax collector, standing far off, would not even look up to heaven, but was beating his breast and saying, 'God, be merciful to me, a sinner!' I tell you, this man went down to his home justified rather than the other; for all who exalt themselves will be humbled, but all who humble themselves will be exalted."

The messages of the parable:
Jesus did not like self-righteous behavior.
Jesus lifted up the simple, humble faith.
God hears the pray of the one who asks for mercy and gives it.

The intended audience for the parable is clear: *He also told this parable to some who trusted in themselves that they were righteous and regarded others with contempt.* The Contemporary English Version translates it this way: *Jesus told a story to some people who thought they were better than others and who looked down on everyone else.*

In Jesus' parable, the hero is the least likely. Tax collectors then were not highly regarded. They were hired by Rome to collect taxes for... Rome! The money collected from the Jews did not go to repair their interstate highways. The taxes were shipped out of town. People bid for the job of chief tax collector and then exacted the tax plus a tidy profit from the citizens. Most of the offices were filled by Romans, although some natives got the bids. Since both men in the parable were going up to the Temple to pray, we would assume both were of the Hebrew faith. But who would ever figure a tax collector to be the hero of the story?

340

Jesus the master storyteller described self-righteous behavior so anyone could understand. The Pharisee toots his own horn and tells God how good he is – in prayer. Then he expresses his gratitude to God that he is not like other people to whom he looks down upon, especially this tax collector.

Jesus' story transitions to the tax collector: *But the tax collector, standing far off, would not even look up to heaven, but was beating his breast and saying, 'God, be merciful to me, a sinner!'* The Tax Collector stood off in the distance and would not even lift his eyes to God. He essentially prayed, *"God, have mercy on me... I am no damn good!"* The story reassures that God is a loving God to people who stand far off and feel far away: at a distance. When a person feels at a distance from God and thinks of themselves as no damn good, he or she admits to being a sinner and asks God to forgive: *"God, be merciful to me, a sinner."*

A mother once approached Napoleon seeking a pardon for her son. The emperor replied that the young man had twice committed a serious offense twice and justice demanded death. "But I don't ask for justice," the mother explained. "I ask for mercy." "But your son does not deserve mercy," Napoleon replied. The mother again pleaded, "Sir, it would not be mercy if he deserved it. Mercy is all I ask for." "Well, then," the emperor said, "I will have mercy." And he spared the woman's son.

God exalts the humble. The tax collector in his sincere confession approached God with humility and confession. His prayer reminds of the thief on the cross, another least expected hero: *Then he said, "Jesus, remember me when you come into your kingdom."* (Luke 23:42).

The Parable teaches that we need not attempt to win God's approval by our religious behavior. A humble faith pleases God. *He has told you, O mortal, what is good; and what does the Lord require of you but to do justice, and to love kindness, and to walk humbly with your God?* (Micah 6:8). Trying to be a faithful child of God is what pleases God. Indeed, a simple childlike trust and faith is how Jesus described the best pathway into God's way:

Truly I tell you, unless you change and become like children, you will never enter the kingdom of heaven. (Matthew 18:3). It is interesting that Jesus added the phrase *"change and become like children."* That presumes that we possess the capacity to change and to approach God with a simple childlike faith.

Some of Jesus' parables end with a question, to require the listener to think, to consider the message of the story and to respond. Not this time. In this parable, perhaps Jesus wanted to make the message so clear that no one could miss it: *I tell you, this man went down to his home justified rather than the other; for all who exalt themselves will be humbled, but all who humble themselves will be exalted.*

The Psalmist's prayer, like the tax collector's prayer, ever so simply asks... begs God for mercy because he recognizes the need for mercy. That is a step towards healing, wholeness, and entering into the presence of the Divine.

PRAYER: O Lord, have mercy upon me. Forgive me for moments when I do not see my need for your mercy. Forgive me for times when I play the victim, judge or blame others, or falsely exalt myself. Be merciful to me, a sinner. Amen.

ONE-HUNDRED-AND-TWENTY-FOUR

Our help is in the name of the Lord, who made heaven and earth.
124:8

Psalm 124 is the Psalmist's prayer of thanksgiving for Israel's deliverance. He enumerates the times when Israel was in trouble, but God delivered them and helped them. His Psalm applies to his personal experience as well as ours. Look back at all the times God has helped you and offer God your thanksgiving, for *"Our help is in the name of the Lord."* The Psalm reminds of Isaac Watt's classic hymn <u>*O God, Our Help in Ages Past*</u>:

O God, our help in ages past,
Our hope for years to come,
Our shelter from the stormy blast,
And our eternal home.

Under the shadow of Thy throne
Thy saints have dwelt secure;
Sufficient is Thine arm alone,
And our defense is sure.

Before the hills in order stood,
Or earth received her frame,
From everlasting Thou art God,
To endless years the same.

A thousand ages in Thy sight
Are like an evening gone;
Short as the watch that ends the night
Before the rising sun.

Time, like an ever-rolling stream,
Bears all its sons away;
They fly forgotten, as a dream
Dies at the opening day.

O God, our help in ages past,
Our hope for years to come,
Be Thou our guard while life shall last,
And our eternal home.

May this hymn be your song for today. Sing it, hum it, say the words, and pray it.

PRAYER: *O God, our help in ages past, Our hope for years to come, Our shelter from the stormy blast, And our eternal home.* My help is in you, O God. As I look back and count even a few of the times you helped me, my gratitude overflows. Thank you, Dear Lord. Amen.

Those who trust in the Lord are like Mount Zion, which cannot be moved, but abides forever.
125:1

Ralph Waldo Emerson wrote "All I have seen teaches me to trust the Creator for all I have not seen." Again, it is a mountain which reminds the Psalmist to trust in the Lord. A great hymn that sings of trust in God is *My Faith, It Is an Oaken Staff.* Sing a song of trust, as presented with contemporary lyrics from The New Century Hymnal (Cleveland: Pilgrim Press):

My faith, it is an oaken staff, the traveler's well-loved aid.
My faith, it is a song of trust, sustains me undismayed.
I'll travel on and still be stirred by silent thought or social word.
By all my perils undeterred, a pilgrim unafraid.

My faith, it is an oaken staff, O let me on it lean.
My faith provides the ground of hope, supports a purpose keen.
Your Spirit, God, upon me send, that I may be what you intend.
With patient courage, we'll contend as radiant saints serene.

One of the favorite lines is *My faith, it is a song of trust, sustains me undismayed.* Your faith sustains you so that you can withstand, bear, endure, weather and even thrive undismayed when you face adversity. That is the song of one who trusts in the Lord, for then you are like Mount Zion, which cannot be moved, but abides forever.

PRAYER: O Lord, my God, I trust in you. I find myself placing complete trust in banks, in planes, in doctors, in technology, in government, and in complete strangers, but then turn around and forget to trust in you. Grow my faith so that every day I renew my trust in you. Amen.

ONE-HUNDRED-AND-TWENTY-SIX

When the Lord restored the fortunes of Zion, we were like those who dream. Then our mouth was filled with laughter, and our tongue with shouts of joy;
126:1, 2

God restores. God restored Job after he suffered. Even in the midst of one tragedy after another striking Job, he remained steadfast to his faith. One of his greatest lines which is perhaps one of the most faith-filled in the Bible, is:
"And he said, 'Naked I came from my mother's womb, and naked shall I return. The LORD gave, and the LORD has taken away. Blessed be the name of the LORD.' In all this Job did not sin or charge God with wrong." (Job 1:21, 22)

The story of Job is a complex and mysterious story. In the end, God restored Job. Job accepts that God is in control, and he says: *"I know that thou canst do all things, and that no purpose of thine can be thwarted."* Then, God restored to Job all that he had before, with new prosperity and a new family: *"And the LORD restored the fortunes of Job, when he had prayed for his friends; and the LORD gave Job twice as much as he had before... He had also seven sons and three daughters."* Job lived to a ripe old age, happy and fulfilled.

God restores. God restored Job. The Lord restored Zion, wrote the Psalmist. And the Bible tells how God will restore you. The book of 1st Peter (1 Peter 5:10) assures that *"After you have suffered for a little while, the God of all grace... will himself restore, support, strengthen, and establish you."* We cannot know the nature of how God will restore us. That is why faith and hope is the foundation for our trust that God will restore us. Does it mean the pain of loss or hurt will go away? No. But God will supply us with that which we need mend, to adapt, to manage, and to move forward.

Ralph Waldo Emerson said *"It is the wounded oyster that mends its shell with pearl."* The most extraordinary thing about the oyster is this: irritations like a grain of sand get into his shell. He does not like them. He tries to get rid of them. When he cannot get rid of them, he settles down to make of them one of the most beautiful things in the world. He uses the irritation to do the loveliest thing that an oyster ever has a chance to do. He creates a pearl. God can turn the hurts in your life into a thing of beauty and help you to create a new beautiful life. God restores.

PRAYER: God who restores, hear my prayer asking for your healing touch to my hurts which still ache. I know I'll never understand the how's or why's of what happened to me, but I trust in you to restore me, support me, strengthen me and establish me so that I may journey forth into my future with renewal and joy in my life. Thank you, Dear God. Amen.

It is in vain that you rise up early and go late to rest, eating the bread of anxious toil; for he gives sleep to his beloved.
127:2

When anxious or worried, it is hard to sleep. The Psalmist pays tribute to God for giving sleep to his beloved. You are God's beloved, and even if you toss and turn from anxiety, God gives you sleep – although sometimes it feels like forever when we cannot get to sleep.

In the 121st Psalm, the writer tells how God is your keeper and that God neither slumbers nor sleeps. When you are reassured that God is awake and watching over, you are able to let go of some of the anxiety and trust that God is keeping you. The Lord is your keeper.

Jesus talked about how he gives rest to those who are weary. He said *"Take my yoke upon you… you will find rest for your souls."* This is one of the warmest and most beautiful invitations in the bible: *"Come to me, all you that are weary and are carrying heavy burdens, and I will give you rest. Take my yoke upon you, and learn from me; for I am gentle and humble in heart, and you will find rest for your souls. For my yoke is easy, and my burden is light."* (Matthew 11:28-30)

You do not need to pull your burden or face your anxiety alone. You have a partner in Jesus, a yokefellow, to share the load. Then the burden is light.

One of the main events at county fairs is the ox pulling contest where a couple oxen are teamed up to a wooden yoke. A chain is linked from the ring of the yoke to the cement block load, which is named the *burden*. The race is to determine how far and how fast the oxen can pull the burden. That is how they plowed the field or pulled the wagon, yoked together, but today the oxen pull the burden to demonstrate their strength and to please the crowd.

The burden, usually cement blocks, is so heavy that the two oxen can barely pull it and certainly one could not pull it alone.

A modern-day carpenter who had visited the holy lands noted that both he and Jesus shared the same trade. He was asked, *"What did carpenters make in Jesus' day?"* He replied that they made little furniture – perhaps a table, a trunk for storage or a door. They used little furniture in the way we do today. They did not make houses, for houses were not made of 2" by 6" studs with plywood sheathing. *"Mostly,"* he said, *"they made farm implements. And many of those,"* he added, *"were ox yokes."* It is likely that Jesus made ox yokes in the carpenter's shop in Nazareth during the silent years of his teens and twenties. When he invites you to *"Come... take my yoke upon you"* he is using an image which he has wrapped his hands around.

Consider the physics of an ox yoke. There are two holes, one for each animal. That is named the *oxbow*. The oxen pull together, in tandem, so that the load is shared. Neither could pull the burden alone, but together they can. Imagine if only one animal had to wear this contraption. It would be off-balanced. Uncentered.

An iron ring is fastened to the center of the oxbow. A rope or chain is hooked to that. The thing they pull – be it a plow, a wagon or any kind of load – is named the *burden*. A heavy burden cannot be pulled by one ox alone. A heavy burden cannot be pulled comfortably if the yoke does not fit easy.

From his crafting of yokes, Jesus offered his comforting and reassuring invitations: *"Come to me, all you that are weary and are carrying heavy burdens, and I will give you rest. Take my yoke upon you, and learn from me; for I am gentle and humble in heart, and you will find rest for your souls. For my yoke is easy, and my burden is light."*

Even the sound of his words sooth the restless soul: COME... REST... GENTLE... EASY... LIGHT.

COME TO ME. Jesus invites you. He is the source of strength, renewal and refreshment.

CARRYING HEAVY BURDENS. Carrying a burden is not necessarily a bad thing. A burden can be a responsibility we shoulder. Or it could be a problem, a worry, a challenge or a difficulty.

I WILL GIVE YOU REST. The word *rest* does not mean a brief coffee break. It does not mean not having to do any work or idleness. We would not want that. Idleness is more boring and stressful than work. Rest here means to make fresh again, to RE-fresh. The rest he gives restores your inner nature, as in Psalm 23 *"He restores my soul."* Rest means to make new, as in *"if anyone is in Christ, he or she is a new creation... the old has passed away, behold, the new has come."* (2 Corinthians 5:17). When you are without rest, things can feel like they are falling apart. Paul wrote to the Colossians (1:17) that *"in him all things hold together."* The rest Jesus gives renews your strength for the journey. In the verse, Jesus did not place limits on how many times you can come to him. He did not say you could come to him only once or twice. Picture Jesus with open arms and upturned palms offering you this invitation whenever you *"are weary and are carrying heavy burdens."* Whenever you are anxious. Whenever you are worried. Every time.

TAKE MY YOKE UPON YOU. Since the yoke is a metaphor, why not be a bit fanciful with the imagination? Imagine the oxbow with two holes in it. Place your head in one of the holes and look over to see Jesus in the other. You and he pull your burden together, in tandem. The load is shared between you. Alone, you could not pull the weight. You would be off-centered and unbalanced. The load would be too heavy. But yoked together, you and he can pull any burden you have.

FIND REST FOR YOUR SOUL. The body needs rest and so does the soul. When your soul is rested and renewed you are able to surge forward with energy, vitality, and a strong spirit. Center your spirit and find your spiritual balance. Jesus gives rest.

You do not have to earn it, pay for it, deserve it or do anything except receive it. Ask and it will be given to you. Seek and you will find. Sometimes people find it hard to receive gifts. Learn to receive graciously and accept his gift of rest for your soul.

MY YOKE IS EASY. Easy here means well-fitting like a comfortable favorite pair of slippers or clothes in which you relax. The yokes were hand-crafted and tailor-made to fit the ox so they did not chafe or irritate. When you and Jesus are pulling your burden together, the yoke is tailor-made to fit you and feels comfortable. There is the reassurance that together "Jesus and I can do this."

What is the burden that you are worried about? What are you anxious about? What is making you weary? Allow Jesus to share your heavy load. Place your head in one side of the yoke and sense his presence in the other side. With him pulling with you, the burden is light and you will have his gift of rest and renewed strength. Jesus will help you pull your burden.

You are God's beloved. Jesus helps you pull your burden and gives you rest for your soul. The Psalmist likewise reminds that God is watching over you and gives you sleep. Rest and sleep, with anxiety and burdens entrusted into God's hand.

PRAYER: Loving God, when I toss and turn and cannot sleep, remind me that you do not slumber, for you are awake and watching over me. Help me to take the things that are bothering me and place them into your hand, so that I may let go and find sleep. When I am anxious, reassure me that I need not pull my burden alone, for Jesus is by my side in the yoke pulling with me. Amen.

Happy is everyone who fears the Lord, who walks in his ways.
128:1

We saw in Psalm 111 that the word fear does not mean fear. The word *fear* is an ancient word with a beautiful meaning. It does not mean being scared or afraid. A loving, compassionate God would not wish for believers to be afraid of God. The true meaning is "to revere." That makes sense. To revere the Lord is the beginning of wisdom, a phrase used by the writers of the Psalms and the Book of Proverbs. Now the Psalmist tells how those who revere the Lord and who walk in God's ways are happy. The Hebrew word for *happy* also means *blessed*, and that is an important distinction, for they have different shades of understanding.

One of the Bible's most beloved teachings about *blessed* is known as The Beatitudes, found in Matthew 5, from the introduction to Jesus' Sermon on the Mount. The Beatitudes are the nine verse which begin with the words *"Blessed are..."* Blessed. The Greek word is *makarios* which means *"fortunate, well off, or happy."* Here are the Beatitudes:
Blessed are the poor in spirit, for theirs is the kingdom of heaven.
Blessed are those who mourn, for they will be comforted.
Blessed are the meek, for they will inherit the earth.
Blessed are those who hunger and thirst for righteousness, for they will be filled.
Blessed are the merciful, for they will receive mercy.
Blessed are the pure in heart, for they will see God.
Blessed are the peacemakers, for they will be called children of God.
Blessed are those who are persecuted for righteousness' sake, for theirs is the kingdom of heaven.
Blessed are you when people revile you and persecute you and utter all kinds of evil against you falsely on my account. Rejoice and be glad, for your reward is great in heaven, for in the same way they persecuted the prophets who were before you.

One translation of the bible actually used the word *"happy"* instead: *"How happy are the humble-minded, for the kingdom of Heaven is theirs!"* (J. B. Phillips). We applaud efforts to bring ancient language into our contemporary understanding, but *happy* does not seem to have the same depth or richness as *blessed*. The word *happy* comes from the root word *hap* which means luck or chance. For those who walk in God's ways, the result is not luck or chance. People who feel blessed know they are blessed by God, which makes this different than the emotion of happiness. Anyone can experience an emotion of happiness, but only people of faith can know they are blessed by God.

Two of the Beatitudes are about being persecuted. It is hard to imagine people being happy about being persecuted, but it can be understood how they might feel blessed when others *"utter all kinds of evil against you falsely on my account."*

There is a beautiful simplicity to the Psalm *"Happy is everyone who fears the Lord, who walks in his ways."* The Psalmist reminds that those who walk in God's ways will feel blessed. Those who revere God will be blessed. May you be blessed!

PRAYER: Almighty God, guide my feet to walk in your ways. I love you, adore you and revere your holy name. Thank you for blessing me. Indeed, I feel blessed as I aspire to walk humbly with you. Amen.

The Lord is righteous; he has cut the cords of the wicked.
129:4

Why is Psalm 129 in the Bible? It is a prayer for the downfall of
Israel's enemies. The Psalmist prayers for them to *"be like the
grass on the housetops that withers before it grows up."* It is a
challenge to find inspiration from this Psalm. Fortunately, our
understanding of God's nature and character has evolved. We
have come to know God as a God of second chances, a God who
gives grace and who forgives. Perhaps the most amazing prayer of
forgiveness came from Jesus' lips, on the cross: *Then Jesus said,
"Father, forgive them; for they do not know what they are doing."*
(Luke 23:34). That is a prayer that sounds God-like. That is the
nature of one who taught *Love your enemies and pray for those
who persecute you, so that you may be children of your Father in
heaven.* Perhaps Psalm 129 is in the Bible to illustrate how the
hurt caused by an adversary can fuel anger and wishes that they be
cut off from the love of God. But, of course, that is an impossible
prayer, for the love and grace of God cannot be limited.

This Psalm does not sound like the loving, compassionate God
who is full of mercy and kindness. Throughout the bible, God
favors the word *"all."* God's way is a loving, arms-outstretched,
palms open, welcome that is inclusive. It is inconsistent with the
bible's teachings to think that God would condemn those who
know God or love God by a pathway or name different from the
Psalmist's experience. Jesus spoke far more of his coming not to
condemn but to save… to make whole. He changed a worldview
of God from judgmental and condemning to one of compassion
and forgiveness, as when he likened God to the parent of the
prodigal son. The loving parent welcomed his son home again and
did not even demand an accounting, but without a word, ran out to
him and embraced him with a hug heard around the world. That is
what God is like, said Jesus. Forgiving. Embracing. Not
condemning. From the bible's point of view, the word *"all"* is at
the center of God's heart.

354

Jesus said in John 12:32
"And I, when I am lifted up from the earth, will draw ALL people to myself."

Paul wrote to the Romans (11:32)
"For God has imprisoned all in disobedience so that he may be merciful to ALL."

He wrote to the Corinthians (1 Cor 15:22)
"For as all die in Adam, so ALL will be made alive in Christ."

And to his young friend Timothy (I Tim. 2:4-6) Paul explained how God desires
"ALL to be saved and to come to the knowledge of the truth." Paul tells of Christ Jesus *"who gave himself as a ransom for ALL"* (1 Tim. 2:4-6).

The nature of God is found in the word *"all."* The Lord our Shepherd desires the inclusion of all in the flock. God's desire is captured by the word *"all."* No one or no interpretation can limit God's grace, love, compassion or mercy because God cannot be limited. God's grace cannot be limited. God's love and inclusion cannot be limited. To limit God is impossible.
Enemies of Israel, enemies of America, enemies of any nation, enemies of the truth, or even enemies of God may do significant harm. The damage they do enflames our anger and enmity. We hate their behavior and actions. It is appropriate for us to tell God how mad we are at them and to guide us to know how to regard them. But it is not for us to pray for God to cause their downfall or to destroy them. We can understand when people feel that way, but we are bound to a God who radiates love, grace, mercy and forgiveness – even to our enemies.

PRAYER: Loving God, help us to know how to feel about people who destroy, be it truth or lives. We hate their words, their actions, their arrogance and their success. Help us to grow in your way of not hating the person but hating their behavior. Teach us to overcome evil with good. Amen.

I wait for the Lord, my soul waits, and in his word I hope.
130:5

The Psalmist waits. Waiting is a common word in the Bible. Waiting upon the Lord. Isaiah (40) wrote *"Those who wait for the LORD shall renew their strength, they shall mount up with wings like eagles."* One character in the Old Testament who developed waiting into a fine art is the prophet Habakkuk. What he did, when he did not know what to do, can inspire you for times when you do not know what to do.

Habakkuk was in Judah, the region west of the Dead Sea. They were the best of times, they were the worst of times. Judah had just experienced the exhilaration of the glorious days of a great king named Josiah. Perhaps they called it Josiah-mania. His leadership was marked by freedom, prosperity and a great religious revival. You might say they enjoyed a rising stock market, increasing property values and a bustling job market. The future looked bright. They had money, they had time and to what would you guess they turned? Materialism. Idols. Worship of the wrong things. Habakkuk called them to be good, to be righteous. That fell upon disinterested ears. His listeners were apathetic about spiritual matters. Apathy about the spiritual can be a by-product of prosperity.

Judah's old enemy, the Assyrians, had fizzled out. The threat was gone. But there is always an enemy. It almost seems like if a nation does not have an enemy it invents one. Enter the Babylonians, also known as the Chaldeans. Now the media broadcasts a new threat to Judah's good times. How does Judah respond? Rather than seeking a non-violent resolution to the threat, rather than by turning to communication and searching for a win-win solution, Judah turns directly to violence.

The dependence upon violence frustrates Habakkuk as he sees his people going the wrong way. Why, he cries, does violence rule rather than justice? Why do his people worship idols rather than Yahweh? Habakkuk does not know, but he is supposed to know because he is a prophet. He is expected to have the answers. He ought to be able to tell people what to do and how to act in those uncertain times.

So, Habakkuk goes up on the ramparts to wait for an answer from God. Ramparts are walls, like the wall surrounding a walled city or the wall around a castle. Habakkuk needed direction, did not have a map and so he went up to keep watch on the rampart and to wait upon the Lord: *I will stand at my watch post, and station myself on the rampart; I will keep watch to see what he will say to me, and what he will answer concerning my complaint... If it seems to tarry, wait for it; it will surely come.* (from Habakkuk 2).

Wait upon the Lord. Action is portrayed here not as one who has the answers but as one who knows how to wait upon God for them. Many of us are not good at waiting. We want to see the time-line, the strategic plan, the goal and the expected outcomes. We want to see more of the map. We want a GPS to display a picture of the road to follow and a voice to tell us where to turn. Waiting upon the Lord? When it feels like you are living between trapezes in the air with nothing to hang onto, waiting is not what you have in mind.

When God answered Habakkuk, God said *"For there is still a vision for the appointed time...*
If it seems to tarry, WAIT for it. It will surely come." Might that be the bible's message for you? When you are between trapezes, indecisive or uncertain about what to do next, God says to you: *Trust me. Have faith. Wait expectantly. Trust ME.* There is still a vision for the appointed time. It may seem like it is not coming according to your timetable, but wait for it.

The word *wait* in the bible is a synonym for the word *trust*. When facing an unknown future, remind yourself that waiting and trusting is frequently the best response. In so much of your life you have been taught to take initiative and to act. In uncertainty, learn that it is not completely up to you but to you and God. Live by faith.

PRAYER: Dear God, I can be impatient. I want to know more of the plan and the timetable. When I do not know what to do or which course of action to take, teach me to wait upon you, to hope in your word, to trust that you will lead, and to live by faith. Amen.

But I have calmed and quieted my soul, like a weaned child with its mother; my soul is like the weaned child that is with me.
131:2

The Psalmist frequently turned to God for his sense of inner peace or to have the Lord restore his spirit. This time, he took responsibility for his own self-care: *"I have calmed and quieted my soul."* A great lesson is there for us, for there are times we ask God to do something for us that we should do for ourselves. It is as though we ask God to calm and quiet our inner being and God responds "First you take responsibility for taking better care of yourself."

We know, for example, the importance of getting exercise, hydration, and participating in calming activities that reduce stress. We need to do those for ourselves. Research indicates the importance of sleep. If we choose to get a good night's sleep, we reap benefits. If we make self-defeating choices which reduce sleep, we suffer consequences. Sleep is vital for learning and memory, and lack of sleep impacts our health, safety, and longevity.

Consider the impact of sleep based on research studies at the Division of Sleep Medicine at Harvard Medical School:
"The quantity and quality of sleep have a profound impact on learning and memory. Research suggests that sleep helps learning and memory in two distinct ways. First, a sleep-deprived person cannot focus attention optimally and therefore cannot learn efficiently. Second, sleep itself has a role in the consolidation of memory, which is essential for learning new information."

"A lack of adequate sleep impacts learning and memory. When we are sleep deprived, our focus, attention, and vigilance drift, making it more difficult to receive information. Without adequate sleep and rest, over-worked neurons can no longer function to coordinate information properly. We lose our ability to access previously learned information.

In addition, our interpretation of events may be affected. We lose our ability to make sound decisions because we can no longer accurately assess the situation, plan accordingly, and choose the correct behavior. Judgment becomes impaired."

The Psalmist did not say how he calmed and quieted his soul, but there is a good chance he went into nature, perhaps as he prayed, sang, meditated or simply walked. Thomas Moore in his book *Meditations* wrote *"At the sight of nothing, the soul rejoices."* Multitasking does not calm and quiet the soul. Take brief sabbaticals during your day when you do nothing, to allow your soul to rejoice.

An article by Deborah Ward in *Psychology Today* offered told about benefits from walking in nature. First, walking somewhere quiet provides a reprieve from the noise that taxes our sensitive nerves. Second, spending time alone rewards us with the peace of only our own thoughts for company. You need solitude on a regular basis. Third, natural elements like plants, trees, water, and sunlight have been said to absorb negative energy. Perhaps we feel calmer around them simply because they are part of the living world and so we feel connected to them, and yet they do not make any demands on us except to appreciate them. Fourth, walking provides a significant benefit because it helps to relieve stress. Brisk walking boosts endorphins, the feel-good hormones that improve your mood and lower stress and mild depression. Walking gives you more energy, which also improves your positive feelings. Fifth, walking through green spaces can put the brain into a meditative state, allowing you to pay attention to the world around you, while creating the calmness needed for reflection. It's in this calm, quiet reflective state where our creativity can flourish.

A story is told of a group of high-power business executives who decided that they wanted to go on a safari to Africa. They thought they would enjoy the adventure of an exotic wilderness, see some wild animals in their own habitat, and be challenged to the rigors of finding big game. They purchased the right safari wardrobe, secured their plane tickets, and headed off to the Dark Continent.

When they arrived, they realized that although they had incredible self-confidence and skill, they needed to hire guides to lead them into the bush. They contracted with some local natives to serve as guides and the next day they set out for their hunt.

The business executives plowed into their adventure the way they charged into their careers. They decided that they would take the lead out in front and the native guides would follow them. A guide suggested that having the guides follow may not be the wisest approach because the executives did not know the terrain. But that is the way the executives wanted it: Out in front, charging onward and upward. The native guides followed, carrying the executives' packs.

As the executives rushed into the bush, they started to get ahead of the guides. That is okay, they thought. They will catch up. They hurried ahead, anxious to get to their destination. After all, these were goal-driven achievers. They got further and further ahead and soon they were out of sight of the guides. They continued charging into the forest. After a while it seemed like they were going in circles. Inevitably they became lost.

The executives sat down and waited. They wondered how far behind the guides were. They wondered even if the guides would come after them. They waited... impatiently. Finally, off in the distance they saw through their binoculars the silhouette of the guides approaching over a distant hill. The guides were heading their direction but they were not hurrying. Their wait continued.

The guides finally caught up. The executives chastised them: Where were you? What took you so long? Why didn't you hurry? When they had a chance to speak, the guides explained, through their interpreter. They said *"We tried to walk faster but then we decided that we could not walk faster than our souls could go."*

Your soul can only go so fast. Then your effectiveness, mood and even your health diminishes. Like the Psalmist, pursue activities that calm and quiet your soul. Walk, but not faster than your soul can go.

PRAYER: Slow me down, Lord. Gently nudge me to take responsibility to calm and quiet my soul. Increase my motivation to get rest, take brief vacations of solitude, hydrate, get exercise, and walk in nature. O Divine Shepherd, lead me to lie down in green pastures. I know you can restore my soul, but let me do for myself that which reduces stress, busy feelings, and anxiety. And when I'm not so good at self-care or get too lazy, push me out the door into the beauty of the earth. Amen.

ONE-HUNDRED-AND-THIRTY-TWO

For your servant David's sake do not turn away the face of your anointed one.
132:10

This Psalm is about the Psalmist's belief that Zion is God's eternal dwelling place and that David
the king is God's anointed. Anointing is the practice of rubbing oil on a person, usually on the head. *"You anoint my head with oil,"* says Psalm 23. In the Hebrew Scriptures, prophets were anointed, priests were anointed, and royal leaders like kings were anointed. King David was anointed. This practice of anointing meant to consecrate for the office. The Apostle Paul believed that followers of Jesus were anointed by the Holy Spirit: *"It is God who establishes us with you in Christ and has anointed us..."* (2 Corinthians 1:21). It this case anointing came to mean dedicated to the service of God.

The literal translation of the Hebrew word *mashiach* (messiah) is *anointed*. *Messiah* means *anointed*. When *Messiah* is translated into Greek, the word is *Christos*, meaning "the anointed one." Christians believe that Jesus was anointed by God, chosen by God, and sent by God into the world so that the world may be *made whole* (*sozo*, also translated as *saved*). When asked by the Samaritan women at the well if he was the Messiah, Jesus answered that he was: *"The woman said to him, 'I know that Messiah is coming' (who is called Christ). 'When he comes, he will proclaim all things to us.' Jesus said to her, 'I am he, the one who is speaking to you'."* (John 4:25, 26). Three revealing words: *I am he.*

Recall that Jesus, God's anointed, was born in the city and of the lineage of David – Bethlehem. Here lies a special connection between Jesus and David. They are relatives. They are both anointed and consecrated or made holy for service to God in the highest order. They were both called King, although not in the same way. They shared another connection, as shepherds. David the shepherd boy tended his flocks.

David likened God as a shepherd in his most famous Psalm (23): *"The Lord is my shepherd."* Jesus chose as his identity the image of a shepherd, tending God's flock and leading people to God: *"I am the good shepherd. The good shepherd lays down his life for the sheep. The hired hand, who is not the shepherd and does not own the sheep, sees the wolf coming and leaves the sheep and runs away – and the wolf snatches them and scatters them. The hired hand runs away because a hired hand does not care for the sheep. I am the good shepherd. I know my own and my own know me."* (John 10:11-14). So, in the shadow of the Shepherd's staff is found the symbol of David, of Jesus, and of God.

In Psalm 23, the Psalmist transformed this rich and profound idea of anointing into a soothing metaphor for how the Lord your Shepherd can anoint you. *Thou anointest my head with oil* (King James Version).

You might wonder why in the world would a shepherd anoint a sheep's head with oil? Perhaps you conjure images of anointing the forehead with a holy oil to sooth or to symbolize God's healing touch. Does it suggest for you some sort of religious ritual? Actually, the meaning is basically about bugs.

Years ago, I moved to Maine and was out mowing the lawn on a calm sunny summer morning. An itch caused me to swat my arm and then another until I looked down to see blood trickling down my arm. What caused it? Black flies. In Maine they are known as *"no-see-ums"* because they are so small, they are hardly seen. Small as they may be, they can be severely irritating and will keep even dedicated fishers off the ponds and ardent campers out of the woods just to avoid them. No-see-ums are what prompts this verse.

Phillip Keller, who was a sheep herd manager and who wrote a book about the Psalm from the shepherd's point-of-view, says that for the sheep man *"summer time is fly time."* Hordes of insects appear with the warm weather. Only people who have kept livestock are aware of the serious problems for animals presented by insects in the summer.

Flies are everywhere in the summertime and the worst of these are tiny little bot flies or nasal flies. The nasal flies buzz about the sheep's head, attempting to deposit their eggs on the damp, mucous membranes of the sheep's nose. Keller explained that if the nasal flies succeed, the eggs will hatch to form small, slender, worm-like larvae which work their way up the nasal passages into the sheep's head. They burrow into the flesh and create an intense irritation and inflammation. So, the sheep try anything to get rid of the irritation. They will deliberately beat their heads against trees, rocks, posts or brush. They will rub them in the soil and thrash around against woody growth.

If you have ever been chased by a bee or a wasp, you know what it is like to run away from them. Keller told how in extreme cases of intense infestation, a sheep may run itself to death in a frenzied endeavor to gain relief from the aggravation. And so, to prevent this from happening in the first place, the shepherd creates a homemade mixture of oil, tar and spices to spear over the sheep's nose and head as protection against the nasal flies. It works, and keeps the flies from getting up the sheep's nose. The shepherd anoints the sheep's head with oil to prevent the nasal flies from bothering the sheep.

Up your nose is a yucky picture! Yet, how often do we use the phrase *bugged*? People bug us. Don't bug me. Pressures bug us. It does not have to be big stuff. It is the little things that can bug you, raise your stress level, and make you miserable. Richard Carlson wrote a book with a perceptive title that said: <u>*Don't Sweat the Small Stuff – and it's all small stuff*</u>. Indeed, it really is the little things, like tiny bot flies, that can bug you most.

We seem most able to confront and deal with big challenges. It is the little things that bug us. Never underestimate the power of the small stuff to get up your nose, under your skin, make you unhappy and cause you to worry. The small stuff can kill you... physically or spiritually. *Thou anointest my head with oil* is a picture of irritations in your life and how the small stuff bugs you and can drive you to distraction.

365

Behavioral scientists who study how people worry indicate that most worry is wasted. In fact, worrying only makes things worse and is bad for health. Jesus knew how people worried. He taught *"So do not worry about tomorrow, for tomorrow will bring worries of its own. Today's trouble is enough for today"* (Matthew 6:34)

Like sheep, we cannot stop many of our worries. We are not skilled at allowing today's trouble to be sufficient for today, for we like to add tomorrow's worries to the mix as well. Like sheep, we cannot help ourselves and need the shepherd to anoint our heads with oil to keep the small stuff from bugging us.

Notice that a sheep cannot anoint its own head. It relies on the shepherd to care for it in this way. That is a good message for you, to realize that you need the Shepherd to help you keep the little things from bugging you. You cannot do that for yourself. Not only that, the anointing does not last once and for all. You need it constantly. When small stuff is bothering you, go to the Shepherd. Then, that Divine oil soothes your head, calms your spirit, and refreshes your soul so that you feel safe to lie down in green pastures and rest beside still waters.

The Shepherd understands how the small stuff can stress you out, make you anxious, and bother you, so God anoints your head with oil which transforms your behavior, mood and attitude from distraction to peace. When you find it difficult to cope, invite the Shepherd to apply the oil of God's spirit to your mind. The Serenity Prayer reminds that God gives you serenity to accept what cannot be changed, courage to change what should be changed, and wisdom to distinguish the one from the other.

David was anointed as a king. Jesus, of the house and lineage of David, was The Anointed One. Messiah. Christ. Prophets, priests and everyday people have been anointed as they dedicate their lives in service to God.

And the Lord your Shepherd anoints you to keep the little things from bugging you and driving you crazy with worry, so that your spirit may be calmed and your soul refreshed.

PRAYER: You, Lord, are my Shepherd. When I get so bugged with small stuff that it takes away the qualify of my life, the creativity of my efforts, and the concentration of my mind, please anoint my head with oil to prevent the little things from irritating me. May I focus my eyes upon you, for when my eyes are upon the Shepherd, they are not upon the worries or problems that annoy. Amen.

ONE-HUNDRED-AND-THIRTY-THREE

How very good and pleasant it is when kindred live together in unity!
133:1

In this short Psalm, the Psalmist observes the blessed of unity, of kindred living together in unity. Kindred. Family. Unity? In families, unity is most certainly good, pleasant and blessed but in reality, it is also rare.

Sometimes people look around at other families and think they see the appearance of pleasant unity. Beneath the surface, there is often brokenness. Every family, at least in the extended family, carries some hurt. We might be inclined to think that there is no "normal" family, but one will come along to dispel our generalization, so it is safer at least to think that a great many families suffer some pain, often quietly.

Consider, for example, the basic cultural bond of unity: marriage. The American Psychological Association notes: "*Marriage and divorce are both common experiences. In Western cultures, more than 90 percent of people marry by age 50. Healthy marriages are good for couples' mental and physical health. They are also good for children; growing up in a happy home protects children from mental, physical, educational and social problems. However, about 40 to 50 percent of married couples in the United States divorce. The divorce rate for subsequent marriages is even higher.*" Counting divorces is not an exact science, for many states do not report their divorce rate, but overall, it is high. It would be safe to say that between a third and a half of all marriages fail. The impact on children and other family members increases the number of kindred who do not live together in unity.

There are marriages that continue, but family unity is hurt by children who estrange themselves from their parents, parents who will not speak to a child, brothers and sisters who become alienated, and all kinds of other strained family relationships that hurt. So, people learn to cope.

Some move on in healthy directions. Others suffer open wounds that will not heal. And who could not agree with the Psalmist's observation? *How very good and pleasant it is when kindred live together in unity!* It is good, but in reality, it is rare.

When there is not unity, there is brokenness. The Psalmist also knows that *"The Lord is near to the brokenhearted, and saves the crushed in spirit."* (34:18). We are comforted and strengthened to know that even in our valleys of dark shadows, God is with us. We join with the Psalmist to celebrate where there is unity in our kindred, and we ask God to be near when there is brokenness.

PRAYER: Loving God, thank you for the unity I have experienced with my family. Where there has not been unity, I ask for your healing touch. I pray for reconciliation where possible, healing from brokenness, and fortitude to move forward. Where my spirit is crushed, let your spirit renew me and make me whole again. Amen.

Come, bless the Lord, all you servants of the Lord, who stand by night in the house of the Lord! Lift up your hands to the holy place, and bless the Lord.
134:1, 2

This brief Psalm again blesses the Lord. A large portion of the Psalms praise God, which reminds us too to fill our prayers with praise. One of the best ways to praise God is with song. Consider the words of a poem by St. Francis of Assisi, transformed into song by William H. Draper and titled *All Creatures of Our God and King*. May these words guide you into prayer:

All creatures of our God and King,
Lift up your voice and with us sing,
Alleluia! Alleluia!
Thou burning sun with golden beam,
Thou silver moon with softer gleam!
O praise Him! O praise Him!
Alleluia! Alleluia! Alleluia!

Thou rushing wind that art so strong,
Ye clouds that sail in heav'n along,
O praise Him! Alleluia!
Thou rising moon, in praise rejoice,
Ye lights of evening, find a voice!
O praise Him! O praise Him!
Alleluia! Alleluia! Alleluia!

Thou flowing water, pure and clear,
Make music for thy Lord to hear,
O praise Him! Alleluia!
Thou fire so masterful and bright,
That givest man both warmth and light.
O praise Him! O praise Him!
Alleluia! Alleluia! Alleluia!

And all ye men of tender heart,
Forgiving others, take your part,
O praise Him! Alleluia!
Ye who long pain and sorrow bear,
Praise God and on Him cast your care!
O praise Him! O praise Him!
Alleluia! Alleluia! Alleluia!

Let all things their Creator bless,
And worship Him in humbleness,
O praise Him! Alleluia!
Praise, praise the Father, praise the Son,
And praise the Spirit, Three in One!
O praise Him! O praise Him!
Alleluia! Alleluia! Alleluia!

PRAYER: Dear God, I lift up my voice to bless your name and praise you. Alleluia! May I worship you in humbleness and never grow weary of praising your holy name. Throughout this day, may this thought be on my mind: I praise you. I praise you. Alleluia! Amen.

ONE-HUNDRED-AND-THIRTY-FIVE

Praise the Lord, for the Lord is good; sing to his name, for he is gracious.
135:3

Barbara was one of the most gracious people I have ever met. She was always kind, helpful, courteous, uplifting, and generous. In conversations, she focused upon the other person rather than talking about herself. You know someone like that, don't you? When you think of the word *gracious*, who pops into your mind? When we meet a gracious person, she or he radiates a goodness and gentleness which inspires us to try to become more like them.

Graciousness is defined by beautiful words: courteous, kind, pleasant, polite, civil, chivalrous, well mannered, decorous, civilized, tactful, diplomatic. When someone is a good loser, in a sport or at an attempt to achieve a goal, we say that they are gracious in defeat and we admire them – not so much for their success, but for their graciousness. In the world of faith, a gracious person is merciful, forgiving, compassionate, kind, kindly, lenient, pitying, forbearing, humane, mild, tenderhearted, sympathetic and giving of grace. Full of grace. A gracious person is a graceful person, someone who at least attempts to not hurt others' feelings with clumsy words or thoughtless deeds. To live in grace is to walk lightly and leave the world blessed by your presence.

God is gracious, wrote the Psalmist. The Hebrew word for *gracious* means to bend or stoop to an inferior. Imagine a picture of God bending or stooping to an inferior... tenderly, lovingly, forgiving, accepting… God bending down to you, just as you are, with grace. The New Testament word *grace* means the undeserved or un-earned forgiveness and acceptance of God. A good synonym for grace is the word *anyway*. No matter what you have done or have not done, no matter what mistakes you have made, God forgives you *anyway*, loves you *anyway*, and accepts you *anyway*. That is grace. Bending or stooping over to you, God gives you mercy and is gracious to you.

Gracious is what God is like, with all the beautiful words listed above. For that, the Psalmist praises God and so should we. We are the recipients of God's grace, kindness, compassion, forgiveness, forbearance, courteousness, pleasantness, leniency, tenderness, sympathy, empathy and goodness. God stoops to you and is gracious to you. For all of that, praise God!

The Lord bless you and keep you.
The Lord make his face to shine upon you, and be gracious to you.
The Lord lift up his countenance upon you, and give you peace.
(Numbers 6:24-26)

PRAYER: Thank you, Gracious God, for your graciousness to me. I feel unworthy of it and am deeply grateful for your gift of grace. Lord, help me to be a more gracious person. I didn't seem to come packaged that way. It is not in my nature. Infuse me with your spirit, inspire me and teach me how to be more compassionate, forgiving, merciful, kind and empathetic with others. Slow me down to gaze into another's eyes and see them as a good person whom you love. And perhaps once in a while, may another see in my eyes an acceptance, empathy and a grace that flows out of you into me. Amen.

ONE-HUNDRED-AND-THIRTY-SIX

O give thanks to the Lord, for he is good, for his steadfast love endures forever... who divided the Red Sea in two, for his steadfast love endures forever;
136:1, 13

Psalm 136 gives thanks to the Lord, lists things God has done and after each item repeats the refrain *for his steadfast love endures forever.* One of those items, found in verse 13, tells how the Lord divided the Red Sea in two. If people were asked to name some of God's miracles, that would be among the top answers.

Miracles, signs and wonders in the bible are undeniably a part of the bible's story, designed to glorify God, to show God's compassion and to encourage faith. There are miracles of nature, like parting the Red Sea or walking on water. There are miracles of healing. Most dramatically, in the New Testament, there is the raising of the dead.

With miracles, you could get so hung up about how and why they happened that you miss the message. Every time you come to a miracle in the bible, ask yourself: What's the message? Consider the parting of the Red Sea. Forget for the moment whether it was the Red Sea or the shallow, narrow, muddy Reed Sea just a bit north of the Red Sea, which is a more likely place for the Hebrews to have traveled lightly through the swampy mud while the heavy armored Egyptian chariots literally got stuck in the mud. It is like there are places where you could toss a rock over the Mississippi River at its narrowest places.

A deeper truth illustrated by the Red Sea story is that God opens unseen paths for you. When you are up against an impasse, when your back is against the sea with no place to turn and no escape route in sight, God can open unseen paths for you and lead you through to safety.

374

When your way is unseen, it requires blind trust, which is the meaning behind Hebrews 11:1: *"Now faith is the assurance of things hoped for, the conviction of things not seen."*

There is always hope. *"We,"* said Paul, *"look not to the things that are seen but to the things that are unseen, for the things that are seen are transient, but the things that are unseen are eternal."* That kind of hope cannot be dashed, for you have placed your times in God's hand.

America's earliest African-Americans had a saying: *"When there's no way out, God makes a way out of no way."* That is a message from the Red Sea story. When you can see no way out, God can make a way out of no way.

A story is told about a painting titled *Checkmate.* It is a picture of Mephistopheles and Dr. Faust which depicts the Mephistopheles – the chief devil in the Faust legend – sitting on one side of the chessboard and Faust sitting on the other side. All of the pieces are gone except the king, the queen and one rook for Faust. The devil has him cornered and he has a smirk on his face. There are no more moves. There is no way out. Faust is in trouble. The devil is just waiting for him and in the painting, you can read his lips as he mouths the word *"checkmate."*

A group toured the gallery where the painting hung. They studied at the picture as the tour guide explained how much the painting cost, who painted it, what the different textures were, how long it took to paint it, and other artistic details. Then the group moved on to another area. Nobody noticed that when the group moved on, one person stayed right there in front of that painting and kept staring and pacing back and forth. The man was scrutinizing the painting and sensed that something was not right about it. As he paced back and forth, the group moved away and was two corridors away when all of a sudden echoing through those marble halls they heard this man hollering at the top of his lungs: *"It's a lie! It's a lie! The king has another move."* Nobody knew that the man in the museum was the reigning international chess champion from Russia.

As a master he could see what the ordinary chess player could not see: there was another move for the king. It was not checkmate.

Are there not moments in your life when you feel checkmated? You become stuck, like a sheep entangled in thorns. You see no clear way out of your dilemma or conflict. Then along comes the Shepherd to untangle you. The King of Kings had another move that you could not see. When the Lord opens unseen paths for you and guides you into another move, that seems like a miracle. For you, it may feel like a parting of the seas. And then, like the Psalmist, you are led to proclaim *O give thanks to the Lord, for he is good, for his steadfast love endures forever.*

PRAYER: O Lord my Shepherd, when I am backed up against the sea with no way out, I pray for you to lead me into a way out of no way. When I get entangled in thorns and am unable to free myself, come to me with your Shepherd's staff to free me from challenges where I cannot free myself. There have been so many times in my life, O God, where you have led me in a new direction which I could not envision. I give thanks to you, O Lord, for you are good and your steadfast love endures forever. Amen.

ONE-HUNDRED-AND-THIRTY-SEVEN

By the rivers of Babylon – there we sat down and there we wept when we remembered Zion. On the willows there we hung up our harps. For there our captors asked us for songs, and our tormentors asked for mirth, saying, "Sing us one of the songs of Zion!"
137:1-3

By the rivers of Babylon – there we sat down and there we wept when we remembered Zion. This is a lament over the destruction of Jerusalem. It is a folk song. There is no other Psalm like this, which sings a hauntingly beautiful folk song... *"By the waters of Babylon..."*

Zion was Jerusalem, which David had conquered for the Jews. Babylon, 550 miles across the desert to the west, was where these Jews were held captive and tormented. Zion was their homeland, now plundered by the enemy. They were held captive in a foreign land, by the rivers of Babylon, and the men holding them captive ordered them to sing a folk song about their homeland of Zion – sort of like, from The Sound of Music: *"Edelweiss, Edelweiss, Bless my homeland forever."*

Babylon is smack dab in the middle of the cradle of civilization, at the place where civilization began, in the valley of the Tigris and Euphrates Rivers. Today it is called Iraq, bordering on Iran. Before it was known as Iraq and Iran, it was called Babylon.

Babylon was the capital city of ancient Mesopotamia.

Babylon was then the largest and most beautiful city in the Middle East, with its renowned Hanging Gardens and massive walls.

Babylon was one of the seven wonders of the ancient world. The Greek historian Herodotus (484-425 BC) reported that Babylon's splendor surpassed any city of the known world. AAA would have given it a five-star rating.

In the greatest city of the ancient world, the Jews were held in captivity by the waters of Babylon – hundreds of miles from their beloved homeland of Zion. *By the waters of Babylon, there we sat down and wept, when we remembered Zion.*

On the willows there we hung up our lyres. There were willow trees along the shores. Lyres were stringed musical instruments. *For there our captors required of us songs, and our tormentors... saying, "Sing us one of the songs of Zion!"* It was an order. The guards had heard the evocative melodies of their homeland. Now their tormentors required them to sing songs of Zion.

People who are oppressed have folk songs. They have stories, heroes, jokes, and memories. It is not something you get over, as POW's can tell you. You learn to move on, but the memories, folk songs, and stories are always there.

There is a modern song based on Psalm 137 by Boney M, a Euro-Caribbean vocal group created by German record producer Frank Farian. It is titled *By the Rivers of Babylon*. Look it up on the internet, listen to it and you will not be able to stop singing it. The lyrics, from the Psalm, go like this:

By the rivers of Babylon, there we sat down
Yeah we wept, when we remembered Zion

By the rivers of Babylon, there we sat down
Yeah we wept, when we remembered Zion

When the wicked
Carried us away in captivity
Required from us a song
Now how shall we sing the Lord's song in a strange land

When the wicked
Carried us away in captivity
Requiring of us a song
Now how shall we sing the Lord's song in a strange land

Yeah, yeah, yeah, yeah, yeah let the words of our mouth and the
meditations of our heart
Be acceptable in thy sight here tonight

Let the words of our mouth and the meditation of our hearts
Be acceptable in thy sight here tonight

By the rivers of Babylon, there we sat down
Yeah we wept, when we remembered Zion

By the rivers of Babylon, there we sat down
Yeah we wept, when we remembered Zion

By the rivers of Babylon (dark tears of Babylon)
There we sat down (you got to sing a song)
Yeah we wept, (sing a song of love)
When we remember Zion (yeah yeah yeah yeah yeah)

By the rivers of Babylon (rough bits of Babylon)
There we sat down (you hear the people cry)
Yeah we wept (they need their god)
When we remember Zion (ooh, have the power)

By the rivers of Babylon, there we sat down
Yeah we wept, when we remembered Zion.

PRAYER: God of all peoples, I pray today for people who are oppressed or held captive. It is hard to believe in this modern day that there are still slaves, held against their will. I pray for those who have had to move away from their homeland to escape threats, danger, oppression or violence. Be with them, cradle them in your loving arms, and guide them to safety. O Lord, make me an instrument of your peace and your welcome... an extravagant welcome to those in need or seeking shelter. Amen.

ONE-HUNDRED-AND-THIRTY-EIGHT

On the day I called, you answered me, you increased my strength of soul.
138:3

Your spirit strength has more to do with your ability to endure or even thrive under adversity than anything else. When the Psalmist did not have enough strength of soul, he called upon God and God increased the strength of his spirit. Perhaps you have witnessed people of faith who faced insurmountable obstacles or heart-wrenching challenges who somehow were able to remain strong and to maintain a positive attitude. This is because of strength of soul.

This Psalm reminds of a gem from Paul's Letter to the Romans (5:3-5): *"We also boast in our sufferings, knowing that suffering produces endurance, and endurance produces character, and character produces hope, and hope does not disappoint us, because God's love has been poured into our hearts through the Holy Spirit that has been given to us."*

At first blush, what you encounter is a long, wandering sentence that runs on, so that by the time you get to the end, you forgot the beginning. But then, as you internalize it, you begin to appreciate the rhythm, the poetic pattern and the journey on which this verse leads you.

The Revise Standard Version begins *"We rejoice in our sufferings…"* That is enough to stop you in your tracks. When it comes to suffering, rejoicing is not the first activity that comes to mind. If anything, we rejoice when we are not suffering or when suffering has passed by. But to rejoice in your suffering? That begs for an explanation and Paul provides it.

Paul is addressing people of faith. People of faith suffer like anyone else. By becoming a Christian, a person does not escape the same sort of challenges that all people encounter.

However, the person of faith possesses an attitude that changes how they see the difficulties. Paul detailed this in another poetic pattern when he wrote to the Corinthians (1 Corinthians 4:8-10):
"We are afflicted in every way, but not crushed;
perplexed, but not driven to despair;
persecuted, but not forsaken;
struck down, but not destroyed;
always carrying in the body the death of Jesus,
so that the life of Jesus may also be made visible in our bodies."

People of faith will not be crushed, will not be driven to despair, will not be destroyed. People of faith who possess a strength of soul recognize the bad but look to the good, acknowledge there is darkness but bask in the light, grieve from loss, but find comfort and strength beyond their own, and they worry about what they see, but hope in the unseen. Even when people of faith experience the worst, they cling to their trust that the best is yet to come, because God is good... all the time. All the time... God is good.

Now Paul addresses his gem to the Romans:
"We rejoice in our sufferings,
knowing that suffering produces endurance,
and endurance produces character,
and character produces hope,
and hope does not disappoint us..."

Suffering, Paul writes, produces endurance. The Greek word Paul used for *endurance* is "hupomone," which means more than endurance. A good translation for *"hupomone"* is *fortitude*. Suffering produces an attitude of fortitude. *"hupomone"* is the spirit which believes it can overcome. Fortitude is the strength of soul which does not passively endure but which actively overcomes the choices and difficulties of life. *"hupomone"* is the hope that everything in life is material which God can use for God's glory and for your betterment. Suffering produces an attitude of fortitude, and fortitude produces character, and character produces hope.

When Beethoven was threatened with deafness he said: *"I will take life by the throat."* That is *"hupomone."* Fortitude. A woman going through a difficult time was told by a friend: *"Sorrow colors life, doesn't it?"* *"YES,"* she replied, *"and I propose to choose the color."* That is an attitude of fortitude. That is the attitude of people of faith who believe that adversity will make you stronger and that suffering produces an attitude of fortitude.

Helen Keller has one of the best definitions of *hupomone*, of fortitude. She said: *"Although the world is full of suffering, it is also full of the overcoming of it."*

Cripple him, and you have a Sir Walter Scott. Bury him in the snows of Valley Forge, and you have a George Washington. Raise him in abject poverty, and you have an Abraham Lincoln. Inform her she will never read beyond the third-grade level nor learn to speak because she became deaf at the age of 18 months, and you have a Heather Whitestone, Miss America. Blind him in a freak boxing accident, tell him to stay home and accept his dependence upon others, and watch how Morris Frank creates "The Seeing Eye" organization to train seeing-eye dogs for the blind. Strike him down with infantile paralysis, and he becomes a Franklin D. Roosevelt. Burn him so severely in a schoolhouse fire that the doctors say he will never walk again, and you have a Glenn Cunningham, who set a world's record in 1934 for running a mile. Burden her with one of the worst demons known to humankind, with bi-polar illness manic-depressive – and Patty Duke wins three Emmy Awards – one for portraying Helen Keller in the movie "The Miracle Worker." Call him a slow learner, retarded, lazy, and write him off as uneducable and you have an Albert Einstein. Let improper medical treatment blind her at age six, and you have a musician – Fanny Jane Crosby – who wrote more than 8,000 hymns and songs. *"This is my story, this is my song..."* she wrote in her hymn *"Blessed Assurance."*

People with a strength of soul learn to...

Use disappointment as material for patience.
Use success as material for thankfulness.
Use uncertainty as material for perseverance.
Use danger as material for courage.
Use praise people give us as material for humility.
Use ingratitude of others as material to remind ourselves to say "Thank you" to God.
Use rejection as material for determination.
Use suffering as material for fortitude.

No matter what happens to you, when God's love is poured into you, everything is material and can be used by God for good. And when strength of soul is lacking, call upon God and God will strengthen you. We have this hope because we are people of faith. Knowing in our hearts that suffering produces an attitude of fortitude could lead even to rejoicing in our sufferings.

Strength of soul provides an attitude of fortitude when dealing with problems. Consider adopting this credo as your own for when you face problems:

I will be a different person when this problem is past. I will be a wiser, stronger, more patient person or I will be sour, cynical, bitter, disillusioned, and angry. It all depends on what I do with this problem. Each problem can make me a better person or a worse person. It can bring me closer to God, or it can drive me away from God. It can build my faith or it can shatter my faith. It all depends on my attitude. I intend to be a better person when this problem leaves me than I was when it met me.
(from Robert Schuller, Move Ahead with Possibility Thinking)

PRAYER: Generous God, thank you for all the times you have strengthened my spirit and infused me with an attitude of fortitude to deal with opportunities as well as difficulties. I am glad to know that I can call upon you, again and again, for increased strength. Charge my polarity in a positive direction so that I will face my future with wisdom, strength, patience and faith. When faced with a problem, guide me to intend to be a better person when the problem leaves me than I was when it met me. Thank you, Dear God. Amen.

O Lord, you have searched me and known me. You know when I sit down and when I rise up; you discern my thoughts from far away. You search out my path and my lying down, and are acquainted with all my ways. Even before a word is on my tongue, O Lord, you know it completely. You hem me in, behind and before, and lay your hand upon me. Such knowledge is too wonderful for me; it is so high that I cannot attain it.
139:1-6

Psalm 139 is a prayer and a poem. It is a favorite Psalm. Try this exercise: Go through and circle the pronouns that relate to the first-person singular – I, me, my, mine. Then circled the pronouns or titles that relate to God – you, yours, O Lord. Forty-nine times this short Psalm uses the first-person singular pronoun I, me, my, or mine. You see why this is such a personal Psalm. Thirty-five times the Psalm uses a pronoun or title that relates to God. This is a Psalm about you and God. It is like the title of a classic book by Martin Buber titled *I – Thou*. That is what Psalm 139 is, an I – Thou relationship. New versions of the bible use the word *You* instead of *Thou*, but there is a poetic beauty to the old word *Thou*: *O LORD, thou hast searched me, and known me. Thou knowest my downsitting and mine uprising, thou understandest my thought afar off.*

The Psalm has a fascinating organization to it.

Verses 1- 6 are about the OMNISCIENCE of God. Omniscience means God is all-knowing. This section focuses upon God's knowledge: what does God know? The psalmist thinks about that and meditates on the idea of how God knows everything: *O LORD, you have searched me and known me.* Sometimes you wish you were understood. This section affirms that God not only knows you but understands you. God knows what you are going to say before you say it... *Even before a word is on my tongue, O LORD, you know it completely.*

Verses 7-10 are about the OMNIPRESENCE of God. Omnipresence means God exists everywhere. *Where can I go from your spirit? Or where can I flee from your presence?* Perhaps there are times you might like to flee from God's presence, to hide behind some Kryptonite lead-lined wall where even Superman could not see you. The idea of being watched all the time is unsettling. That does not seem to be what the Psalmist is saying here – it is not that he wants to flee, but rather, if he were to flee or to be far away, God would be even there. If you were to sail to uncharted waters, as you may feel you when you find yourself in territory where there is no map – into problems, complexity, conflict, lack of control, uncertainty – God will be even there. *If I take the wings of the morning, and dwell in the uttermost parts of the sea; Even there shall thy hand lead me, and thy right hand shall hold me.*

Verses 11 and 12 are about DARKNESS and LIGHT, a common theme throughout the bible. *If I say, "Surely the darkness shall cover me, and the light around me become night," even the darkness is not dark to you; the night is as bright as the day, for darkness is as light to you.* The Psalmist testifies to his belief that God created the light and the darkness. Darkness is a symbol for the unknown. What if darkness should cover him? It may never happen, but what if it does? That is a worry for all of us. Behavioral scientists have documented time and again how most of what you worry about will never happen. And Jesus taught *Do not worry about tomorrow, for tomorrow will bring worries of its own... let the day's own trouble be sufficient for the day.* When darkness appears to cover us or to cover things that go wrong in our lives, in our nation, in our church, in our school, in threats to our safety or peace, we wonder if darkness could win. Even there, affirms the Psalmist, God's light will lift you up because in God's presence, the night is as bright as the day.

Verses 13-18 are about GOD YOUR MAKER. *For it was you who formed my inward parts; you knit me together in my mother's womb. I praise you, for I am fearfully and wonderfully made. Wonderful are your works; that I know very well.* Here is the creation story in poetry, reaffirming as in Genesis that God created the world and that everything God creates is good. Because God created you, that means that there is something sacred and holy about your body. God formed your inward parts, says the Psalmist, even before you were born. *Your eyes beheld my unformed substance.* Imagine a time when you were an unformed substance. God knew you even then and formed you from a formless void.

Verse 23 and 24 are the climax to this Psalm prayer, about YIELDING TO GOD'S LEADING. Everything else has led up to this pinnacle. Psalm 139 concludes by a surrendering of the Psalmist's own will, a yielding to God's will, and a readiness to be led. *Search me, O God, and know my heart; test me and know my thoughts. See if there is any wicked way in me, and lead me in the way everlasting.* These verses remind of the hymn *Spirit of the Living God*:

Spirit of the Living God,
Fall a-fresh on me.
Spirit of the Living God,
Fall a-fresh on me.
Melt me, mold me,
Fill me, use me.
Spirit of the Living God,
Fall a-fresh on me.

The Psalm and the hymn are interwoven...
Try me and know my thoughts. MELT ME.
See if there be any wicked way in me. MOLD ME.
In your book were written all the days that were formed for me. FILL ME.
Lead me in the way everlasting. USE ME.

May that be our prayer, inspired by the poetic beauty of Psalm 139.

PRAYER: O Lord, you have searched me and known me. You formed me and made me and now you know me. You know my thoughts and my words – I pray to have thoughts and use words which glorify you. You are with me wherever I go and if I am in a tough place, even there your hand leads me and you hold me. Dear God, lead me in the way everlasting. Melt me, mold me, fill me, use me. Spirit of the Living God, fall afresh on me. Amen.

I know that the Lord maintains the cause of the needy, and executes justice for the poor.
140:12

When God judges, God will favor those who helped people in need: The NRSV translates it: *"Truly I tell you, just as you did it to one of the least of these who are members of my family, you did it to me."* (Matthew 25:40). What we do to the "least of these" we do to God. Conversely, what we do not do to those in need, we fail to do to God.

You cannot solve every social problem or meet every human need, but you can do something for a few with whom you come in contact. This is known as Starfish Theology, derived from this story: Two men walked along a beach where hundreds of starfish had been washed up by the tide. One of the men picked up a starfish and flung it back into the water. As he tossed it back to the sea, the other man said, *"What's the point of doing that? There are too many starfish on the beach. What difference does it make?"* His friend answered, *"It makes a difference to that one!"*

When we help one of "the least of these" we make a difference to that one. You cannot send money to every need, mend all the hurts or write legislators about every issue. It is possible to get overwhelmed by all the starfish on the beach or suffer compassion burnout by all the problems in the world, but if you could make a difference to one, it matters to them and it matters to God... because what you do to the child, you do to the parent.

Think about people who have helped your child or grandchild. They did it for them, yes, but you consider that they also did it for you. On the flip side, think about someone who hurt your child or grandchild. You take that personally and consider that they also did it to you. What you do for the child, you do for the parent. What you do to the child, you do to the parent.

What you do for God's beloved children, the weakest and the least, you do for God. The reverse is true too: what you do not do to God's children, you do not do to God. It is a profound story with a simple meaning.

Where do you start with so much need in the world? Emily Dickinson considers that question with her poem:
If I can stop one heart from breaking,
I shall not live in vain;
If I can ease one life the aching,
Or cool one pain,
Or help one fainting robin
Unto his nest again,
I shall not live in vain.

You start with the starfish on the beach in front of you and you make a difference to that one.

John Wesley reminded people of faith to:
Do all the good you can,
By all the means you can,
In all the ways you can,
In all the places you can,
At all the times you can,
To all the people you can,
As long as ever you can.

A story about how St. Francis tells how he was walking on a road through the woods. He saw in the distance a man coming in his direction. As the man drew closer, Francis could see that he was a leper, with fingers missing and his face disfigured. He had compassion on the man. He looked at the leper. Their eyes met. He smiled. As they passed, Francis muttered a prayer asking God to bless the man. A few steps later he stopped. He turned and looked back. The man was looking back at him, but what Francis saw was not the leper he had passed on the road but the face of Jesus himself.

When we help those in greatest need on the margins of our society, perhaps we too will look back and see the face of Jesus himself. Perhaps you will hear him say: *"Whenever you did one of these things to someone overlooked or ignored, that was me – you did it to me."*

PRAYER: I know, O Lord, that you maintain the cause of the needy and you desire justice for the poor. I also know that you want me to do the same. Otherwise, what good is my faith? And yet, Dear God, I do not know where to start or what to do. Help me to start wherever I am to do all the good I can. Lead me to opportunities to join you in caring for the needy and the poor. Teach me how to be most helpful. Change my heart so that I truly desire to care for those who are overlooked or ignored. Amen.

ONE-HUNDRED-AND-FORTY-ONE

Set a guard over my mouth, O Lord; keep watch over the door of my lips.
141:3

An office manager taped this verse to her desk as a reminder of her daily prayer: *"Set a guard over my mouth, O Lord; keep watch over the door of my lips."* When asked why this verse, she answered that she had a tendency to not listen well, to speak too quickly without thinking and then to get angry or make others angry. So, she prayed before each new day that God would set a guard over her mouth and keep watch over the door of her lips. To intend to the right attitude leads to the right behavior. She knew it, you know it and I know it: our tongue can be the ambassador of ill will or of blessing.

Solomon in Proverbs (15:1) cast it ever so memorably: *"A soft answer turns away wrath, but a harsh word stirs up anger."* James (1:19, 20) captured it this way: *You must understand this, my beloved: let everyone be quick to listen, slow to speak, slow to anger; for your anger does not produce God's righteousness.* Later in the book of James (4:11a) is a similar verse: *"Do not speak evil against one another, brothers and sisters."* Jesus said the same: *"Don't pick on people, jump on their failures, criticize their faults— unless, of course, you want the same treatment. That critical spirit has a way of boomeranging"* (Matthew 7:1, *The Message*).

You can't get the toothpaste back into the tube, it is said about people who speak an unkind word which they later regret. Once it is out there, the damage has been done. And so, perhaps the office manager demonstrated the wisdom of Solomon and the poetry of the Psalms as she appropriated this verse as her daily preventative mantra: *Set a guard over my mouth, O Lord; keep watch over the door of my lips.*

PRAYER: O Lord, I have got to watch my tongue. Words pop out of my mouth without thinking of how they might affect another. I know I can't make excuses. I must be accountable for the words I use. Let kindness rule my heart and my tongue and if I can't say something nice, please set a guard over my mouth. Amen.

Look on my right hand and see – there is no one who takes notice of me; no refuge remains to me; no one cares for me. I cry to you, O Lord; I say, "You are my refuge, my portion in the land of the living."
142:4, 5

There is no one who takes notice of me. These are forlorn words, when it feels like no one cares or even notices you.

There are personal feelings we are reluctant to admit: feeling rejected. Feeling lonely, even in a crowd of people. Feeling left out, ignored, not valued, or neglected. Have you ever been in a crowd where you felt invisible, like no one noticed you or even saw you, let alone paid any attention to you? Have you ever walked up to folks who are talking and stand there and they don't even look at you or acknowledge you? Are there moments where it feels like even family or friends treat you like you don't exist? Have you not wondered, even in a passing thought, if you have made any real difference or contributed in some significant way… or if anyone cares?

Our personal package comes with great built-in ego defense mechanisms to help protect our egos from being vulnerable: We've got denial. Rationalization. Intellectualization. And yet, down deep, there may be moments when we feel a little bleak, especially when it feels like no one cares or takes notice of you. That is the feeling captured in Psalm 142.

Can you imagine the depths of feeling abandoned or neglected, as when Jesus on the cross cried out: *"My God, my God, why have you forsaken me?"* Or the Apostle Paul, experiencing failure after failure, shoved out of town, and ostracized. He wrote to Timothy (2 Tim 4:16): *"…no one came to my support, but all deserted me."* Similarly, the Psalmist wrote with soulful passion *"There is no one who takes notice of me… no one cares for me."*

The Psalmist continues: *"I cry to you, O LORD; I say, 'You are my refuge, my portion in the land of the living'."* If you are hurting, you do not want pie-in-the-sky promises about how everything will be alright when you get to heaven. You are concerned about the now, in the land of the living. The Land of the Living is where God is your refuge. A Scottish proverb says *Be sure to live your life, because you are a long time dead.* Live your life in the present. Learn from the past and relish the best of it, but do not live there. Look forward to the future, and plan well, but do not live there. Live in the present, in the land of the living. In the land of the living, today, God is your refuge. Feeling like no one cares or takes notice of him, the Psalmist turned to his ever-present refuge, to God. *You are my refuge, my portion in the land of the living.* There is a saying: *"Don't tell God how big the storm is. Rather, tell the storm how big your God is!"* When you have no place else to go, go with the Psalmist to a place of refuge.

There is no one who takes notice of me; no refuge remains to me; no one cares for me. The Psalmist, who crafted one of humankind's greatest works of literature, felt that way. People at every level of occupation, economic status, location, gender, race, sexual orientation, religion, achievement, success or any other characteristic can feel that way. You can feel that way. When you do, seek refuge in the safe harbor of God's arms, for God's knows you, notices you, cares for you, and loves you. When no one takes notice of you, God speaks to you: *"You are precious in my sight, and honored, and I love you."* (Isaiah 43:4).

PRAYER: Thank you, Dear God. Thank you, for being with me when I am brought low or are feeling like no one takes notice of me. Thank you for reminding me anew that I am your beloved child and that you care about me. When I am feeling not valued, like the Psalmist, guide me to take some time to lift up another person and make him or her feel valued, noticed, and cared for. Amen.

ONE-HUNDRED-AND-FORTY-THREE

Let me hear of your steadfast love in the morning, for in you I put my trust. Teach me the way I should go, for to you I lift up my soul.
143:8

Teach me the way I should go. This may be one of the most prayed requests. If there is anything that people of faith believe, it is that God guides us. *"The human mind plans the way, but the LORD directs the steps,"* wrote the author of Proverbs (16:9). We frequently ask God to lead us, to guide us, to teach us the way we should go, and to direct our steps. A high prayer is to ask God to teach us the way to be a good person and a faithful child of God. We need God to teach us the way we should go with decisions, whether it is about a career choice, a major purchase, a relationship or any decision where we stand in need of God's leading. Many times, we make decisions using our mind. Other times it is our heart which leads us to make choices. Blaise Pascal, French mathematician and theologian, said *"The heart has its reasons of which reason knows nothing."* Both heart and mind are integral to decision-making.

When we invite God to teach us the way we should go, we are well-served to understand the process of decision-making. This is because it is helpful to have God's guidance at each stage of the process and not just at the last minute. Consider a four-step decision-making process:

THINKING UP IDEAS AND POSSIBILITIES. This is like internal brainstorming. An actual decision is intentionally deferred in this stage while you think up all the possible ideas, ideals and dreams. The goal here is to cast a wide net. Do not rule out anything or impose limitations or reasons why something is not possible. Your goal is to come up with a long list of ideas to fuel the decision-making process. In this stage, invite God to teach you the way you should go and help you to dream up possibilities.

GATHERING INFORMATION. This is the homework. Research the ideas and possibilities. You cannot choose that which you do not know exists, so dig into information to see what may be out there to choose from. Defer making a choice or ruling out decisions in this stage. Discover what is required to pursue options you are considering. In this stage, invite God to lead you to sources of information which can direct you in the way you should go.

WEIGHING ALTERNATIVES. Here is where you narrow down the choices to compare them. Understand that rarely is there a perfect choice. For everything you get, you give up something else. Some compromise is almost always a necessity. Weigh the top choices in terms of your interests, skills, needs and values. In this stage, invite God to help you to see clearly as you consider to pros and cons of each possibility.

MAKING THE CHOICE. This is where you press the submit button. You have thought up ideas, gathered information, considered the strengths and weaknesses of each choice, and now the time comes to make the choice. In this stage, ask God to help you to make the right choice and to teach you the way you should go.

Do you see the value of inviting God to guide you in each stage of making a choice? There is an old saying "Pray to God, but row to shore." You need to row, to do your part. But then, it is our heartfelt belief that God directs our steps, God leads, and God teaches us the way we should go. God guides.

This belief is reflected by the lyrics of William Williams in his hymn *Guide me, O Thou great Jehovah*:
Guide me, O Thou great Jehovah
Pilgrim through this barren land
I am weak, but Thou art mighty;
Hold me with Thy powerful hand
Bread of heaven, bread of heaven
Feed me till I want no more;
Feed me till I want no more

Open now the crystal fountain
Where the living waters flow;
Let the fire and cloudy pillar
Lead me all my journey through.
Strong Deliverer, strong Deliverer
Be Thou still my Strength and Shield;
Be Thou still my Strength and Shield

When I tread the verge of Jordan
Bid my anxious fears subside;
Death of death and hell's destruction
Land me safe on Canaan's side
Songs of praises, songs of praises
I will ever give to Thee;
I will ever give to Thee.

PRAYER: O Thou Great Jehovah, I pray that you would teach me the way I should go. When I need to make an important decision, let me not forget to invite you to guide me and direct my steps in each stage of the decision making. Teach me too, O God, the way to becoming the person you desire me to be. Amen.

ONE-HUNDRED-AND-FORTY-FOUR

O Lord, what are human beings that you regard them, or mortals that you think of them? They are like a breath; their days are like a passing shadow.
144:3, 4

This is the existential question, set within a prayer: what is humankind, God, that you take notice of them? It occurs within a psalm-prayer that essentially asks God to smite his enemy, deliver him from those out to harm him and then asks God to supply him with all kinds of good things. While it is unlikely that we face the danger of swords pointed at our chests or a battalion of enemies seeking our demise, there are times when we are besieged by problems, challenges, failures, or serious threats to our well-being. Perhaps it is in our most dangerous of times that we ponder the big questions of life: What is the purpose of life, what is the purpose of my life, why am I here, or does my life make any difference? In the valleys, we wonder about God and humans: who are we that you are mindful of us?

Many of the Psalms are peppered with the first-person singular pronoun: I, me or mine. They are poems and songs about our personal, individual relationship with the Divine. Down deep inside, we want to know more than answers to philosophical questions. Our questions are personal: O Lord, who am I that you take notice of me? Do you know me, God? You are so big... the biggest... and I am so small, even insignificant. And yet, do you know me? Care for me? Have my back in difficult times? Love me? It is the emotional bond we seek.

When you know that God, your God, is there for you with all of God's unconditional love, acceptance and support, then you know you can thrive under any circumstances. In the best of relationships, including and especially marital relationships, the basis of love is not a give-get arrangement but an emotional bonding of mutual support and affirmation. Now we consider the highest relationship ever – the relationship between you and the Divine.

The best relationship, if we can take our clue from human relationships, will be more of an emotional bond between you and God rather than a "what can I get" relationship. From you, God desires your love, following, and trust. What you desire from God is that God knows you personally, loves you, supports you, and holds you tight in God's affectionate and embracing arms – an emotional bond.

In the classic play *Fiddler on the Roof*, Tevye's daughters talk about falling in love. Falling in love is a new concept in a Jewish village centered upon tradition. Tevye then is curious. He wonders if his wife Golde, who married him as an arrangement agreed upon by their parents, loves him. And so, he asks her:

Tevye: Do you love me?
Golde: Do I what?
Tevye: Do you love me?

Golde: Do I love you?
With our daughters getting married and this trouble in the town,
You're upset. You want out. Go inside. Go lie down.
Maybe it's indigestion.

Tevye: Golde, I'm asking you a question. Do you love me?
Golde: You're a fool!
Tevye: I know. But do you love me?

Golde: Do I love you?
For twenty-five years, I've washed your clothes,
Cooked your meals, cleaned your house,
Given you children, milked the cow.
After twenty-five years, why talk about love right now?

Tevye: The first time I met you was on our wedding day. I was scared.
Golde: I was shy.
Tevye: I was nervous.
Golde: So was I.

Tevye: But my father and my father said we'd learn to love each other.
So, now I'm asking, Golde...
Tevye: Do you love me?
Golde: I'm your wife!
Tevye: I know. But do you love me?

Golde: Do I love him?
For twenty-five years, I've lived with him,
Fought with him, starved with him.
For twenty-five years, my bed is his.
If that's not love, what is?

Tevye: Then you love me?
Golde: I suppose I do.
Tevye: And I suppose I love you, too.
Together: It doesn't change a thing, but even so,
After twenty-five years, it's nice to know

That, in a way, is what we want to know. Not the philosophical question, but the question of emotional bond: O Lord, who am I that you would know me and love me? You already know the answer, but the overwhelming awe of God's love for you prompts the question as an expression of praise and thanksgiving.

PRAYER: O Lord, thank you for knowing me and loving me. You, Creator of the Universe, and me, a speck whose days are like a passing shadow, you love me and I love you. O God, help me to learn to know you better and to love you more. Amen.

The Lord is good to all, and his compassion is over all that he has made.
145:9

The word compassion is rich with meaning. It means empathy, sympathy, kindness, gentleness, tenderness. It comes from the root words meaning to suffer together, to be with the other when he or she is hurting, to feel for the other.

God has compassion, reassures the Psalmist. God is big enough to have compassion over all that God has made and personal enough to have compassion for you when you are hurting.

Consider a sample of verses from the bible telling of God's compassion:

Sing for joy, O heavens, and exult, O earth; break forth, O mountains, into singing! For the Lord has comforted his people, and will have compassion on his suffering ones.
Isaiah 49:13

He will again have compassion upon us; he will tread our iniquities under foot. You will cast all our sins into the depths of the sea.
Micah 7:19

When he saw the crowds, he had compassion for them, because they were harassed and helpless, like sheep without a shepherd.
Matthew 9:36

When he went ashore, he saw a great crowd; and he had compassion for them and cured their sick.
Matthew 14:14

Then Jesus called his disciples to him and said, "I have compassion for the crowd, because they have been with me now for three days and have nothing to eat; and I do not want to send them away hungry, for they might faint on the way."
Matthew 15:32

Moved with compassion, Jesus touched their eyes. Immediately they regained their sight and followed him.
Matthew 20:34

When the Lord saw her, he had compassion for her and said to her, "Do not weep."
Luke 7:13

So he set off and went to his father. But while he was still far off, his father saw him and was filled with compassion; he ran and put his arms around him and kissed him.
Luke 15:20

The verse about compassion in Luke 15 comes from Jesus' Parable of the Prodigal Son. Actually, the word *prodigal* is not in the bible and the story is really more about the father than the son. In some ways, the Parable is one of the most important teachings of Jesus because it comes in answer to the question "What is God really like?" God is like this, answered Jesus. God is like a compassionate and loving parent who welcomes the wayward child home again.

Because this Parable, from the Son of God, tells about God's nature and character, it is of great significance. This is what God is like! The most important verse in this most important parable is like a library of theology scrunched into one verse, for this is at the heart of God's nature: *But while he was still far off, his father saw him and was filled with compassion; he ran and put his arms around him and kissed him.*

Observe: In the most important teaching about God in the most important story in the bible, what words are spoken? Not a word.

The father had compassion. He forgave. He gave his child undeserved mercy. This son squandered a lot of money, a whole inheritance. People who do not own anything cannot appreciate how hard parents work to save what they have. This young man blew it and yet his father accepted him and loved him anyway. Like God, who is a parent of compassion.

What did the father say? What words did he speak? Nothing. He did not use words. He did not speak. There is no sentence coming out of the compassionate father's mouth. He did not ask for explanation, excuses, reasons or an accounting. He did not bawl out or give advice. He did not threaten or punish. He did not grill about behavior, values, mistakes or beliefs. He did not even give his son a chance to apologize. He did not talk. This is incredible. He did not speak!

This is the HUG HEARD AROUND THE WORLD: *his father saw him and was filled with compassion; he ran and put his arms around him and kissed him.*

That is what God is like. Compassionate.

PRAYER: Thank you, Compassionate God, for loving me, for being with me when I hurt, and for your gift of compassion to me. When I stray away from you and long to return, welcome me with your embracing arms wrapped around me. I long to feel your compassionate hug. And then, dear Lord, may I be an instrument of your compassion with others. Amen.

Praise the Lord! Praise the Lord, O my soul! I will praise the Lord as long as I live; I will sing praises to my God all my life long.
146:1, 2

This could be the cover title for the Book of Psalms: Praise the Lord. Out of the Psalmist's heart flows his everlasting song of giving God glory: *I will praise the Lord as long as I live. I will sing praises o my God all my life long.*

His songs of praise raise the bar for our prayers to God. Let them remind us in every prayer to praise God and to love God so much that we desire to sing praises as long as we live. Sometimes it is easier for us to praise God in song, as in the hymn *Father, We Praise Thee*:

Father, we praise thee, now the night is over;
active and watchful, stand we all before thee;
singing we offer prayer and meditation:
thus we adore thee.

Monarch of all things, fit us for thy mansions;
banish our weakness, health and wholeness sending;
bring us to heaven, where thy saints united
joy without ending.

All-holy Father, Son and equal Spirit,
Trinity blessed, send us thy salvation;
thine is the glory, gleaming and resounding
through all creation.

PRAYER: All Holy God, hear my song of adoration and praise to you. Hallowed by Thy name. To you be all glory. May my things, words and actions glorify you. Amen.

He heals the brokenhearted, and binds up their wounds.
147:3

Healing the brokenhearted means that God heals and binds up emotional wounds. Those are the ones which hurt the most. These are wounds that might have been caused by a relationship breakdown – a failed or failing marriage, a child or parent who hurt us, a friend who said something or violated a confidence, a colleague who betrayed us, a person we love who was not there when we needed them, or another who has abused us. Open wounds ache and sometimes will not heal. Time does not heal all wounds, but it allows us perspective to move forward. How blessed when we pray and ask God to heal a part of our heart which is broken and God binds up our wounds.

There is a beautiful story in the gospels about a woman with a physical hurt. Often in the New Testament when there is healing, it is about Jesus touching a person to heal them. This story is different because it is the woman who reached out to teach Jesus. The bible says: *"Now there was a woman who had been suffering from hemorrhages for twelve years; and though she had spent all she had on physicians, no one could cure her."* (Luke 8:43).

Twelve years is a long time to suffer. This is not someone sick with the flu. Where do you think she hurt? Hemorrhages? Probably in the stomach: pain, discomfort, agony. Maybe a form of a bleeding cancer. Did you ever have a bad stomach ache? She could not enjoy going places, doing things, or could not concentrate even on her family because she was always in pain. She had to plan her day around how her stomach would feel. People who suffer chronic pain tell how there is not a minute of the day they are not aware of it. It dominates their life. For twelve years, this woman hurt.

There would be no point trying to diagnose her. The story says she had visited all the doctors. She tried everything.

Have you ever had to bounce from one doctor to another and perhaps try Chiropractic, acupuncture, prescriptions, herbs and vitamins, pain management clinics... and nothing helps? For a dozen years, she tried it all.

Now she hears that Jesus is coming to her town. She had heard of his wonderful works. She heard reports that he healed lepers, restored sight to the blind, and the lame threw away their sticks. She had heard what he had done for others. It did not take long for her to wonder *"What if I could touch him?"*

This dialog, though edited, is inspired by a sermon titled "The Touch of Faith" from the late Peter Marshall, former pastor of the New York Avenue Presbyterian Church in Washington, D.C.

It was all the woman could think about as her thought turned into a plan. It would be bold and require daring action. Her heart thumped, but it was worth trying. It could only fail and she was no stranger to failure. Can you imagine her thinking: *Touch Him... yes... just to touch him. There would be no harm in that! Would it bother him? He is said to be a kind man, gentle, full of compassion.* She decides to do it.

The day arrives. The incident took place in a city street. Perhaps it looked like a narrow and twisted street packed with a crowd of excited people who appeared to be waiting for a parade to pass their way. The sounds and smells of its bazaars and pavement stalls joined with the noise and confusion of an eastern market place. It was busy, hot, crowded, and animated.

Here is my only chance, she thinks. *He's coming this way. He will pass quickly and soon he will be gone. I must push through to touch him.* The woman thinks: *I cannot touch him on the head – that would be inappropriate. On the hand? That would be too personal. Give him a hug? I could not get that close.* But, she thinks, there could not be any harm in touching his robe as he passes. It would be enough, just to touch the border of his robe.

I must touch him. I must attempt this one last hope. She pushes her way through the mass of people standing shoulder-to-shoulder. With the persistence of despair, she struggles in that dense crowd. People get in her way unaware of her need. He must not pass so near and yet so far away.

You can imagine her diving under the legs of the crowd as he approaches. The moment arrives and with split second timing, she reaches out and with trembling finger she touches him.

She did it! Mission accomplished. She touched the fringe of his garment. She touched the fringe of his robe and like an electric shock there surged back into her the rich glow of health and vitality.

She faded back into the crowd, unnoticed, she thought. But he knew. Jesus recognized the one magnetic touch of faith amid the pushing and shoving press of the crowd. He stopped dead in his tracks, turned around, and asked that amazing question: *"Who touched me?"*

The question seemed ridiculous. His disciples asked, *"What? What do you mean who touched you? Hundreds are crowding around you. Everybody is touching you."* Peter said, *"Master, the crowds surround you and press in on you."* How do we know who touched you?

But he knew. He felt the touch. Jesus said, *"Someone touched me; for I noticed that power had gone out from me."*

When the woman saw that she could not remain hidden, she came trembling. Falling down before him, she declared in the presence of all the people why she had touched him and how she had been healed. In tenderness Jesus assured her, *"Daughter, your faith has made you well. Go in peace."*

We long to reach out to touch him in the same way, to heal our broken heart and to bind up our emotional wounds. Perhaps as we keep on reaching out, we will discover our open wounds healing and hear him say "Child, your faith has made you well. Go in peace."

PRAYER: Loving and Compassionate God, I pray for your healing touch. I have open wounds from being hurt by another. I have tried so hard to forgive them, to understand what happened, and to let it go. But the wounds still hurt. I reach out in faith to you and invite you to heal me with your soothing balm. Amen.

ONE-HUNDRED-AND-FORTY-EIGHT

*Praise the Lord from the earth, you sea monsters and all deeps,
fire and hail, snow and frost, stormy wind fulfilling his command!
Mountains and all hills, fruit trees and all cedars! Wild animals
and all cattle, creeping things and flying birds!*
148:7-10

Overflowing with praise, the Psalmist continues his adoration of
the Almighty. Not only does he praise God, but he views
everything in nature as praising God. *You see monsters and all
deeps.* If you have ever been whale watching, you might describe
it as a spiritual experience, to see these great leviathans in their
natural habitat, and with such high intelligence. They praise the
Lord. So do the elements of nature: snow, frost and wind. Trees,
wild animals, cattle, birds and even creeping things like bugs
praise God. It is hard to think of spiders, ants and mosquitos
praising God. But of course, all of these have been created by God
and everything God creates, God creates good.

While the Psalm is a metaphor for all nature praising God, there is
something sacred about the notion. Imagine looking at everything
which God has made to see the plants and animals, insects and
mountains, whales and dust mites praising God. It changes how
you look at nature, because all nature joins you in offering praise
to God.

The Psalm reminds of the beautiful hymn *Fairest Lord Jesus*,
which proclaims Jesus as the ruler of all nature.

*Fairest Lord Jesus!
Ruler of all nature!
O Thou of God and man the Son!
Thee will I cherish,
Thee will I honor,
Thou, my soul's glory, joy, and crown!*

411

Fair are the meadows
Fairer still the woodlands,
Robed in the blooming garb of spring;
Jesus is fairer,
Jesus is purer,
Who makes the woeful heart to sing!

Fair is the sunshine,
Fairer still the moonlight,
And all the twinkling starry host;
Jesus shines brighter,
Jesus shines purer,
Than all the angels heav'n can boast!

All fairest beauty,
Heavenly and earthly,
Wondrously, Jesus, is found in Thee;
None can be nearer,
Fairer, or dearer,
Than Thou my Savior art to me.

Perhaps the last stanza captures the Psalm well: All fairest beauty, heavenly and earthly, wondrously, Jesus, is found in Thee. May everything that breathes, praise the Lord. Praise God. Amen.

PRAYER: Creator God, give me fresh lenses to look at all of your creation, from the largest to the tiniest, to see them praising you, their creator. This makes them sacred. May I treat all that you create as sacred, good, and belonging to you. Amen.

ONE-HUNDRED-AND-FORTY-NINE

For the Lord takes pleasure in his people; he adorns the humble with victory.
149:4

How do I bring you pleasure, Lord? Is it by...
- Loving you with all my heart, soul, might and mind?
- Loving my neighbor, indeed, loving all of your children, no exceptions?
- Praising and adoring you?
- Doing justice, treating all people well and caring for those most in need?
- Loving kindness and trying my best to be kind?
- Desiring to be a good person?
- Walking humbly with you in trust and obedience?
- Radiating an inner light because of the light you place within me?
- Trusting in hope which does not disappoint?
- Accepting your gift of joy to me and living joyfully each day?
- Embracing a sense of inner peace, knowing that no matter what happens, it is well with my soul?
- Having patience with other people and giving them my gift of grace?
- Forgiving others, even when it hurts for me to forgive?
- Aspiring to be faithful to you, realizing that what you want most is for me to be a faithful child?
- Attempting to be strong enough so that I can be a gentle person?
- Controlling me ego needs so that I can focus more upon others rather than calling attention to myself?
- Growing a spirit of generosity within so that I may be a giver in all ways and give something back out of gratitude for what I have received?
- Participating as a member of a faith community to worship you regularly and serve my community?

O my God, if this is what brings you pleasure, I have failed at every one of them! What amazes me is that I bring you pleasure anyway and that you love, accept, and cherish me anyway, just as I am.

PRAYER: May it become one of my highest goals to try to bring you pleasure, O Lord. Thank you for reaching down to me, even before I reach up to you, and for your loving embrace of me, just as I am. Amen.

ONE-HUNDRED-AND-FIFTY

Let everything that breathes praise the Lord! Praise the Lord!
150:6

How fitting that the final Psalm is all about praising God:

*Praise the Lord! Praise God in his sanctuary; praise him in his
mighty firmament! Praise him for his mighty deeds; praise him
according to his surpassing greatness! Praise him with trumpet
sound; praise him with lute and harp! Praise him with tambourine
and dance; praise him with strings and pipe! Praise him with
clanging cymbals; praise him with loud clashing cymbals! Let
everything that breathes praise the Lord! Praise the Lord!*

The Psalms have been completed. Their repetitious songs of praise
have changed us, transformed how we pray, and have given us a
model for celebrating our emotional bond with God. They have
led us into an encounter with the Divine. Music, poetry, nature,
beautify – all collaborate to hallow God's holy name.

Thanksgiving has been another primary theme of the Psalms. How
can we ever thank God for all of the blessings God has given us?
Perhaps the best music to conclude with is the Doxology, for it
summarizes the Psalmist's praise and thanksgiving:

Praise God, from whom all blessings flow;
Praise Him, all creatures here below;
Praise Him above, ye heav'nly host;
Praise Father, Son, and Holy Ghost!

Consider also an inclusive language version:
Praise God, from whom all blessings flow,
Praise God, all creatures here below,
Praise God above, ye heav'nly host,
Creator, Christ and Holy Ghost. Amen.

415

The first line of the Doxology speaks volumes: *Praise God, from whom all blessings flow*. This verse can only be sung by a person of faith, for who else would bother to praise God? Then, it recognizes in the simplest language and shortest words that all of our blessings flow from God. This verse is sung by a person who knows she or he is blessed by God. May it be our concluding thought, song and prayer as we thank God for giving us the Psalms to lead us higher into an encounter with the Divine.

One final hymn serves as our concluding prayer: *Take My Life and Let It Be*.

PRAYER:
Take my life, and let it be,
Consecrated, Lord, to thee;
Take my moments and my days,
Let them flow in ceaseless praise.
Amen!

# # #

About the Author

John Zehring has served United Church of Christ congregations for more than twenty years as Senior Pastor in Massachusetts (Andover), Rhode Island (Kingston), Maine (Augusta) and as an Interim Pastor in Massachusetts (Arlington, Harvard). Prior to parish ministry, he served as a vice president and teacher at colleges, universities, and a theological seminary for more than two decades. He is the author of more than forty books and eBooks. Rev. Zehring graduated from Eastern University and holds graduate degrees from Princeton Theological Seminary, Rider University, and the Earlham School of Religion.

Books by John Zehring

Majestic is Thy Name: Devotions from the Psalms. 2019.

Treasures from Proverbs: GEMS for You from the Book of Proverbs. 2018.

Treasures from Rome: GEMS for You from the Epistle to the Romans. 2018.

Get Your Church Ready to Grow: A Guide to Building Attendance & Participation. 2018.

Beyond Stewardship: A Church Guide to Generous Giving Campaigns. 2016.

Asking for Campaign Support: A Guide for Church Volunteers. 2018.

Clergy Quick Guide to Encouraging Leaders and Staff. Also… evaluating staff and evaluating yourself. 2017.

Hard Sayings of Jesus: Discussions for Curious Christians. 2017.

Clergy Quick Guide to Time Management. 2017.

Pastoral Leadership and Church Administration. 2017.

Miracles? Discussions for Curious Christians about Jesus' Miracles. 2018.

Treasures from James: GEMS for You from the Epistle of James. 2017.

Eulogies, Introductions and Special Occasion Speeches: Tips for When You Are Asked to Speak Well of Another. 2017.

Treasures from Galatia: GEMS for You from the Epistle to the Galatians. 2017.

Lent Discussions for Curious Christians: Conversations in the Purple Season. 2017.

Favorite Parables from Jesus of Nazareth. 2016.

Anxious? A Booklet of Bible Verses for When You Feel Anxious. 2016.

Clergy Guide to Sermon Preparation: Including 40 Sermon Ideas and Outlines. 2015.

Mount Up with Wings: Renew Your Strength. 2015.

Jesus' Sermon on the Mount: Matthew 5, 6 and 7. 2015.

Visiting on Behalf of Your Church: A Guide for Deacons, Care Teams and Those Who Visit. 2015.

The One Minute Beatitude: A Brief Review of Jesus' Beatitudes. 2015.

Seven Mantras to Shape Your Day: Bible Verses to Improve How You See Things. 2015.

Psalm 23: An Everyday Psalm. 2015.

By the Golden Rule. Torture is Always Wrong. 2014.

Public Speaking for Executives. Leaders & Managers. 2014.

Clergy Guide to Making Visits. 2014.

Clergy Public Speaking Guide: Improve What You
Already Do Well. 2014.

Clergy Negotiating Guide: Don't Sell Yourself Short.
2014.

Treasures from Philippi: GEMS for You from the Epistle
to the Philippians. 2014.

What the Bible Says About Homosexuality: A Bible Study
for Progressive People of Faith. 2014.

Did He Hit Her? A Compassionate Christian Response to
Abusive Relationships. 2014.

To Know God Better And To Love God More: Messages
for Your Spiritual Journey. 2014.

You Can Run A Capital Campaign: A Guide for Church
Leaders. 1990.

Work Smarter -- Not Harder: A Manual for Development
Officers. 1986.

WORKING SMART: The Handbook for New Managers.
1985.

Careers in State and Local Government. 1980.

Preparing for W*O*R*K. 1981.

Making Your Life Count. 1980.

IMPLICATIONS: Case Studies for Ethical and Spiritual
Development. 1980.

Get Your Career In Gear: How To Find Or Change Your
Lifework. 1976.

Made in the USA
Middletown, DE
14 April 2019